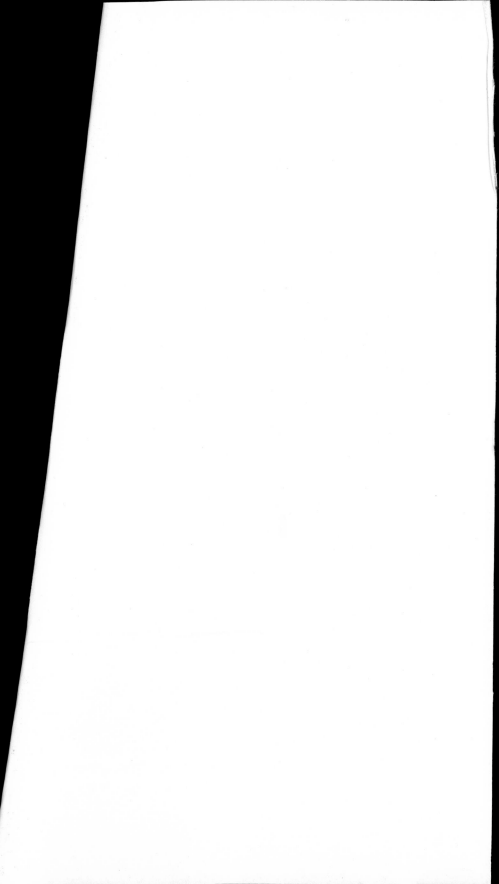

The Walter P.
Memorial

Manifest Destiny and Empire

Manifest Destiny and Empire American Antebellum Expansionism

BY
Robert W. Johannsen
John M. Belohlavek
Thomas R. Hietala
Samuel J. Watson
Sam W. Haynes
Robert E. May

EDITED BY
Sam W. Haynes and Christopher Morris

Published for the University of Texas at Arlington by
Texas A&M University Press
COLLEGE STATION

The paper used in this book meets the minimum requirements
of the American National Standard for Permanence
of Paper for Printed Library Materials, Z39.48–1984.
Binding materials have been chosen for durability.

Library of Congress Cataloging-in-Publication Data

Manifest destiny and empire : American antebellum expansionism / by
Robert W. Johannsen . . . [et al.] ; edited by Sam W. Haynes and
Christopher Morris. — 1st ed.

       p.   cm. — (The Walter Prescott Webb memorial lectures ; 31)

   ISBN 0-89096-756-3

   1. United States —Territorial expansion.   I. Johannsen, Robert
Walter, 1925– .   II. Haynes, Sam W. (Sam Walter), 1956– .
III. Morris, Christopher, 1958– .   IV. Series.

E179.5M32   1997

973—dc21   97-25072

                                             CIP

To Virginia Garrett

CONTENTS

PREFACE

The essays in this volume were presented in March, 1996, for the Thirtieth Walter Prescott Webb Memorial Lectures, held annually at the University of Texas at Arlington. These lectures, all devoted to the theme of early U.S. expansionism, seek to bring into sharper focus the territorial ambitions of Americans—both policy makers and private citizens—in the decades prior to the Civil War. While approaching this subject from different perspectives and lines of inquiry, these essays underscore a peculiarly American paradox, for it was during the nineteenth century that the United States emerged as a hemispheric power, even as it grew increasingly unsure of its very identity as a nation.

This year's Webb Lecturers have written and researched widely on the subject of Manifest Destiny and American empire. Robert W. Johannsen is J. G. Randall Distinguished Professor of History at the University of Illinois, Urbana-Champaign. His many books include *Stephen A. Douglas* (1973) and *To The Halls of the Montezumas: The Mexican War in the American Imagination* (1985). Thomas R. Hietala is an associate professor at Grinnell College and the author of *Manifest Design: Anxious Aggrandizement in Late Jacksonian America* (1985). Sam W. Haynes is an associate professor at the University of Texas at Arlington. He is the author of *Soldiers of Misfortune: The Somervell and Mier Expeditions* (1990), and *James K. Polk and the Expansionist Impulse* (1996). John M. Belohlavek is a professor at the University of South Florida. He has written *George Mifflin Dallas: Jacksonian Patrician* (1977) and *Let the Eagle Soar! The Foreign Policy of Andrew Jackson* (1985). Samuel J. Watson received his Ph.D. from Rice University in 1996 and is an adjunct professor at the University of St. Thomas, Houston. His contribution to this volume won the 1996 Webb-Smith Essay Competition. Robert E. May is a professor at Purdue University. His books include *The Southern*

Dream of a Caribbean Empire, 1854–1861, and *John A. Quitman, Old South Crusader* (1985).

On behalf of the UTA department of history, we would like to acknowledge several benefactors and friends of the Webb Lectures. C. B. Smith, Sr., an Austin businessman and former student of Walter Prescott Webb, generously provided the endowment that makes possible the annual presentation and publication of the lectures. Additional support came from the Rudolf Hermanns Endowment for the Liberal Arts. The loyal support of Jenkins and Virginia Garrett of Fort Worth is long and ongoing. Once again, we thank them. President Robert Witt supported our efforts by generously providing a reception in honor of the lecturers. Thanks also go to Stanley Palmer, interim department chair, for his many helpful suggestions as we planned this year's lectures, and to Steven Reinhardt, tireless chair of the Webb Lectures.

We dedicate this volume to Virginia Garrett. Her interest in the history of U.S. expansion into the Southwest led her to collect hundreds of items that document it. Her generosity led her to place those documents among the UTA Special Collections, where they may be used by others who share her interests.

Sam W. Haynes
Christopher Morris

Manifest Destiny and Empire

Introduction

Robert W. Johannsen

Although destiny and mission have a pedigree that predates the nation itself, it was not until the early nineteenth century that profound changes in American life were combined with the idealism of the nation's revolutionary beginnings and with currents of European Romanticism to produce a popular romantic nationalism that gave new meaning to the idea of progress. Fundamental to the feelings of national superiority generated by romantic nationalism was the conviction that American territorial expansion was inevitable, that the nation's providential destiny—its Manifest Destiny—decreed an extension of the ideals of its founding charter throughout the entire continent. The notion was all the more credible because American settlers, traders, and missionaries were already on the move to far distant areas of North America. John L. O'Sullivan's first uses of the phrase *Manifest Destiny* were in response to population movements that were already underway in Texas and in the Oregon Country. Thus, Manifest Destiny became and has remained virtually synonymous with territorial expansion.

American territorial expansion before the Civil War is the theme of the essays which follow, comprising (with two exceptions) the Thirty-First Annual Walter Prescott Webb Memorial Lectures, sponsored by the University of Texas at Arlington. Five scholars whose work has been devoted to the study of national expansion, have each examined Manifest Destiny from a different perspective. The result is a perceptive and authoritative portrayal of the uses to which Manifest Destiny has been put and of the meanings the concept has had to past and present generations since O'Sullivan first penned the words. O'Sullivan's own meaning, however, is too often forgotten, a problem that my opening chapter seeks to redress. It seems a fitting place to begin.

John M. Belohlavek, biographer of Polk's vice president, George Mifflin Dallas, and author of a long-needed study of Jacksonian foreign policy, focuses on Caleb Cushing, New England intellectual, politician, diplomat, and soldier, as a prominent figure in what he calls the "new historiography of American empire," that is, the study of Manifest Destiny's racial motivations. Based on a careful examination of Cushing's diary and letters, his many public lectures, and his published articles, Belohlavek's study reveals an individual whose arguments for American superiority carried a strong and caustic element of Anglo-Saxon racialism, mixed with a Whiggish concern for ordered progress. Convinced that America's destiny demanded that the United States "people, cultivate, and civilize" the continent, Cushing challenged Britain's rival pretentions in the Maine and Oregon controversies, advocated Texas annexation, and was an ardent supporter of the Mexican War for which he raised a New England regiment of volunteers. He was probably best known, however, for his diplomatic service as envoy to China and for his negotiation of the first U.S. commercial treaty with the Chinese Empire in 1844. Cushing's vision for America was consistent, Belohlavek concludes, although his arguments for racial and cultural superiority, his militarism, and his failure to express outrage at slavery have overshadowed his virtues and dimmed his reputation in our time.

Thomas R. Hietala emphasizes the inadequacy of the phrase *Manifest Destiny* to convey the "actual dynamics" of territorial expansion, for it "obscures more than it clarifies." Expressions of democratic ideals, he insists, merely cloaked "rank prejudice"; while behind the notions of providential destiny were the "grasping fingers" of mortals like James K Polk, Stephen A. Douglas, and John L. O'Sullivan. (Hietala prefers *manifest design* to *Manifest Destiny*, a phrase also first used by O'Sullivan, when he wrote of the "manifest design of Providence in regard to the occupation of the continent.") Hietala continues the indictment of the expansionists set forth in his earlier study. Racial prejudice and ethnocentrism were principal motivating factors behind the removal of Native Americans and the war upon the Mexicans, but they were not the only ones. Ambitions for economic advantage, new markets, and seaports, a fear of manufacturing and urbanization, and the need to "quell dissent" by dispersing America's poor over large areas also drove territorial expansion. Hietala, however, points out that not all of America's voices were raised in support of expansion. Among its critics were Henry David Thoreau, New York banker Philip Hone, and especially George

Catlin, the painter of Native Americans in the 1830s. Catlin wrote of the "grand and irresistible march of civilization," but he also was disturbed by the desolation it left behind.

Studies of territorial expansion have emphasized the contributions of explorers, traders, missionaries, miners, town builders, and farmers but have paid little attention to one of the more important groups in the westward-moving procession, the soldiers who served in the United States Army. Samuel J. Watson's essay, winner of the annual Webb-Smith Essay Contest, seeks to fill this gap by exploring the role of the army's officer corps as "agents of empire," from the end of the War of 1812 to the opening of the Mexican War. In his discussion of the attitudes held by the officers toward U.S. foreign policy, Watson finds a declining enthusiasm for territorial expansion. His search of the diaries and letters of the officers revealed a surprising lack of comment on the expansionist issues of the 1840s. The officers generally seemed indifferent to the political debates generated by expansion and rarely expressed any of the "republican or other ideological sentiments" usually identified with Manifest Destiny. Until the outbreak of the Mexican War (a war many of them had not expected to fight), they appeared to be more concerned with the boredom of camp life, their health, and their separation from wives and families. Watson concludes that while the officers had a stake in "orderly national expansion," they were unwilling to take the risks of "urging or precipitating it."

The complexity of the Texas annexation issue, Sam W. Haynes correctly observes, has been generally ignored by historians who have studied annexation from the perspective of the sectional conflict over slavery. Haynes offers, as a significant dimension of the "tangled dynamics of the annexation, debate," the widespread and very real fear that Great Britain intended to block annexation, turn Texas into a British protectorate, and thus effectively counter U.S. expansion. Anglophobia, to be sure, has been a missing ingredient in most discussions of Manifest Destiny. One need only recall that it was the interference of Europe's monarchies that first inspired O'Sullivan to use the term Manifest Destiny. Haynes's essay is a convincing response to those historians of American expansion, like Frederick Merk, who have routinely dismissed the fear of British designs in North America as a shibboleth or as mere propaganda in support of the expansionists' goals. The danger of the British threat to American national interests gained credibility from the schemes, presumably with the sanction of the British foreign office, of Charles Elliot, Britain's diplomatic respresentative in Texas. Haynes has skillfully presented what he calls the "vectors of Anglophobia": the fear of a

British plot to abolish slavery in Texas, a concern for Britain's commercial rivalry with the United States, the anxiety of republicanism's defenders that a monarchical system might appear on the southern borders, and a fear of British encirclement that linked the Texas question with American interests in Oregon and California.

What of Manifest Destiny in the period between the Mexican War and the Civil War? In the final essay, Robert E. May offers a spirited yet discerning review of filibustering activities from the late eighteenth to the mid-nineteenth centuries. Building upon his impressive record of scholarly publications, he probes the contributions which filibustering made to American expansion and explores the relationship between filibustering and Manifest Destiny. Filibustering, that is, "private expeditions to foreign domains," reached epidemic proportions during the decade following the Mexican War, capturing the country's imagination and influencing virtually every medium of popular expression. How, May asks, can this "filibustering addiction" be explained? Supported by an exhaustive research in a wide range of manuscript and published sources, May finds answers in the dislocations of social and economic change, the thirst for romance and high adventure, the lure of monetary gain, and (for Southerners) an effort to strengthen slavery at a time when slavery was under mounting attack. But more significantly, he suggests, the ideology of Manifest Destiny, the fusion of expansion with the democratic mission, inspired the filibusters. Furthermore, Manifest Destiny provided a racial justification for their expeditions, extending the institutions of republican government while also regenerating less fortunate peoples. In the end, however, May concludes in this original and provocative study, Manifest Destiny not only failed to enhance expansion but actually inhibited it.

The Meaning
of Manifest Destiny

Robert W. Johannsen

Any discussion of Manifest Destiny must inevitably begin with the obliga-
tory bow to John Louis O'Sullivan.[1] A New York journalist of Irish descent,
confident and optimistic in temperament, O'Sullivan was an outspoken
champion of Andrew Jackson's Romantic democracy; like so many others of
his generation, he saw the "hand of Providence in the workings and will of
the majority." In 1837, the year Jackson left the presidential office, O'Sullivan
founded with the help of his brother-in-law the *United States Magazine and
Democratic Review* (commonly called simply the *Democratic Review*). The
journal's purpose, he wrote, was "to strike the hitherto silent string of the
democratic genius of the age and the country." Under his able editorial tute-
lage, the *Review* quickly became what one historian of the period has termed
the "liveliest journal of the day." As the spokesman for both small-*d* democracy and the large-*D* Democracy, O'Sullivan published a remarkably eclectic
array of articles, reflecting his own interest in the creation of a uniquely
American national literature. As the publicist of American Romanticism, he
was the first to recognize and publish the work of Nathaniel Hawthorne
(with whom he maintained a lifelong friendship) and Walt Whitman and
numbered among his authors William Cullen Bryant, Henry David Thoreau, Ralph Waldo Emerson, Edgar Allan Poe, George Bancroft, John Green-
leaf Whittier, and others—a veritable roster of American Romanticism.[2]

It was in the columns of the *Democratic Review,* during the summer of
1845, that O'Sullivan first penned the words *Manifest Destiny.* They were em-
bedded in an article justifying the annexation of Texas, calling little attention

to themselves, and easily missed in the reading. The article, simply titled "Annexation," appeared at a critical moment in the Texas story. Four months before, Congress had set the annexation process in motion with the passage of a joint resolution inviting the independent republic to join the American Union. At the same time, James K. Polk assumed the presidency, pledging to bring the congressional action to its successful conclusion. Although there was little doubt that Texans would accept the invitation, critics in the United States (principally abolitionists who feared the admission of another slave state) continued to oppose annexation. Of greater concern to annexation's supporters were the desperate maneuvers undertaken by British and French emissaries in Texas, presumably with the sanction of their home governments, to frustrate annexation; it was against this unwarranted interference by Europe's monarchies that O'Sullivan expressed indignation. These nations, he charged, have intruded

in a spirit of hostile interference against us, for the avowed object of thwarting our policy and hampering our power, limiting our greatness and checking the fulfilment of our manifest destiny to overspread the continent allotted by Providence for the free development of our yearly multiplying millions.[3]

The appearance of the phrase *Manifest Destiny* at this time caused hardly a ripple, perhaps because voters in Texas approved annexation and elected a constitutional convention at the same time the article appeared. Texas was admitted to the Union as a state the following December.

O'Sullivan's second use of the phrase in the New York *Morning News* on February 27, 1845, in what David Pletcher has called "the most famous editorial of the decade," elicited a quite different response. The *Morning News* had been established during the 1844 presidential campaign by Samuel J. Tilden, a young New York Democrat, and O'Sullivan to promote the fortunes of the party in the election. Following Polk's narrow victory, Tilden withdrew from the paper, leaving O'Sullivan in sole charge.

Public attention in the meantime had shifted to the Oregon boundary dispute with Great Britain, an issue fraught with a good deal more anxiety than the Texas question, for it posed a very real threat of war with one of the world's major powers. The dispute had been simmering for years, kept from boiling over only by an unsatisfactory joint occupation agreement. When President Polk, in his December, 1845, message to Congress, recommended that the joint occupation agreement be terminated, thereby forcing a negotiated settlement, the lines were drawn between the opposing claims of the two countries. O'Sullivan stood with the expansionists who insisted that all of Oregon, from the forty-second parallel to 54 degrees 40 minutes north latitude, was rightfully American. Once again he framed his argument in providential and moral terms, albeit in a more belligerent tone than he had used just six months before:

> Away, away with all these cobweb tissues of rights of discovery, exploration, settlement, continuity, etc. To state the truth at once in its neglected simplicity, we are free to say that were the respective cases and arguments of the two parties, as to all these points of history and law, reversed—had England all ours, and we nothing but hers—our claim to Oregon would still be best and strongest. And that claim is by the right of our manifest destiny to overspread and to possess the whole of the continent which Providence has given us for the development of the great experiment of liberty and federated self-government entrusted to us.

To O'Sullivan, America's providentially sanctioned right of destiny superseded all claims that looked to history and law, providing a "higher law" which would govern U.S. behavior.[4]

The response was immediate, as Manifest Destiny found its way into the congressional debates, where it gave added fervor to the spread-eagle oratory of the expansionists and new intensity to the nation's territorial aspirations. It is not possible to measure its impact on the final resolution of the boundary crisis. Shortly after O'Sullivan's editorial appeared, there were unmistakable signs that Britain's hard-liners were softening their stand. Negotiations were soon underway, and in June, 1846, a new agreement was drawn between the two countries, extending the boundary along the forty-ninth parallel, which after all had been the traditional American position.

The editorial was to be O'Sullivan's valedictory statement. In mid-May, 1846, he was ousted from the *Morning News,* and a few weeks later he sold his interest in the *Democratic Review.* His legacy, however, was unmistakable. He had provided a catchphrase for a concept that was as old as the nation itself, even older. In that sense, the hapless New York journalist exerted an influence beyond measure on generations of historians, politicians, polemicists, and writers of all sorts who have used, misused, even abused the phrase he unwittingly contributed to the American idiom. Indeed, it has been taken for granted to such an extent, twisted and turned to fit so many circumstances, that it has assumed a life of its own. Much of its original meaning and intent has hence been lost.

What has not been generally recognized, if it is known at all, is that there was nothing in O'Sullivan's statements to suggest territorial expansion by force, as some latter-day historians have insisted. His Manifest Destiny was nonviolent. As a New York legislator in 1841, he had proposed the creation of a Congress of Nations that could resolve international disputes peaceably, a proposal that placed him near, if not within the ranks of, the American peace movement. His last words for the *Morning News* deplored the outbreak of the Mexican War (as befit a supporter of Martin Van Buren), but like many of those who were disturbed by the war, he soon came to terms with it because he felt it would benefit both nations in the long run.[5]

Because O'Sullivan employed *Manifest Destiny* with reference to the annexation of Texas and the adjustment of the Oregon boundary dispute, the phrase has been narrowly applied to territorial expansion alone. The operative word, however, was *Destiny.* By adding the adjective, O'Sullivan was simply saying that the nation's destiny was "obvious to the understanding."[6] The belief that the United States was guided by a providential destiny, in other words, that the nation had a preordained, God-sanctioned mission to fulfill, formed a significant element in American Romantic thought. O'Sullivan's words reflected the boundlessness, the rejection of limits on national as well as individual development, and an impatience with anything that restrained or inhibited progress that characterized what the Romantics called the "spirit of the age." In both his statements of Manifest Destiny, he used the language of Romanticism, objecting in the first instance to the "thwarting . . . hampering . . . limiting . . . checking" efforts of the European monarchies, and in the second instance rejecting the limitations of history and law that blocked the nation's mission to possess the continent God had provided for the development of "the great experiment of liberty and federated self-government" he had "entrusted to us." It was destiny, moreover, that tied territorial expansion to the American mission. Mission and expansion were inseparably linked by Manifest Destiny.[7]

O'Sullivan's paean to destiny and mission, without which his Manifest Destiny can be only imperfectly understood, appeared in one of his most revealing tributes to the promise of Romantic America, the often overlooked article "The Great Nation of Futurity," published in the *Democratic Review* in 1839, six years before he coined his famous phrase.[8]

"Our national birth," he announced at the outset, "was the beginning of a new history." Separated from the past by their adoption of an "untried political system," Americans connected only with the future. "The far-reaching, the boundless future," he declared, "will be the era of American greatness." To O'Sullivan, the "everlasting truth" of the Declaration of Independence, the founding charter of the United States, was in its articulation of "God's natural and moral law of equality." America, he asserted, "is destined to manifest [note the juxtaposition of words] to mankind the excellence of divine principles." That was the nation's mission. "We are the nation of human progress, and who will, what can, set limits to our onward march?" The answer was indisputable: "No earthly power can," for "Providence is with us." There were no limits.

Although the truth upon which the nation's political and social system was founded would "work out [America's] glorious destiny," O'Sullivan warned that there were still some circumstances that threatened to inhibit progress. It was the "tendency to imitativeness" among the country's intellectual and literary spokesmen that was "subversive of originality of thought, and wholly unfavorable to progress." Too many Americans were behind "the mind and movement of the age in which they live." In keeping with his purpose in the *Democratic Review,* he issued a vigorous call for an American national literature, one that would "breathe the spirit of our republican institutions" and be imbued with the "elevating principle of equality." When, he asked, would the country's literature "assert *its* independence, and speak the soul—the heart of the American people . . . inspired by the magnificent scenery of our own world, imbibe the fresh enthusiasm of a new heaven and a new earth, and soar upon the expanded wings of truth and liberty?" In his own soaring rhetoric, O'Sullivan struck a refrain that had been voiced at least since Noah Webster had admonished Americans to be as independent in their literature as they were in their politics.

The mission of democracy was also the mission of The Democracy. The future of the nation, O'Sullivan contended, lay with the "mechanical and agricultural population," wherein beats the national heart. His Jacksonian persuasion permeated his language. He inveighed against the power and privilege of moneyed interests that "shrink to nothing when brought in conflict against the rights of individuals." O'Sullivan's faith was in the "virtue, intelligence and capability of the people."

O'Sullivan concluded his peroration with an effusion of Romantic sentiment as he summoned his fellow Americans to heed the responsibilities that the nation's mission and destiny imposed upon them. "We must onward to the fulfilment of our mission—to the entire development of the principle of our organization—freedom of conscience, freedom of person, freedom of trade and business pursuits, universality of freedom and equality. This is our high destiny. . . . All this will be our future history, to establish on earth the moral dignity and salvation of man—the immutable truth and benefi-cence of God."

There is an Emersonian ring to O'Sullivan's statements that not only be-speaks a familiarity with the sentiments of the Concord sage but also ac-knowledges a substantive influence. Just a month before Manifest Destiny was first introduced to its readers, the *Democratic Review* published an en-thusiastic review of Emerson's volume of essays, its authorship attributed simply to "A Disciple." "No man is better adapted than Emerson," the re-viewer concluded, "to comprehend the spirit of the age and to interpret its mission." It was a time when the "range of observation both in space and time is infinitely expanded," when men aspire "to a future that shall confirm the great idea of unlimited progress"; Emerson was its spokesman, prophet, and philosopher. One recent scholar has concluded that Transcendental thought, of which Emerson was the principal representative, gave Manifest Destiny its ideological base, by popularizing geographical determinism, the active role of Divine Providence in the nation's destiny, the natural progress of the human race, and the superiority of the Anglo-Saxon race in promot-ing that progress.[9]

Early in 1844, Emerson sharpened his Romantic appeal when he ad-dressed the Boston Mercantile Library Association with a lecture he titled "The Young American," in which he called upon the country's young men to assume the leadership in fulfilling the national mission. "In every age of the world," he pointed out, "there has been a leading nation," one whose citizens were dedicated to just and humanitarian goals. "Which should be that nation," he asked, "but these States?" And "who should be the leaders, but the Young American?" The United States, "new-born, free, healthful, strong . . . should speak for the human race." He urged Young America to take advantage of the unifying power of America's remarkable technological development—"Railroad iron is a magician's rod, in its power to evoke the sleeping energies of land and water"—and its expanding trade and com-merce to build "a new and more excellent social state than history has recorded" and to create a "high national feeling" and "lofty counsels that rightfully stir the blood." Guided by a "sublime and friendly Destiny," the United States, he said, is the "country of the Future . . . a country of begin-nings, of projects, of vast designs, and expectations. It has no past: all has an onward and prospective look." Emerson reminded his audience that "the bountiful continent is ours, state on state, and territory on territory, to the waves of the Pacific sea."[10]

Although the concept of Manifest Destiny was not new to mid-nineteenth-century America, its impact on popular thought during those midcentury years was. It drew sustenance from the pervasive currents of a popular Romanticism, and credibility from the dynamic political, social, and economic changes in American life that were spawned by a new spirit of optimism and self-confidence. Manifest Destiny combined a fervent, idealistic, even mystical expression of Romantic nationalism with the realistic, practical consequences of extraordinary technological and economic developments as well as an unprecedented movement of Americans to distant parts of the continent. Indeed, it was the latter that gave the former its credibility. The dramatic expansion of the United States in the 1840s, the realization of the long-sought-for "ocean-bound republic," marked the apogee of American Romanticism; and it was the war with Mexico that seemed to win a place for the United States in the sweep of world history.

Manifest Destiny must ultimately derive its meaning and significance from the cultural environment of which it was a primary ingredient. To ignore the historical and cultural context is to court oversimplification, if not downright distortion. It has not been an easy prescription. "A vast complex of ideas, policies, and actions is comprehended under the phrase 'Manifest Destiny,'" Ernest Lee Tuveson has written. "They are not, as we should expect, all compatible, nor do they come from one source."[11]

Not only were the lives of Americans changing rapidly and dramatically in a myriad of economic and social ways—the rise of an industrial establishment and the mass production of consumer goods, technological improvements in transportation and communication, the growth of cities, and an increasing flow of immigrants from Europe—but midcentury Americans were also reaching out beyond their borders to learn more of other lands and peoples, all of which gave impetus to expressions of Manifest Destiny. The expansion of commerce, an increase in travel made possible by steam power on sea and land, and a heightened interest in exploration were carrying Americans to the far corners of the globe. Clipper ships shortened the time between the East Coast and China, while large bulky wagons lumbering to northern Mexico turned the Santa Fe trail into a busy highway. Fur traders and mountain men roamed the northern and central Rockies, gradually penetrating the Pacific Northwest and California, while a flourishing coastal trade brought New England merchants to California's shores. Whaling vessels from New England's ports carried the American flag into the Pacific and Indian oceans.

The government followed with an active promotion of global exploration to expand knowledge of some of the world's remote areas, to strengthen American commercial activity, and, perhaps most important, to demonstrate the ability of a republic to pursue peaceful expansion with vigor and energy. The most ambitious effort was the United States Exploring Expedition, or Wilkes Expedition, comprising six naval vessels on a four-year voyage around the world, surveying and charting the west coast of South America, California, and the Oregon Country, the islands of the Southwest Pacific, and the waters of Antarctica, making contact with native peoples wherever possible. The expedition returned in 1842, loaded with an extensive collection of geological and botanical specimens. Naval expeditions to the Pacific Northwest, the Amazon Basin, Paraguay, and the west coast of Africa and the overland expeditions of John C. Frémont, beginning in 1842, expanded the horizons of Americans while stirring their romantic interest in nature, landscape, and native peoples.

At the moment O'Sullivan first employed the phrase *Manifest Destiny*, in the summer of 1845, three thousand Americans, drawn principally from the states of the Mississippi valley, were on the Oregon Trail moving to new homes in the lush western valleys of Oregon. Their arrival in Oregon would more than double the American population; by the following year, the number of emigrants from the United States had risen to seven thousand, and would continue to increase. A provisional government had been organized along the lines of an American state, replacing an earlier make-shift apparatus, in anticipation of a speedy admission to the American Union. At the same time, the number of Americans who had arrived in California by the overland trail reached four hundred, swelling the American population in that area. The numbers showed no signs of diminishing in subsequent years.

In the United States, a publication explosion made possible by steam-powered rotary presses and other technological advances, the development of a common public school system, and one of the highest literacy rates in the world brought all this activity within the reach of most Americans, adding credibility to even the most extravagant claims of Manifest Destiny's spokesmen. Countless travel narratives, one of the most popular literary forms of the time, enabled Americans to experience the world vicariously and to draw their own conclusions concerning their national identity and destiny.

The conjunction of Romanticism's emphasis on boundlessness, the republic's expanding role in the world, the movement of Americans to new and permanent homes in the far reaches of the continent, the advances in the economic and political environment that seemed to add up to progress, the humanitarian reform efforts to sweep away the obstacles to perfection, and the democratization of religious belief and salvation all gave impetus to the many and varied voices of Manifest Destiny. "The spirit of the time," wrote Emerson, "is felt by every individual with some differences—to each one casting its light upon the objects nearest to his temper and habits of thought."[12]

A belief in Manifest Destiny cut across partisan and sectional lines; Whigs as well as Democrats, Southerners as well as Northerners expressed it. Narrowly perceived as territorial expansion or viewed more broadly to encompass virtually every area of human behavior, Manifest Destiny moved Americans to aggressive action against their neighbors, or confirmed their passivity. Some were willing to risk war in order to achieve destiny's ends, others (like O'Sullivan himself) looked to peaceable negotiation and agreement. Still others advocated a do-nothing policy, like John C. Calhoun's famous gloss on Manifest Destiny as a policy of "wise and masterly inactivity," leaving the fulfillment of the American mission to the nation's "hardy pioneer stock," the thousands of settlers who were carrying American civilization to the shores of the Pacific. As one alarmed Briton warned, the real danger from the United States was "in the Settler . . . not in their Armies and Navies."[13]

For many reformers and Utopian visionaries, Manifest Destiny was racially motivated. Abolitionists, for example, rejected territorial expansion in the interest of slavery as Manifest Destiny gone wrong, while they found its justification in what they regarded as nobler ends, like the triumph of the Anglo-Saxon racial mission. Theodore Parker, the influential clergyman-abolitionist and co-editor with Emerson of the *Massachusetts Quarterly Review,* lauded the Anglo-Saxon race as the "most formidable and powerful" the world had ever seen before which all inferior races (he had Mexicans and Indians in mind) would inevitably be swept aside. The day was not far distant, he predicted, when the continent would fall to the "superior race, with [its] superior ideas and a better civilization." Parker's view was echoed later by James Russell Lowell when he declared that "it is the manifest destiny of the English race to occupy this whole continent."[14]

Of the many spokesmen for Manifest Destiny, none stands out like Stephen A. Douglas. The personification of Young America, Douglas made destiny and mission an everyday creed, combining the idealistic currents of

American Romanticism with a hardheaded political realism. He was not a systematic thinker in an abstract sense, and he rather distrusted ideologues whose commitments were usually focused on narrow goals. But he had a feeling for what he called the "spirit of the age" or the "genius of progress." "From early youth," he once recalled, "I have indulged an enthusiasm, which seemed to others wild and romantic, in regard to the growth, expansion, and destiny of the republic." He never lost that enthusiasm, although it was severely tested during the dark days of the secession crisis.[15]

As a member of the House of Representatives and as a U.S. senator from Illinois, Douglas bent his efforts toward converting that enthusiasm into positive legislative achievement. During his eighteen years in the national legislature, he dedicated himself to the fulfillment of the nation's democratic mission. The American Revolution, which severed the ties with a declining and decadent monarchical Europe and established a new, as yet untried republican government, made manifest a new and unique role in the world for the United States. Democracy, he declared, had a "mission to perform ... of progress in the arts and sciences—in the science of politics and government—in the development and advancement of human rights throughout the world." It was an awesome charge, one that required vigilance and exertion, perpetual action and undying energy, for the democratic process was not only fragile but also constant prey to the reactionary forces of European monarchism.[16]

To Douglas, the prospects for national growth were limitless. "You cannot fix bounds to the onward march of this great and growing country. You cannot fetter the limbs of the young giant. He will burst all your chains. He will expand, and grow, and increase, and extend civilization, Christianity, and liberal principles."[17] Taking stock of the nation's condition at the century's midpoint, he concluded that the United States had progressed faster and farther than any other country in the world, a sure sign that it was guided by a friendly providential destiny.

When Douglas first entered Congress in 1843, he carried with him a legislative program that called for the encouragement of migration to the far West, the planting of colonies along the trails, a free land policy for the settlers, the creation of territorial governments, and the construction of a Pacific railroad. He advocated the immediate annexation of Texas, demanded "all of Oregon" to 54°40' north latitude, supported the Mexican War (at one point considering volunteering as a soldier), and was disappointed that more territory had not been taken from Mexico in the treaty of peace. Territorial expansion carried out God's plan for the United States, in keeping with his intention to set aside the continent for the culture of republican principles.

There was more to Douglas's Manifest Destiny, however, than the extension of the nation's boundaries to the Pacific. The American mission demanded that the United States become the first nation in the world in the cultivation of the arts and sciences, in agricultural development, in maritime commerce, and in manufacturing. He sang the praises of the nation's inventive genius (which he attributed in part to a policy of unrestricted immigration) and recognized in technology—the "power of great conceptions, the aspiration and the will, the mental faculty and the manual skill"—a key element in the national destiny. Douglas was one of the first to support a system of national industrial universities that would enhance the United States's role as the center of the world's agricultural production and as the world's leading industrial nation. He was an active promoter of the magnetic telegraph and of railroad construction. To the amusement of his congressional colleagues, he sought appropriations for "aerial navigation," the construction of immense steam-powered balloons that could speed people and goods across the country. His concern for the promotion and dissemination of practical scientific knowledge was reflected in his long tenure as a regent of the Smithsonian Institution.

For all of Douglas's efforts, his vision of an expanding United States and his many attempts to translate that vision into programs and policies ultimately fell short of realization. After its peak at midcentury, Romanticism wavered and gradually lost much of its appeal. Boundlessness gave way to a new sense of limits, as sectional controversy tightened its grip on the thought and emotions of a nation that appeared to be drifting. Douglas died in 1861, a saddened and disappointed man; America's mission was unfulfilled, and the Union, the agent of progress, was itself in jeopardy. It is ironic that Douglas died just as the Civil War was getting underway, for it was the war between the sections that provided a new and vital forum for questions of Manifest Destiny and mission.[18]

A final irony, by way of a postscript: In February, 1859, a little over a month after he was defeated in his bid for Douglas's U.S. Senate seat, Abraham Lincoln addressed an academic audience at Illinois College in Jacksonville on the subject of "Discoveries, Inventions, and Improvements." The lecture apparently revealed his irritation at having been beaten by Douglas, for it began with an uncharacteristic outburst of sarcasm and mockery against Young America and Manifest Destiny.

"We have all heard of Young America," Lincoln began. "He is the most current *youth* of the age. Some think him conceited, and arrogant; but has he no reason to entertain a rather extensive opinion of himself? Is he not the inventor and owner of the *present*, and sole hope of the *future?*" A far-reaching commerce, Lincoln continued, provided Young America with the world's products. The latest technology was at his beck and call: steam power was "panting, and impatient" to carry him everywhere "in no time," and the "lightening" stood "ready harnessed to take and bring his tidings in a trifle less than no time."

Young America, Lincoln went on,

> owns a large part of the world, by right of possessing it; and all the rest by right of wanting it, and *intending* to have it. . . . Young America has "a pleasing hope—a fond desire—a longing after" teritory [*sic*]. He has a great passion—a perfect rage—for the "new." . . . He is a great friend of humanity; and his desire for land is not selfish, but merely an impulse to extend the area of freedom. . . . He knows all that can possibly be known; inclines to believe in spiritual rappings, and is the unquestioned inventor of "Manifest Destiny." His horror is for all that is old, particularly "Old Fogy"; and if there be any thing old which he can endure, it is only old whiskey and old tobacco.[19]

There was more, but these excerpts capture the lecture's tone. What is interesting is that while Lincoln ridiculed Young America's concept of Manifest Destiny, he was at that very moment embracing notions of destiny and mission that bore a striking resemblance to those of Manifest Destiny's spokesmen. Convinced that the United States was in danger of being converted into a slave empire, Lincoln issued an urgent call to heed the nation's destiny as a bastion of freedom and its mission to extend the promise of the Declaration of Independence, elevating Manifest Destiny to a lofty plane of republican virtue and morality. Every people, he declared in the language of the Romantic, expresses some "*central idea*," some basic principle from which all thoughts radiate. "The theory of our government," he contended, "is Universal Freedom." America's "genius" was embodied in its founding document, linking the hearts of liberty-loving men everywhere.[20]

Lincoln's embrace of Manifest Destiny and mission sustained his efforts to preserve the Union through the darkest days of the Civil War and offered hope to both a beleaguered people and those beyond our borders who saw in the Union's cause the promise of freedom for all mankind. It takes no great leap of the imagination to recognize that the most enduring statement of America's Manifest Destiny and mission was contained in those 272 words Lincoln uttered on the battlefield at Gettysburg on November 19, 1863.

NOTES

1. The best study of Manifest Destiny is still that of Albert K. Weinberg, *Manifest Destiny: A Study of Nationalist Expansionism in American History* (Baltimore: Johns Hopkins University Press, 1935; paper ed., Chicago: Quadrangle Books, 1963). Other studies are Ephraim Douglass Adams, "Manifest Destiny—An Emotion," in *The Power of Ideals in American History* (New Haven: Yale University Press, 1913), pp. 65–97, old but still useful; Edward McNall Burns, *The American Idea of Mission: Concepts of National Purpose and Destiny* (New Brunswick, N.J.: Rutgers University Press, 1957); Frederick Merk, *Manifest Destiny and Mission in American History: A Reinterpretation* (New York: Alfred A. Knopf, 1963); Norman A. Graebner, *Empire on the Pacific: A Study in American Continental Expansion* (New York: Ronald Press, 1955); Graebner, ed., *Manifest Destiny* (Indianapolis: Bobbs-Merrill, 1968); David M. Pletcher, "Manifest Destiny," in Alexander DeConde, ed., *Encyclopedia of American Foreign Policy*, 3 vols. (New York: Scribner, 1978), vol. 2, pp. 526–34; Ernest Lee Tuveson, *Redeemer Nation: The Idea of America's Millennial Role* (Chicago: University of Chicago Press, 1968); Reginald Horsman, *Race and Manifest Destiny: The Origins of American Racial Anglo-Saxonism* (Cambridge, Mass.: Harvard University Press, 1981); Anders Stephanson, *Manifest Destiny: American Expansionism and the Empire of Right* (New York: New York University Press, 1995); Michael A. Morrison, "The Eclipse of Manifest Destiny: The Ideology of American Expansion, 1844–1860," (Ph.D. dissertation, University of Michigan, Ann Arbor, 1989).

2. Robert Dean Sampson, "'Under the Banner of the Democratic Principle': John Louis O'Sullivan, the Democracy and the *Democratic Review*" (Ph.D. dissertation, University of Illinois, Urbana-Champaign, 1995), p. iii; Arthur M. Schlesinger, Jr., *The Age of Jackson* (Boston: Little, Brown, 1945), p. 372. Sampson's study is the best, most complete scholarly account of O'Sullivan's life and career.

3. [O'Sullivan,] "Annexation," *Democratic Review* 17 (July and August, 1845): 5–10, quotation, 5.

4. David M. Pletcher, *The Diplomacy of Annexation: Texas, Oregon, and the Mexican War* (Columbia: University of Missouri Press, 1973), p. 320; New York *Morning News*, December 27, 1845. See also two articles by Julius W. Pratt: "The Origin of 'Manifest Destiny,'" *American Historical Review* 32 (July, 1927): 795–98; and "John L. O'Sullivan and Manifest Destiny," *New York History* 14 (July, 1933): 213–34.

5. Sampson, "'Under the Banner of the Democratic Principle,'" pp., 181–82, 369–73.

6. Noah Webster, *An American Dictionary of the English Language* (New York: Harper and Brothers, 1845), p. 515.

7. Frederick Merk has taken an opposite position, insisting that Manifest Destiny (a trap into which the nation was led in 1846) and mission (idealistic, self-denying, a true expression of the national spirit) were separate and distinct, a position that cannot withstand close scrutiny. Merk, *Manifest Destiny and Mission in American History*, p. 261.

8. [O'Sullivan,] "The Great Nation of Futurity," *Democratic Review* 6 (November, 1839): 426–30.

9. "Emerson's Essays. By a Disciple," *Democratic Review* 16 (June, 1845): 589–602, quotations, 591, 602; Donald V. Gawronski, "Transcendentalism: An Ideological Basis for Manifest Destiny" (Ph.D. dissertation, St. Louis University, 1964), abstract in *Dissertation Abstracts* 25, no. 8 (February, 1965): 4663.

10. Ralph Waldo Emerson, "The Young American," *The Dial*, 4 (April, 1844): 484–507, reprinted in Robert W. Johannsen, ed., *Democracy on Trial* (2d. ed., Urbana: University of Illinois Press, 1988), pp. 4–18, quotations, 15, 12, 17, 18; John Q. Anderson, "Emerson's 'Young American' As Democratic Nobleman," *American Transcendental Quarterly* no. 9 (Winter, 1971): 16–20.

11. Tuveson, *Redeemer Nation*, p. 91. Tuveson, in seeking an answer to his question "When Did Destiny Become Manifest?," suggests the 1771 publication of Timothy Dwight's *America: or, A Poem on the Settlement of the British Colonies.* See ibid., p. 103.

12. Emerson "to the Reader of the Dial," July, 1840, in *Uncollected Writings* (New York: Lamb Publishing Co., 1912), pp. 32–33.

13. Calhoun, quoted in Charles M. Wiltse, *John C. Calhoun: Sectionalist 1840–1850* (Indianapolis: Bobbs-Merrill, 1951), pp. 107–108; Charles Elliot to Aberdeen, June 15, 1845, Ephraim Douglass Adams, ed., "British Correspondence Concerning Texas, XX," *Southwestern Historical Quarterly* 20 (October, 1916): 186.

14. Theodore Parker, "A Sermon of War, June 7, 1846," in *The Collected Works of Theodore Parker Vol.* 4, ed. Frances Power Cobbe (London: Trübner and Co., 1863), pp. 23–24; James Russell Lowell to Thomas Hughes, September 13, 1859, *Letters of James Russell Lowell*, 2 vols., ed. Charles Eliot Norton (New York: Harper and Brothers, 1894), Vol. 1, p. 296. See also Horsman, *Race and Manifest Destiny.*

15. *Washington Union*, January 9, 1853; Springfield *Illinois Daily Register*, April 8, 1851.

16. *Washington Union*, January 11, 1852.

17. *Congressional Globe*, 33 Congress, 1 Session, Appendix, 337 (March 3, 1854).

18. Robert W. Johannsen, "Stephen A. Douglas and the American Mission," in *The Frontier, The Union, and Stephen A. Douglas* (Urbana: University of Illinois Press, 1989), 77–102. See also John Higham, *From Boundlessness to Consolidation: The Transformation of American Culture, 1848–1860* (Ann Arbor: William L. Clements Library, 1969).

19. Second Lecture on Discoveries and Inventions, February 11, 1859, in Roy P. Basler, et al., eds., *The Collected Works of Abraham Lincoln*, 9 vols. (New Brunswick, N.J.: Rutgers University Press, 1953), Vol. 3, pp. 356–63.

20. Robert W. Johannsen, "Abraham Lincoln and the Universal Yankee Nation," in *Abraham Lincoln within the Context of American Culture: Papers from the Fifth Annual Lincoln Colloquium, October 20, 1990* (Springfield, Ill.: Lincoln Home National Historic Site, 1991), pp. 14–25.

Race, Progress, and Destiny

CALEB CUSHING AND THE

QUEST FOR AMERICAN EMPIRE

John Belohlavek

*It happens that men, nations, races, may, must, will perish
before us. That is inevitable. There can be no change
for the better save at the expense of that which is.
Out of decay springs fresh life.*

Caleb Cushing
Newburyport, April 23, 1857

This harsh, even brutal, vision of American expansion is not the view of a turn-of-the-century social Darwinian, but that of an antebellum Massachusetts politician, diplomat, reformer, and intellectual, Caleb Cushing. In a nation that prides itself on its domestic social liberalism—including progressive attitudes toward race, class, and gender—and its international democratic mission, Cushing's words rub raw our historical consciences. We have long exulted and agonized over the impact of "manifest destiny," the divinely ordained imprimatur that empowered the United States to expand across the continent. More recently, scholars such as Thomas Hietala and Reginald Horsman have sought to redefine America's destiny. Hietala contends that spread-eagle Americanism resulted from a calculated and rational "design," rather than a more ephemeral "destiny," while Horsman links the Anglo-Saxon roots of U.S. racism to expansion.[1]

Caleb Cushing figures prominently in this new historiography of American empire. No public figure argued the case for America's role in the world with more intellectual prowess, with more rhetorical skill, and—unfortunately—with a more caustic racial edge. Cushing's lengthy and controversial career serves as a mirror of both the man and a young republic struggling to define an identity as it sailed the treacherous waters from "union" to "nation."

Caleb Cushing, the scion of a prominent Massachusetts shipping family, was born in 1800 and graduated from Harvard at the age of seventeen. Possessing an eclectic mind that ranged widely from the sciences to the arts, he was a master botanist and a brilliant linguist. Certainly, he could have remained in Cambridge and commenced a teaching career. Instead, he entered the law, establishing a thriving practice in his hometown of Newburyport. A well-advised marriage to Caroline Wilde, the daughter of a state supreme court justice, solidified Cushing's career. A successful run for the state legislature at the age of twenty-four only whetted the young barrister's appetite for politics. He began his national career with a failed bid for Congress in 1826, but perseverance paid off in an eventual triumph as an anti-Jacksonian in 1834.

Cushing brought with him to the House of Representatives a reputation that had already made him a boy wonder in New England. Observers often described him as a handsome man of presence—standing almost six feet tall with strong manly features, dark brown hair, and hazel eyes. Two decades of public service as a legislator, diplomat, soldier, and cabinet member only enhanced that reputation. His contemporaries stood in awe of his intellect. Essayist Ralph Waldo Emerson, who did not suffer fools lightly, considered him the most eminent scholar of the era, while abolitionist cleric Wendell Phillips commented, "I consider Mr. Cushing the most learned man now living." House member Robert Winthrop wrote of his compatriot's "wonderful versatility . . . and prodigious intellectual and physical energy." Embodying the essence of the stereotypical Puritan, the indefatigable Cushing apparently needed only four hours of sleep a night.[2]

While Cushing impressed many of his contemporaries with his mental agility and rapier tongue in argument and debate, he often alienated those same individuals, who also perceived him as arrogant and self-serving. Politically unpredictable, he moved from one party to another, seemingly in response to a higher call that only he heard. Many depicted him as un-principled. Washington observer Benjamin B. French viewed Cushing as Machiavellian—"brilliant and cold as an icicle. A man of splendid intellect and of the best possible education, but of unbounded ambition." Senator Thomas Hart Benton of Missouri, a grizzled Democratic veteran, dubbed the New Englander as "unscrupulous, double-sexed, doubled-gendered, and hermaphrodite in politics with a hinge in his knee, which often crooks, that thrift may follow fawning." Poet James Russell Lowell satirized Cushing, who served as an officer in the Mexican war, in the *Biglow Papers:* "Gineral C. is a dreffle smart man; He's ben on all sides thet give places or pelf; But consistency still wuz a part of his plan,—He's ben true to one art and thet is to himself." John Quincy Adams, a fellow Harvard graduate and Whig member of the House of Representatives, lacerated his colleague with the simple observation, "Cushing has no moral principle."[3]

Historians have presented the same mixed image. Johanna Shields, who has examined Cushing as congressman, portrays him as a maverick, "mildly romantic" in politics, immodest, highly ambitious, and very intellectual. Roy F. Nichols, who has written widely on the mid-nineteenth-century Democratic Party, admits that the energetic Cushing possessed "vast learning on all subjects . . . and fairly dripped with erudition." He also exhibited "no stable principles, with a perverted instinct for seeking the winning side, who could change horses at will." In his history of the presidency of Franklin Pierce, Larry Gara describes Attorney General Cushing as the "Richelieu" of the administration, praising him for his hard work and the prestige and influence he added to the office. Diplomatic historian Paul Varg calls Cushing "an extremely able man" with a penchant for taking provocative positions. His talent and independent spirit, however, could not overcome his abrasiveness.[4]

Cushing emerges from the pages of nineteenth-century documents and twentieth-century texts as brilliant, complex, and unpredictable. Unfettered by party loyalty or long-term devotion to domestic issues such as national banks or protective tariffs, he did maintain one intense commitment—to the Union and its unlimited expansion. In 1821, the youthful Cushing delivered a July 4 oration in Newburyport in which he extolled "the constitutional and republican principles of the Federal Union universally disseminated, as the only method of giving a stable foundation to freedom, and delivering the world from the horrors of war." A decade later, as the shadow of nullification loomed large, Cushing told a hometown audience, "This Union is a vast fabric of political forethought, sagacity, and comprehension."

The Founding Fathers, through the letter and spirit of the Constitution, represented "the master minds of the new world."

Cushing believed that the unity of the United States ensured mankind's hope for free institutions and free government. If the Union failed, the impact had global dimensions. His "union" blended conveniently into nationhood. Nationhood was engendered by birth, but fostered by the ties of domestic life, community, and mutually protected and promoted interests. Cushing attributed Greek and Roman greatness to this "fiery, intense, all-pervading spirit of nationality, of patriotism, of zeal for country." "In the New World," he emphasized, "nationalism belongs to the very condition of man." Society logically improved by beginning with individuals, progressing to nations, and thence to mankind.

For Cushing, the United States's rise to national greatness, prosperity, freedom, and stability could be explained in one word: *land*. While other factors (race and religion among them) may have influenced American growth, Cushing stressed, "land is the footstool of our power; land is the throne of our empire." He saw the vastness of the continent as the generator of successful manufacture and commerce, but also as "the safety-valve for all the pentup passions and explosive or subversive tendencies of an advanced society." Although he refused to predict in 1850 where American empire might end, he warned that to "check it, stop it, shut it up, force it back upon itself" would jeopardize the Union.

An integral link existed between religion and the true progress of nations. In an 1838 address, Cushing conceded that although the Egyptians, Greeks, and Romans achieved advancements in the arts, knowledge, and government, they lacked the "elementary ingredient" of Christianity, which "has done and is doing so much more than any other single agent for the refinement and cultivation of the human race." He contrasted the "barbarism and social debasement" of Africa and Asia with the justice, humanity, and rule of law making itself felt in the courts of western Europe. Praising the status of women under Christianity, he noted that Western women were invested "with a sort of halo of immunity and respect" not found in Turkey or India. Christianity elevated the soul, promoted moral growth, and advanced modernity.

The United States emerged, not surprisingly, as "the highest civilization of Christendom." Americans demonstrated their superiority to Europeans in political institutions, scientific knowledge, and moral cultivation. Protestantism combined with constitutional liberty to create an American culture that encouraged both material and moral greatness. Cushing proudly compared the United States to those "nations, distanced by us in the race for wealth and power, who gaze on our marvelous progress with admiration and awe." In 1858, he boasted that the Europeans must now contend with the "colossal power" of the United States and taunted, "who may pretend that we have reached the zenith of our power? . . . The world is witness of our onward and upward progress thus far. But have we culminated? Is the age of our glory gone? Was that light of our power which rose so brightly, to blaze with a superlative splendor for a brief time only on high, and then to go down, leaving but a memorial ray behind it to make its disappearance beyond the mountain tops of death? It must and cannot be!"[7] Divine providence had intervened to place Americans on a fertile continent—a *tabula rasa* in which the wrongs of the old World might be righted, providing them their Christian faith and a strong Constitution as moral and governmental compasses for the long voyage ahead. The journey across North America could not have been completed, however, without the presence of a superior race of Anglo-Saxon peoples. At the age of eighteen Cushing confided to his diary that the Lockean notion of equality was simply word play: Nature, in fact, had given some people higher abilities and therefore higher rights. Thus, equality could never exist in practice. Cushing contended that a strong relationship existed between order and progress in a society. He disdained an unlimited democracy in which less cultivated and educated peoples could participate freely in the political process. To do so would destroy the liberties of the United States and the nation as a model for the rest of the world.

Cushing's doctrine of racial superiority manifested itself in numerous public speeches. In 1859, he angrily attacked the concept of racial equality before the Massachusetts House of Representatives:

> We belong to that excellent white race, the consummate impersonation of intellect in man, and of loveliness in woman, whose power and privilege it is, wherever they may go, and wherever they may be, to Christianize and to civilize, to command to be obeyed, to conquer and to reign. I admit to an equality with me, sir, the white man, my blood and race, whether he be the Saxon of England or the Celt of Ireland. But I do not admit as my equals the red men of America, the yellow men of Asia, or the black men of Africa.[8]

His remarks were met with tumultuous applause from the galleries.

Cushing's racism was, however, inconsistent and calculated. He alternately scorned and praised "inferior races." In 1838, during the midst of the

Cherokee removal crisis, he noted that Native Americans formed "the lowest stage of human condition." A decade before, Cushing had sentimentalized before a local audience, "the red races have melted away before you, as the dew vanished from the hillside beneath the rays of morning." They possessed no redeeming customs or characteristics save the ability to endure pain and suffering with stoic impassion. Some optimists, Cushing noted, applauded the Cherokees' development of a written language. He was not impressed, however, with this modest achievement after three hundred years of red-white contact. Returning to a favorite theme, Cushing attacked Indians for the debasement of women. The Indian could not rise above his present degraded state until "you teach him, until you compel him, if he will not be taught, to love, to cherish, and to respect woman, alike in peace and war."[9]

In 1832, buffeted by pressures from the administration of Andrew Jackson and the state of Georgia, Cushing adopted a new tack in his attitude toward removal. He transformed the Cherokees from "brutal and sottish barbarians" into "persecuted Indians" whose inhumane treatment defiled the national honor. They had established fixed communities and modeled themselves after Anglo society. Cushing consequently endorsed their pleas against the legal onslaught of Georgia in the United States Supreme Court. He lauded the bravery of the Seminoles of Florida and chided the Democrats for waging war against these "poor wretches." "Go, if ye dare, and ask of Oseola [sic], whether the red man wants courage or physical force to defend his native land." Nevertheless, he prophesied that Indians would inexorably be overwhelmed by more civilized whites. An absence of laws, inferior political organization, and the holding of common property doomed the Native American.

By the 1850s Cushing conceded that New Englanders may have been "needlessly severe" in their treatment of the native population, but he decried those who were mawkish about the Indians. Finding no real Hiawathas or Minnehahas among Massachusetts Indians, Cushing reaffirmed the "decrees of destiny" and the role of Anglo-Saxons "to cheer the hopes of mankind and spur on the system of progress."[10]

Cushing vacillated much less about African Americans. After a youthful flirtation with the Haitian slave revolt of the 1790s during which he praised the intellectual capacities of the black rebels, he settled onto a more politically viable path of denouncing slavery without advocating black equality or rights. The institution contradicted both Christian morality and democratic principle, creating a "plague-spot" that oppressed the liberties of blacks and dampened the spirit of enterprise of whites. "Slavery consigns the southern states to perpetual weakness and to perpetual discontent," Cushing declared in 1839, while liberty strengthened and enriched the North. Legendary black abolitionist Frederick Douglass told an audience, "Caleb Cushing was my first abolition preacher and teacher. . . . It was glorious to hear him, but he was only with us for a while." Cushing condemned slavery as a moral and political evil but argued that fealty to the Constitution prohibited direct interference with the institution in the South.

By the 1830s Cushing firmly embraced African American colonization as a solution beneficial to both races, contending that Christian expatriate slaves formed the greatest hope for the eventual civilization of Africa. His Jeffersonian vision of a republic of white yeoman farmers fell victim to the rise of the cotton kingdom. He doubted whether the nation could afford the huge sums for compensated emancipation and colonization, whether blacks would prosper in freedom, and if the Southern economy would be crippled by the loss of slave labor. Perhaps most important, his service in Congress and accompanying contact with Southern representatives convinced him that abolition tested the stability of the Union. In 1857, amidst the furor over the Dred Scott decision, Cushing denounced the "zealots" who promoted emancipation in spite of the bloody consequences in Haiti, Jamaica, and South America. Arguing that black freedom posed a curse for both races, Cushing warned that anarchy, barbarism, and misery would follow such social experimentation. The preeminence of the Union obliged Cushing and other Yankee contemporaries to swallow the bitter pill of bondage.[11]

In spite of his claim in 1859 that "yellow men" were inferior to whites, Cushing held a more sympathetic view of Asians than of Native Americans or African Americans. His journey to formally open United States relations with China in 1843 carried him across the Asian subcontinent. Cushing perceived Punjab males as "brave, intelligent, high-spirited, and patriotic," and "the women were models of Asiatic beauty and symmetry, of soft manners, and clear, though not dark olive complexion." He wondered, however, how 150 million people could be controlled by 60,000 Englishmen. The answer rested with a combination of forces. The "superior courage and intellect" of the Anglo-Saxons manifested itself in the British masters who militarily weakened the Indians by dividing the country into small principalities. The Indians contributed to their own subservience by perceiving Crown rule as providential destiny and perpetuating the divisive caste system. Cushing gave the English his grudging respect as a ruling race but speculated that the rise of the United States or France as a naval power could one day dislodge Britain from her control of key geopolitical possessions such as Egypt and India.

Although Cushing knew little about Hinduism before his voyage to the Far East, he had developed a deep affection for Chinese language and culture. An accomplished linguist, he taught himself Manchu to facilitate direct communication with the emperor's representatives. As an amateur historian and anthropologist, he observed that Americans tended to focus singularly upon their Greco-Roman roots and forget the existence of an "Asian antiquity." Yet as he traveled through the Middle East, India, and Malaysia, Cushing came to recognize that "the color line" defined other parts of the world as well as America. For the British, the combination of three white races (Celtic, Norman, and Saxon), languages, and laws produced an easy fusion into one people. In Asia (as in America) the races co-existed but were incompatible. Caste, religion, dress, food, legal, and moral codes kept them apart. Islamic conquerors of the subcontinent harbored no hope of melting the races. The European who followed them believed neither in the elevation of these "conquered inhabitants" to a position of equality nor in abdicating their own position of moral and intellectual superiority. Thus, European racism supplanted Islamic racism as a dominant force in the Near and Far East.

Cushing, observant and thoughtful, readily comprehended Chinese surrender to a superior military, not cultural, power. His six months in the Celestial Empire confirmed and expanded his preconceived notions. In October, 1845, Cushing spoke to an attentive lyceum gathering, where he lauded Chinese education, intelligence, and industry. Perceptively noting that the fundamental Chinese moral principle was the relation of authority and obedience between parent and child, Cushing faulted the Chinese for being "too epicurean" in their habits and government. If they could apply stronger discipline to the bureaucracy and develop their military skills, greatness was inevitable.

A quarter-century later, Cushing echoed almost identical sentiments of admiration and respect before a gathering of Chinese and U.S. dignitaries in Boston. He lavished praise upon the visitors, noting that they were a civilized power when "our forefathers were but half naked savages in the wilds of Britain or Germany." Cushing recognized Chinese contributions in literary, intellectual, and scientific pursuits—specifically mentioning printing and gunpowder. He praised the language and the stability of the empire over centuries—while never mentioning, of course, that the Europeans had been nibbling away at the country's periphery. Cushing admired the awesome legacy and power of Chinese culture, although he continued to disregard China's military prowess. Clearly, he envisioned an American empire that would reach across the Pacific ocean and might include in its grasp possessions such as the Sandwich (Hawaiian) Islands. While lacking the civilizing effects of democracy and Christianity, the Chinese demanded and received Cushing's respect and never became candidates for absorption.[12]

Cushing's views on progress, race, and empire formed early and juxtaposed nicely with his political ambitions and his family's involvement in shipping. Entering Congress in 1835, the novice representative from North Essex district quickly impressed his peers as a skilled and erudite, if long-winded, debater. He constantly pummeled the Jackson and Van Buren administrations for their maladroit handling of the economy before and after the disastrous Panic of 1837. Cushing made his mark, however, in foreign, not domestic affairs. During his first term, he was named to the Committee on Foreign Affairs, which he used as a soapbox to advocate United States expansion and simultaneously bash Great Britain.

Slashing at the many-tentacled hydra of the British Empire had become good politics in the United States by the 1830s. The Crown's military but especially economic might could be felt as close as Texas, Mexico, and Latin America and as distant as the Middle East, India, and China. Congressmen with an imperial bent could whip their constituencies into a frenzy with the vision (real or imagined) of Her Majesty's agents clipping the wings of the soaring American eagle. Addressing a Springfield audience in 1839, Cushing reproached the Democratic administration for its "gross and monstrous neglect" in not protecting United States interests on the West Coast. He called on Washington to move aggressively so the nation might attain its "natural boundary" on the Pacific ocean and give American merchants access to the enormous Asian markets.

In addition, the United States must guard the area from Great Britain, which was "ready enough at all times to lay her grasping hand upon every spot on the face of the globe which by fraud or force she can wrest from its true proprietors." Cushing denounced the methods of English imperialism, which forced people of alien religion, race, and language into a global empire in which they had no ties or interests. He contrasted Britain with Russia, endorsing the Czars' plan of annexing adjoining territory and drawing the predictable comparison with the United States in North America. Praising the various branches of the so-called Teutonic race (Dutch, German, Swedish, Saxon, and Norman) for their hardiness, resolution, perseverance, enterprise, and love of liberty, Cushing concluded: "I consider it the destiny of the United States to people, cultivate, and civilize this Continent; and I anticipate no end of her power until the appointed work be done."[13]

Cushing viewed Great Britain as the hoary, yet powerful, master, desperately seeking to contain its former charge within predefined geographic boundaries. Each time the fledgling republic attempted to expand, it encountered English resistance. Whitehall formed the root of U.S. problems, from meddling in the turn of the century Barbary Wars to intriguing in California and Central America. Fertile ground existed for conflict between the United States and Britain over the U.S. role in the Canadian rebellion, a half-century-old Maine boundary dispute, and the joint occupation of Oregon.[14]

Cushing's prediction of U.S. continental destiny no doubt did little to ease tensions. The abrasive congressman, who, Daniel Webster noted, "always liked to ride a charger," quickly emerged as a champion of the Upper Canada rebellion in 1837 against British rule. Referring to the provinces as "a conquered country," he drew frequent parallels between the U.S. and Canadian revolutions in their quest for self-determination. He derided British rule as "monarchy in its worst form" that had "grossly, wickedly, misgoverned" Canada. Cushing wistfully spoke of the provinces dropping "like a ripe fruit" from the colonial tree. Soon thereafter, a sister republic would evolve, representing an imperial blow to Britain and a boon to the United States. He told a correspondent in 1837 that a Canada free from English control would make the United States "absolutely impregnable to all the powers of Europe." From a strategic vantage point, the independence of Canada was "a thing whose importance it is impossible to exaggerate." Would Canada then become part of the United States? Cushing would not rule out the possibility. He advised that should the United States be drawn into a war with Great Britain over Canada, its government should be ready to act in the spirit of Article 11 of the Articles of Confederation, which provided for the equal admission of the provinces into the Union. Recognizing the explosiveness of Canadian annexation, Cushing quickly advanced the concept of a "Congress of Nations" in North America. The two republics, bonded by race, language, institutions, and ideas, would work together for the common good. "What a noble anticipation!" Cushing exulted, "What a glorious prospect!"[15]

Cushing penned letters to newspapers, wrote articles for journals, spoke in public and in Congress, and corresponded with Canadian rebels in advocacy of the revolution. In an oft-quoted speech, he theatrically implored,

"God of justice, where sleeps thy thunder?" His activities irritated the loyal press in Canada; it labeled his rhetoric as "clap-trap," the product of less than a "polished and shining mind," and dismissed his views as "narrow-minded" and "ignorant." Cushing maintained a regular correspondence with several of the rebellion's chieftains, including William Mackenzie, providing them with inspiration and encouragement, but never suggesting that the Americans would take an active military role. When the insurrection collapsed in 1837, Mackenzie felt betrayed and abandoned. He continued to write to Cushing into the early 1840s in a futile attempt to get the congressman to keep the pot of revolution boiling in Washington. Other issues, however, had displaced the failed rebellion at the fulcrum of Anglo-American relations.[16]

Cushing also emerged in the forefront of the long-standing boundary dispute between Maine and New Brunswick. As tension mounted in 1839, with border incursions fanning the flames of conflict, the congressman from Massachusetts delighted in twisting the lion's tail. He demanded of the British, "no more delays, no more procrastinations, no more diplomatic chicanery" in attempting to secure the Aroostook territory. Cushing strongly endorsed the legal merits of the United States claim, laying out his arguments in the *Democratic Review* in 1838.

He laid blame for the most recent border crisis at the feet of the Crown and its agent, the New Brunswick governor, Sir John Harvey. Again reproving Britain for its "all-grasping spirit of universal encroachment," Cushing warned that the day may soon arrive when the power of the two nations could not coexist on the same continent. He did not believe war would come at this time, but he added with bravado, if it does, "I will be found in the tented field, where death is to be met, or honor won, at the cannon's mouth." Such talk prompted *Democratic Review* editor John L. O'Sullivan to hearken back to the War of 1812 with the half-joking remark, "I hope you Federalists don't intend to kick the country into war again and then abandon it."[17]

Many of Cushing's colleagues viewed his Anglophobia somewhat suspiciously. Fellow Bay State nabob John Quincy Adams remarked, "Cushing thought that inflammatory declamation against England upon all possible topics was the short cut to popularity, and he speechified accordingly." Cushing recognized the resentment, but stood firm. He acknowledged his anti-English reputation to the House in 1839, agreeing that he had spoken on numerous occasions against Great Britain. He had done so, however, not out of hostility to the Crown, but rather because he perceived the United States as the object of its aggression. "Must I conceal it?" he pleaded, "May

I not speak out?" By 1840, the situation intensified and a concerned Cushing opined that war with Britain appeared imminent, but feared the American people were not "greatly stirred."

Fortunately for both powers, the Maine controversy did not escalate into war. Cushing's mentor, Daniel Webster, finally negotiated a settlement on terms favorable to the United States in 1842. Cushing, who blamed the decade-long delay on the diplomatic ineptitude of the Jackson—Van Buren dynasty, doubtless took both patriotic and partisan pleasure in its final resolution.[8]

Cushing further challenged the British on the Oregon issue. Although the two nations had explored the Pacific Northwest in the 1790s, little activity had initially occurred in the region beyond the competition of their respective fur companies. Following the War of 1812, as U.S. interest heightened in the area, diplomats concluded an Anglo-American compromise providing for joint occupancy. This accord became increasingly unsatisfactory, however, with the blazing of the Oregon Trail and accompanying settlement in the Willamette Valley. Cushing viewed the intrigues of the Hudson's Bay and Northwest Fur Companies with the Indians in the region as a Trojan horse for stifling U.S. advancement. He argued vociferously that continued American emigration westward would foster the progress of the Union and provide a safety valve that "frees us from all the dangers of poverty, and discontent, and consequent disorders, which always spring up in a community when the number of its inhabitants has outrun its capacity to afford due recompense to honest industry and ambition."[19]

In an hour-long speech in Congress in May, 1838, Cushing urged the establishment of a military post on the Columbia River to monitor the Indians and protect American commerce and agriculture in the region. Accusing the British of encroachment, he thundered, "Oregon is a country ours by right, ours by necessity of geographical position; ours by every consideration of national safety." Congress dawdled, but Cushing rapidly earned a reputation as a friend of northwestern expansion. The acerbic John Quincy Adams denounced his colleague's "ravenous appetite for the occupation of Oregon," but many Americans shared his hunger. Letters poured in praising the representative's courageous stance and denouncing the "lawless cupidity" of the Hudson Bay Company. Cushing did not falter. In January, 1840, he wrote a lengthy piece for the *North American Review* in which he trumpeted the strategic and commercial value of the territory and argued the possibility of its peaceful takeover.[20]

A more cynical observer might note that Cushing received constant prodding on the Oregon question from his father, who waxed optimistic about the commercial benefits to be gained from taking possession of Oregon and the entire West Coast. The family actively traded in the region. John N. Cushing divined the local possibilities for fishing, commerce, and agriculture, noting coyly its "nearness to China, Manilla [*sic*], and all the islands in the Pacific." The dutiful son promptly wrote Secretary of State John Forsyth in January, 1840, urging the formal opening of the China Trade.[21]

Unfortunately for the expansionists, joint occupation of Oregon continued through the mid-1840s. After his diplomatic triumph on the northeastern boundary, Daniel Webster appeared briefly optimistic about an Oregon settlement in February, 1843. He sought Cushing's advice on proposed negotiations, but the matter remained stalemated. Webster's resignation and the rapid refocusing of the administration on the Texas question placed the Pacific coast on the back burner.[22]

Cushing's eight years of service in Congress ended in the spring of 1843. While he had distinguished himself on the House Foreign Relations Committee and loyally supported nationalistic Whig economic measures, the political climate had changed dramatically. He endorsed the right of his constituents to petition Congress but had increasing reservations about the wisdom and constitutional validity of the abolitionist cause. Many of his constituents rejected this rather conservative mindset. Cushing also became thoroughly embroiled in the war between embattled President John Tyler and venerable Whig party leader, Senator Henry Clay. Cushing sided with the chief executive. This choice also proved unpopular in northeastern Massachusetts, where voters perceived Tyler as a states-rights turncoat and the wily Kentuckian as the likely choice for the 1844 Whig nomination. Pilloried by the press and under attack in local conventions, Cushing decided not to run for reelection in 1842.

As part of Tyler's inner circle, the so-called "Corporal's Guard," Cushing desired and deserved presidential favor. The Virginian attempted to reward his loyalty with a cabinet seat. In March, 1843, the president submitted Cushing's nomination as secretary of the treasury to the Senate three times—and each time it was soundly defeated. Clay's spear-carriers would have their revenge. Frustrated in his efforts to provide Cushing with a domestic appointment, Tyler considered the foreign options. Certainly, the merchant from Newburyport had long advocated a Chinese mission. In fact, the administration had already planned to dispatch Edward Everett, presently minister to England, on this delicate assignment. Everett's refusal permitted Tyler to select Cushing in his stead. The president slyly waited until the Senate adjourned for the spring session before announcing the controversial appointment.[23]

On May 8, 1843, Secretary of State Daniel Webster sent Cushing his instructions as the new envoy to China. The anti-Tyler press promptly labeled the choice "in opposition to the public will (and) in violation of the law of the land." John Quincy Adams dourly noted that it was Cushing's reward for his obsequiousness, while Henry Clay urged Senate rejection of the nomination. Some New York merchants believed that the blood tie between wealthy and powerful China trader John Perkins Cushing and the new minister provided an immediate advantage to the New England coterie. They sought to discredit Cushing by hinting that he and his family engaged in the illicit opium trade.[24]

Cushing, out of Congress and with no immediate prospects, eagerly grasped the offer. The opportunity presented itself to rebuild his somewhat tattered reputation and simultaneously ensure that the evil British would not monopolize the markets of the orient. U.S. trade with China had been an ongoing concern since the 1780s. The exchange—cotton, lead, ginseng, and opium for tea—had never been formalized. Mutual mistrust and misunderstanding, founded largely on cultural differences, clouded Sino-American relations during this half-century. Treaty protection of American ships, sailors, and goods hardly seemed necessary, however, until the outbreak of the Opium War between China and Great Britain in 1839. The successful prosecution of the war by Her Majesty's forces allowed the Crown access to four new ports. U.S. merchants, already troubled by English dominance in the opium trade, energetically lobbied the Tyler administration for a more vigorous Pacific policy.[25]

Conveniently for the merchants, the president banked his reelection hopes for 1844 on a successful foreign policy. Part of his strategy involved the "Tyler Doctrine," presented in his December, 1842, message to Congress, articulating U.S. commercial expansion into the Pacific. Demands for an independent Sandwich Islands and formalization of the China trade highlighted the doctrine. Webster considered the mission to be more significant than any that had "ever proceeded from this Country & more important than any other, likely to succeed it, in our days." Not everyone agreed. Democratic Senator Thomas Hart Benton ridiculed the venture, asking why Congress should appropriate $40,000 to give a U.S. diplomat the opportunity to "bump his head upon the ground nineteen times." Given specific instructions to avoid the "kowtow" ritual, Cushing clearly hoped to obtain guarantees to place U.S. merchants on an equal footing with those of other nations.

Unfortunately for some of the Yankee traders, the State Department also took an unequivocal position on the drug traffic, warning them not to participate. Many obligingly took the high road of moral indignation and ostensibly denounced the trade but ultimately could not resist the narcotic profits.[26]

Cushing departed the United States on the steam frigate *Missouri*, the most impressive vessel in the Navy, in late July, 1843. The voyage took him through the Middle East and India until he finally arrived in Macao in February, 1844. A war of nerves promptly commenced, a waiting game in which the minister attempted to bring the reluctant Chinese to the bargaining table. Still smarting from the recent humiliation at the hands of the British in the Treaty of Nanking (1842), the emperor understandably hesitated before granting further concessions to a Western power. Cushing exercised tact and patience. By mid-June negotiations began and took only two weeks to complete. Aided by the able medical missionary, Dr. Peter Parker, Cushing achieved his goals: the opening of five Chinese ports, the establishment of satisfactory trade regulations, and the promise of "extraterritoriality" for U.S. citizens living in China. The opium traffic, curiously, remained unresolved. However, reflections of the positive relationship that had quickly developed between Cushing and his Chinese counterpart, Keying, were clear. Keying wrote Cushing, "It is very seldom that persons are found like us two men, the same in heart and united in sentiments." He sent a Tartar cheesecake and a portrait of himself to the American as parting gifts; Cushing responded with a painting of John Tyler. Once back in Newburyport, Cushing christened a new brig the *Keying* and received a letter from the diplomat urging an ongoing correspondence between the two men.[27]

The Treaty of Wang-Hiya, signed on July 3, 1844, opened a new era in Sino-American relations. The jubilant Tyler approached ecstasy at the triumph. Both the president and Secretary of State John C. Calhoun agreed that Cushing should push on and negotiate with Japan. Although somewhat skeptical of the minister's success, both men were well aware that Cushing had earlier warned of English imperial designs to incorporate Nippon in its sphere of influence. Calhoun gave Cushing carte blanche to deal with Japan as he saw fit. Approval of the new mission, however, came too late—the diplomat had embarked on the voyage home in August, 1844.

Caleb Cushing had accomplished his goal. Within the decade Yankee clippers plied the China trade and Matthew Perry opened Japan to United States commerce. Observing in 1845 that no great power dominated the Pacific Ocean, Cushing correctly predicted that the United States would soon fill that void, Thomas Hietala notes that Cushing outlined the essential features of the Open Door policy fifty years before John Hay's celebrated notes appeared. For the shipper from Newburyport, American empire did not stop at the waterline.[28]

Returning home to encounter rising tensions with England, Cushing resumed his place as a leading Anglophobe. In a speech to a Boston Lyceum audience in October, 1845, he denied any harsh personal feelings toward Great Britain and then proceeded to blister the brutality of the British empire. The editors of the Boston *Journal*, who had come to hear the talk, noted Cushing's "fearless and independent tone," which was "somewhat characteristic of the speaker." They praised the "boldness and eloquence" of his words, noting that "he scored England without mercy." Cushing refused to place a definitive limit on American territorial empire, suggesting that it would advance no faster than could be done constitutionally and peacefully after other peoples were prepared to receive U.S. institutions. Recently renowned poet Edgar Allan Poe followed Cushing to the lectern, but the editors, put off by his "somewhat fanciful preface," departed before Poe began his recitation.

After his fall triumph, the Lyceum invited Cushing to return to deliver a lecture specifically on the Oregon crisis. He praised the vigorous, yet conciliatory nature of the James K. Polk administration while attacking the "pretensions" of Great Britain in the Northwest. Cushing urged a bold U.S. policy, confident that England, dependent on Yankee corn and Southern cotton, would be reluctant to fight over so remote an outpost. He defiantly told his audience, "it is not to be tolerated any longer that England should consider this continent the field for indulgence of her insatiable thirst of conquest and colonization." If war came, however, Cushing evinced no fear of Britain's might, suggesting that "there would be found many a gallant captain in the American navy to eclipse the fame of John Paul Jones, and, it may be, to sweep the British channel with a broom at the mast-head." Cushing's remarks received widespread attention in the U.S. and British press. Fortunately, rationality and good sense prevailed on both sides of the Atlantic. By June, 1846, the parties reached a compromise that allowed for a logical extension of the 49-degree boundary from the Rocky Mountains to the Pacific Ocean. This sound settlement enabled officials in Washington to turn their attention to the newly declared war in Mexico.[29]

Mexican-American tensions had increased in the decade since the Republic of Texas had won its independence in 1836. Although the Jackson administration had adopted a hands-off policy regarding the Texan Revolution, U.S. emigrants had led the rebellion against Mexican authority, and the

United States had recognized the independence of the Lone Star Republic in 1837. As a novice congressman from a region with a strong antislavery element, Cushing cautiously approached the Texas question. In May, 1836, he warned against the violation of U.S. neutrality and premature talk of recognition or annexation. But by summer he had joined a minority of New England congressmen who voted to recognize the new republic. The realization that many of his constituents saw Texas as a plot to extend the institution of slavery tempered his enthusiasm. Deluged by correspondence from concerned citizens and wary of voter reaction, he told a correspondent in mid-1837, "My present convictions are adverse to the admission of Texas into the Union."[30]

Torn between loyalty to his anti-Texas constituents and his fear of increased British and French presence in the region, Cushing's "present convictions" began to melt away. By 1839, he advised a Massachusetts audience that U.S. expansion into Mexican territory was inevitable and irresistible. Whether in the form of a separate republic or as part of the United States, lightly inhabited Mexican lands would lure "the daring and hearty pioneer." Sooner or later, that land would become the possession of the Anglo American.

When Cushing vacated his congressional seat in 1843, his departure proved a loss to both the chief executive and the pro-Texas forces. As one Lone Star diplomat noted in his correspondence about Cushing, "Though from the North, he was with us." John Quincy Adams, who opposed annexation, agreed, but from a differing vantage point, labeling his compatriot as "servile or dough-face" on the issue. Tyler finally managed to obtain the absorption of Texas into the Union—in March, 1845, at the conclusion of his administration and too late to have an impact on his presidential fortunes.[31]

While the annexation of the Lone Star Republic doubtless brought Cushing much satisfaction, his imperial mind could not rest with so much Mexican territory at risk. In November, 1845, he penned an oft-reprinted article for the New York *Courier* in which he responded to heightened fears about British and French penetration of California. Particular concerns had arisen over a supposed scheme by which English bankers would redeem their loans to the Mexican government by cashing in a mortgage on California. In words guaranteed to raise the anxieties of U.S. expansionists, Cushing argued that it would be advantageous to the Mexicans to rid themselves of such an unprofitable and disjointed part of the republic for relief of their massive debt. It would also benefit the creditors, who could then control the territory in an "East India Company" arrangement.[32]

Tensions along the Rio Grande River erupted into conflict in April, 1846. Cushing, now a Massachusetts Democratic state legislator, defended the righteousness of the American cause in a war "forced upon us by the violence and folly of the Mexican Republic." With an eye upon the West, rather than the Texas border, he declared, "the occupation of California is, itself alone, an event of the highest importance to the United States." In October, as the war expanded, the representative ominously warned that continued resistance on the part of the Hispanics might mean their victory "or else the end of the Mexican republic." Cushing rapidly emerged as the champion of an unpopular war. Not content with mere words, he urged the appropriation of $20,000 from the legislature for a volunteer regiment. Fellow politicos balked at the cause and the cost, prompting Cushing to lecture them about their duty to country and constitutional obligations. The Boston *Times* called the speech a "most eloquent and logical effort" to incite Bay State patriotism.

Whig legislators remained unimpressed, however, and Cushing angrily resigned his seat and spent $12,000 of his own money to help fund and organize a thousand-man unit. Naturally, he became the colonel. The regiment served in Mexico but never saw combat. Cushing, frustrated by his failure to win laurels on the field, took some solace in his promotion by the president to brigadier-general. Sneering Whigs mocked him, noting that the extent of his wounds was a broken ankle from falling in a ditch and that his greatest gallantry occurred in the pursuit of "the dark eyed Senoritas." Eager Democrats, however, welcomed his political rebirth and twice nominated him (1847 and 1848) for governor. Not surprisingly, he lost both times to Whig George Nixon Briggs.[33]

While Cushing took delight in the confidence of his new party, he reveled even more so in the success of the nation at war. The Treaty of Guadalupe-Hidalgo in 1848 ceded millions of acres of the Southwest and California to the United States. Some Americans had boldly advocated the absorption of all of Mexico into the Union. Cushing's views on annexation of Mexican territory rested on racial destiny. In 1845, he had crossed Mexico en route from his diplomatic mission to China. When he reached Washington, Cushing drafted a lengthy dispatch to Secretary of State James Buchanan in which he detailed his impressions of the Mexican character and climate. A generally flattering portrait of the resources of the nation emerged, but the nature of the people received sharp criticism. Cushing especially noted "the intolerant spirit of the Mexicans, and their ignorance, passion, or indiscretion in dealing with foreigners and foreign governments." Perhaps an attack and robbery by banditti, who stole his papers and personal possessions in the hinterland of Mexico City, negatively affected his views. Two years later, in accepting the Democratic nomination for governor, he remarked that the Mexicans were mired "in that stupid infatuation that characterizes her counsels and which has made of her government a marvel of crazy anarchy, [and] merited the contempt, the scorn of all other nations."[34]

Various correspondents, including historian William Prescott, championed the higher civilization of the Americans in advocating conquest. One writer wondered, "if the sword is drawn the Saxons of the west must ultimately find sleep in the Mexican capital. But what will England say?" Cushing himself pondered the question of the extent of American empire and its impact upon foreign relations and the Union. In 1850, as the nation struggled to resolve the issue of slavery in the new territories and the balance of political power between North and South, he editorialized against the Wilmot Proviso. The debate over slavery in the Southwest seemed a moot point. The institution and the arid climate were incompatible in the Mexican Cession, while beyond the Rio Grande inexpensive peasant labor made slavery unnecessary. "All Mexico needs in order to make her powerful and prosperous," he contended, "is not any importation of inferior races—whether Negro or other—but the organizing and developing energies of the Teutonic mind as we now see it exhibited in all its grand proportion in California, Deseret, and New Mexico." At this point, Cushing clearly weighed the advantages of U.S. annexation of Mexico yet realized that the addition of eight million free, dark-skinned, Catholic, Spanish-speaking people to the country would drastically upset the sectional and cultural balance.[35]

Eight years later, Cushing reevaluated his position, as the United States faced disunion following the debacle of "Bleeding Kansas" and Mexico became embroiled in civil war, inviting intervention from Spain, England, and France. In April, 1858, he told former President Franklin Pierce that an incursion into Mexico might be necessary to unite disputing political factions in the United States and preserve the nation. Six months later Cushing invoked the Monroe Doctrine before a Richmond gathering, telling the crowd that the government had a duty to intervene in Mexico rather than permit any European power to gain sway there. "Unhappy Mexico! . . . Miserable Mexico . . . it is not a question of conquest of a neighboring people, but of their salvation." Cushing did not rule out annexation, but the intense partisan climate of the prewar years doomed such extreme measures to failure.[36]

As Cushing began to see American empire extending beyond the Atlantic and Pacific coastlines in the 1850s, he naturally envisioned the Caribbean—

and especially Cuba—within that redefined perspective. James K. Polk had attempted to purchase the island in 1848 but found Spain reluctant to sell. Filibusters, soldiers of fortune who hoped to profit politically and economically from the capture of Cuba, began periodic invasions from U.S. bases with the tacit approval of many Southerners. The island already possessed a sizable slave population and grew labor-intensive crops. Cushing envisioned the addition of Cuba to the United States as the logical extension of Anglo-Saxon empire. It would also function to help preserve the Union by allowing for Southern expansion. Cushing flirted with the Cuban exile community in the United States—many of whom supported the filibusters and desired U.S. annexation. He became increasingly skeptical of this extralegal and unpredictable method of obtaining the island, however, and soon severed any ties. Instead, he told Edward Everett in 1852 that the Pierce administration would offer to purchase Cuba, and, failing in that effort, would pick a quarrel with Spain and invade the island.[37]

Cushing became the attorney general in the Pierce cabinet in 1853, and his prediction seemed not far off the mark. The president offered $130 million for Cuba, but Spain rejected the proposal. In March, 1854, when Spanish officials seized an American vessel, the *Black Warrior,* in Havana harbor for shipping violations, Cushing and Secretary of War Jefferson Davis began beating the drums for war. A combination of Spanish compromise and northern resistance, however, eliminated any hope that the expansionists might utilize this minor incident to catapult the nation into a conflict. Several months later an editorial appeared in the Washington *Daily Union,* the administration organ, presumably written by the attorney general. Arguing from the premise of self-preservation, the author contended that the United States had the ultimate right to seize the island if purchase failed. In October, 1854, U.S. ministers in Europe, perhaps not coincidentally, offered similar views in the "Ostend Manifesto." Yankees now conjured a "slave power conspiracy" to extend the dark empire into Mexico, Haiti, "and the valley of the Amazon," as well as Cuba. Such fears, combined with the sectional bitterness aroused by the Kansas question, destroyed any efforts to acquire the island. With the prospects of Southern expansion limited by the inability to add lands in Mexico or the Caribbean, the possibility of secession now seemed very real.[38]

Caleb Cushing clearly comprehended the disintegration of his beloved Union—and with it all hope for mankind. As he spoke to a Newburyport crowd in 1857, his voice mirrored a defiant desperation: "men, nations, races, may, must, will, perish before us." Cushing's vision of a lifetime—the United

States as the beacon of liberty and progress reaching across a continent and then seas, subsuming weaker cultures with the benefits of an enlightened Anglo-Saxonism to fulfill a grand global destiny—now seemed in peril. With the exception of an imperfect arrangement with Great Britain that created a stumbling block for American progress in the Isthmus, the United States had moved according to providential design. Now narrow-minded abolitionists placed a sentimental goal of black freedom in the path of that destiny by threatening the nation. Cushing believed that slavery could not be eradicated without war, a war that would destroy the Union.

In 1858, Cushing implored a New York crowd for a revitalized spirit of nationality: "We need only cast our thoughts to a few years forward in the march of events to the time when we shall be a hundred million and forty or fifty confederate states, to see how contemptibly insignificant are the controversies of the hour, how unworthy of the great destinies of the United States." A quarter-century of American politics and diplomacy had not essentially changed Caleb Cushing. He understood the immorality of slavery and its corrosive impact on the nation and its people—black and white—in the 1830s. While never an abolitionist, he vilified the institution and tried to represent his constituents' views fairly in Congress. Cushing withdrew from the antislavery fight when he realized that the crusade threatened a far more important goal—the expansion of the Union. Frederick Douglass felt bitterly deceived by his former hero and lamented in the late 1850s: "Mr. Cushing was then, as now, the same gifted, learned crafty, unscrupulous corrupter of the public heart. . . . (He) loves the Union, but not the objects for which the Union was formed. . . . quotes the great words of the fathers but only to excuse the sins of their children. . . . preserves the form, but murders the spirit of liberty." Initially for Cushing, the evolution of American empire seemed a natural, inevitable phenomenon. It helped him define his own and, more importantly, the nation's identity. After the Mexican War, Manifest Destiny took on additional meaning: it became a vehicle for preservation of the Union. Expansion became the glue that held the nation together.

Cushing fell victim to what historian Hietala calls "anxious aggrandizement." He altered his politics and his party. He abandoned the economic nationalism of Whiggery for the expansionist nationalism of the Democracy. This philosophical metamorphosis won him the sobriquet "opportunist" and the derision of many in the Bay State. Roy F. Nichols suggests that Cushing "was an active candidate for the distinction of becoming Massachusetts' most unpopular citizen."

There is considerable truth in this contention, but such attacks seemed not to scar him. He told a contemporary that without the Union there was nothing: "I have no desire to survive the overthrow of the United States government." Thus he continued undaunted in his pursuit of a higher calling for the United States. Cushing did not stand alone. He represented, perhaps better than anyone else of his generation, spread-eagle Americanism in all of its arrogance and aggressiveness. Cushing's vices—racism, cultural superiority, and militarism—have superseded his virtues—a passion for learning, reform, and the Union in our historical consciousness. His cool, tough demeanor, party shifts, and failure to express—or seemingly feel—the outrage of many Americans over slavery has lowered our estimation of one of the most intelligent and articulate men of his age.[39]

NOTES

1. Kenneth Stampp, *America in 1857* (New York: Oxford University Press, 1990), p. 194; Cushing speech at Newburyport, April 23, 1857, in *New York Times;* Claude Fuess, *Caleb Cushing*, vol. 2 (New York: Harcourt Brace and Co., 1923), p. 194. See also Frederick Merk, *Manifest Destiny and Mission* (New York: Random House, 1963) and *The Monroe Doctrine and American Expansionism, 1843–49* (New York: Random House, 1966); Bernard Weinberg, *Manifest Destiny* (Baltimore: Johns Hopkins, 1935); Bernard DeVoto, *1846:The Year of Decision* (Boston: Little, Brown, 1943); Norman Graebner, *Empire on the Pacific* (New York: Ronald Press, 1955); Thomas Hietala, *Manifest Design* (Ithaca: Cornell University Press, 1985); and Reginald Horsman, *Race and Manifest Destiny* (Cambridge: Harvard, 1981).

2. Caleb Cushing Diary, 1818, Box 198, file 5, Cushing MSS, Library of Congress; Margaret C. Christman, *Adventurous Pursuit: American and the China Trade, 1784–1844* (Washington, D.C.: Smithsonian, 1984).

3. Donald Cole and John McDonough, eds., *Witness to the Young Republic: A Yankee's Journal, 1828–1879*, entry for March 13, 1855 (Hanover, N.H.: University of New England Press, 1989), p. 255; William Meigs, *The Life of Thomas Hart Benton* (1904; New York: Da Capo Press, 1970), p. 511; James Russell Lowell, ed., *The Poetical Works of James Russell Lowell* (Boston: Houghton, Mifflin, 1890), p. 180; C. F. Adams, ed., *The Memoirs of John Quincy Adams*, vol. 11, entry for August 21, 1842 (Philadelphia: J. Lippincott, 1874–77), p. 226.

4. Johanna Shields, *The Line of Duty: Maverick Congressmen and the Development of American Political Culture, 1836–1860* (Westport: Greenwood Press, 1985), pp. 124–126, 180–181; Roy F. Nichols, *Franklin Pierce* (Philadelphia: University of Pennsylvania Press, 1958), pp. 249, 537; Larry Gara, *The Presidency of Franklin Pierce* (Lawrence: University of Kansas Press, 1991), pp. 69–71; Paul Varg, *New England and Foreign Relations* (Hanover, N.H.: University Press of New England, 1983), 161–62.

5. Cushing speeches at Newburyport, July 4, 1821, July 4, 1832, July 4, 1850, Cushing MSS, Library of Congress.

6. Benjamin F. Butler, eulogy on Cushing to the Judges of the Circuit Court (Boston, 1879); Cushing address to the American Institute in New York, October 20, 1836; Cushing speech at Newburyport, July 4, 1850; Cushing address to the Essex Agricultural Society, December 1850, Cushing MSS, Library of Congress.

7. Cushing lecture on American Culture and Institutions, Boston, August, 1834; Cushing "Discourse on Social Influences of Christianity," Providence, R.I., September, 1838; Cushing speech at Newburyport, July 4, 1850; Cushing speech to Tammany Society, July 5, 1858; Cushing speech to Boston Colonization Society, July 4, 1833, Cushing MSS, Library of Congress.

8. Cushing Diary, 1818, Box 198, file 5; Cushing speech before the Library Society of Amherst College, August 23, 1836; Cushing speech to the Massachusetts House of Representatives, February 11 1859, Cushing MSS, Library of Congress.

9. Cushing, "Social Influences of Christianity"; Cushing, address to the American Institute; Cushing, Newburyport address, July 4, 1822, Cushing MSS, Library of Congress.

10. Cushing, January 31, 1831, to Reverend John Cleaveland; Cushing, Newburyport Addresses, March 13, 1832, July 4, 1832; Cushing on the Seminole War, September 19, 1837, *Congressional Globe Containing Sketches of the Debates and Proceedings of the 25th Congress lst Session*, vol. 14, p. 642; Cushing speech on "Material Growth and Territorial Progress," Springfield, Mass., July 4, 1839; Cushing address to the Newburyport Lyceum, November 25, 1857, in the Newburyport *Herald*, November 28, 1857, Cushing MSS, Library of Congress. Cushing later defended the civil rights of Indians, especially in relation to African Americans, in legislative debate. Cushing speech at Newburyport, October 31, 1857; Cushing remarks to the Massachusetts House of Representatives, February 8, 1859, Cushing MSS, Library of Congress. Cushing earlier defended the Cherokee because of politics—his dislike for Andrew Jackson and the Democrats—and the threats to the Constitution and the Union posed by the aggressive states' rights posture of Georgia in violation of national treaties with the Indians.

11. Cushing, "Hayti," *North American Review,* January, 1821, p. 112, January, 1829, pp. 150–166; Cushing to the American Colonization Society, Boston, July 4, 1833, Cushing MSS, Library of Congress; William Freehling, *The Reintegration of American History* (New York: Oxford University Press, 1994), 1149–150; Cushing, "Material Growth and Territorial Progress;" Cushing memo on slavery, ca. 1835, Box 222; J. Flournoy, March 29, 1839, to Cushing; Cushing speech at Faneuil Hall, Boston, October 27, 1857, Cushing MSS, Library of Congress. John Blassingame, ed., *The Frederick Douglass Papers,* Series 1, vol. 3 (New Haven: Yale University Press, 1985), p. 368.

12. Cushing, December 3, 1843, to A. P. Upshur, Dispatches, China, #23, Department of State, National Archives; *Memoirs of John Quincy Adams,* vol. 12, December 29, 1845, p. 227; Newburyport *Herald,* October 13, 1845; Philadelphia *Inquirer,* November 26, 1845; Cushing speech at reception of the Chinese Embassy, Boston, August 20, 1868, Cushing MSS, Library of Congress.

13. Cushing, "Material Growth and Progress"; Kinley J. Brauer, "The United States and British Imperial Expansion, 1815–1860," *Diplomatic History,* 12 (Winter, 1988): 19–37.

14. Cushing, January 30, 1838, to R. Greenhow; J. O'Sullivan, April 4, 1840, to Cushing, Cushing MSS, Library of Congress.

15. D. Webster, April 23, 1842, to E. Everett, Everett MSS, Massachusetts Historical Society; Varg, *Foreign Relations,* p. 137; Cushing, "Material Growth and Progress," T. J. Brown, November 13, 1837, to Cushing; Cushing, December 3, 1837, to Brown (?); Cushing, MSS, Library of Congress; Cushing, July 11–14, 1837, to Gov. E. Everett, Boston *Daily Advertiser.*

16. Cushing editorial, New York *Express,* August 17, 1837; Cushing speech, Boston *Courier,* October 18, 1839; Montreal *Morning Courier,* October 30, 1839; E. B. O'Callaghan, February 7, 1838, to Cushing, Cushing MSS, Library of Congress. In spite of his loyal Whiggery, Cushing wrote for the new and aggressively expansionist *Democratic Review.* See September, 1838, pp. 29–49; J. O'Sullivan, November 11, 1837, January 13, 1838, to Cushing; Cushing, January 11, 1838, to O'Sullivan, Cushing MSS, Library of Congress. Cushing wrote a series of letters on the Canadian question for the New York *Daily Express* under the pseudonym "Nov-Anglus," December 12, 1837—January 2, 1838. William MacKenzie, November 24, 1839, March 9, 1841, February 17, 1843, to Cushing; Cushing, December 26, 1840, to Mackenzie; Cushing, August 11, 1842, to D. Webster; C. Duncombe, September 5, 1842, to Cushing, Cushing MSS, Library of Congress. The best recent work on the subject is Kenneth Stevens, *Border Diplomacy: The Caroline and McLeod Affairs in Anglo-American-Canadian Relation, 1837–1842* (Tuscaloosa: University of Alabama Press, 1989).

17. Varg, *Foreign Relations,* 137; "Poplicola" (Cushing), December 11, 1837, New York *Commercial Advertiser;* Cushing, July 11–14, to Governor E. Everett, Boston *Daily Advertiser;* Cushing remarks, February 25, March 2, 1839, *Congressional Globe,* 25th Congress, 3rd Session, vol. 7, pp. 230, 269. J. O'Sullivan, July 19, August (?), 1838, to Cushing, Cushing MSS, Library of Congress. Massachusetts also had a vested territorial interest in the settlement of the border dispute dating back to the peace treaty of 1783. See Commonwealth of Massachusetts Resolutions concerning the Northeastern Boundary, March 21, 1839, Cushing MSS, Library of Congress.

18. *Memoirs of John Quincy Adams,* vol. 11, December 10, 1841, pp. 37–38; Cushing remarks, March 3, 1839, *Congressional Globe,* 25th Congress, 3rd Session, vol. 7, p. 269. Cushing notes for speech "A Spy in Washington," 1841; Cushing, April 1, 1840, to H. A. S. Dearborn, Chamberlain MSS, Boston Public Library, quoted in Arthur B. Darling, *Political Changes in Massachusetts, 1824–1848* (New Haven: Yale University Press, 1925), p. 260

19. Cushing remarks, March 6, March 9, March 19, May 17, May 22, 1838; *Congressional Globe,* 25th Congress, 2nd Session, vol. 6, pp. 231, 242, 565–70.; Varg, *Foreign Relations,* 168; Cushing, "Material Growth and Progress."

20. *Memoirs of John Quincy Adams,* vol. 9, May 17, 1838, p. 535; vol. 11, January 30, 1843, p. 304; W. Allen, June 3, 1838, to Cushing; S. Whitcomb, June 10, 1838, to Cushing; F. Baylies, June 16, 1838, to Cushing; Cushing, December 26, 1838, to J. Poinsett; W. A. Howard, November 17, 1842, to Cushing; S. Reed, November 26, 1842, to Cushing; G. LeBreton, December 1, 1843, to Cushing, Cushing MSS, Library of

Congress. Cushing remarks, May 17, May 22, 1838, *Congressional Globe,* 25th Congress, 2nd Session, vol. 7, pp. 565–70; Varg, *Foreign Relations,* 168; Cushing, "Discovery Beyond the Mountains," *North American Review* 50 (January, 1840): 75–144. See Frederick Merk, *The Oregon Question* (Cambridge: Harvard University Press, 1967).

21. John N. Cushing, February 2, 1837, December 20, 1838, November 15, 1842, to Caleb Cushing; Cushing, December 8, 1845, to the editors of the St. Louis *Reveille;* Cushing, January 9, 1840, to J. Forsyth, Cushing MSS, Library of Congress; Varg, *Foreign Relations,* p. 168.

22. D. Webster, February 24, 1843, to Cushing, Cushing MSS, Library of Congress.

23. E. Everett, September 3, October 10, 1842, to Cushing; D. Webster, March 12, 1843, to Cushing; D. Webster, March 12, 1843, to T. Curtis, Cushing MSS, Library of Congress.

24. D. Webster, May 8, 1843, to Cushing, Charles Wiltse, ed., *Papers of Daniel Webster: Diplomatic Papers,* Series 3, vol. 1 (Hanover: University Press of New England, 1983), pp. 922–26; *Memoirs of John Quincy Adams,* vol. 11, July 3, 1843, p. 388; H. Clay, January 24, 1844, to J. J. Crittenden, in Melba P. Hay, ed., *Papers of Henry Clay,* vol. 10 (Lexington: University of Kentucky Press, 1991), 4–5; New York *Morning Courier,* January 20, 1844; Varg, *Foreign Relations,* 155–56; C. Hall, November 30, 1844, to J. C. Calhoun, in Clyde Wilson, ed., *Papers of John C. Calhoun* vol. 20 (Columbia: University of South Carolina Press 1991), pp. 405–11.

25. C. W. King, December 29, 1840, July 3, November 12, 1841, to Cushing; J. Balch, March 25, 1840, to Cushing; C. J. Everett, April 6, 1840, to William Wetmore, Cushing MSS, Library of Congress.

26. *Diplomatic Papers of Daniel Webster,* vol. 1, pp. xxv–xxvi, 877–84; Norma Peterson, *The Presidencies of William Henry Harrison and John Tyler* (Lawrence: University of Kansas Press, 1989), 142–43; H. Legare, June 12, 1843, to Paul Forbes; C. W. King, May 29, 1843, to Cushing; John Peters, July 13, December 17, 1843, to Cushing, Cushing MSS, Library of Congress.

27. Varg, *Foreign Relations,* pp. 158, 163–64; Robert Seager, *And Tyler, Too: A Biography of John and Julia G. Tyler* (New York: McGraw-Hill, 1963), p. 211; Cushing, August 10, August 13, 1844, to Keying; Keying, July 26, September 25, 1844, January 23, 1845, to Cushing, Cushing MSS, Library of Congress. The necessity and results of Cushing's mission to China have been extensively debated. William J. Donahue in "The Caleb Cushing Mission," *Modern Asian Studies* 16 (1982): 193–216, praises Cushing, whom he calls an "able diplomat," for the commercial success of the mission. Kenneth Ch'en, "The Cushing Mission: Was It Necessary?," *Chinese Social and Political Science Review* 8 (1939): 3–14, contends the mission was unnecessary since trade rights were already in operation. More traditional sources include Kenneth Latourette, *History of Early Relations between the United States and China, 1784–1844* (New Haven: Yale University Press, 1919); Tyler Dennett, *Americans in East Asia: A Critical Study of United States' Policy in the Far East in the Nineteenth Century* (New York: Barnes and Noble, 1922); John Downs, *The American Trade with the Far East: The China Trade and Its Influence* (New York: Macmillan

Company, 1941); and Richard E. Welch, Jr., "Caleb Cushing's Mission and the Treaty of Wanghia: A Review," *Oregon Historical Quarterly* 58 (December, 1957): 328–57.

28. Tyler, August 3, 1844, to Calhoun, *Calhoun Papers,* vol. 19, pp. 510–11; Calhoun, August 15, 1844, to Cushing, ibid., p. 589; Cushing, August 24, 1844, to Calhoun, ibid., pp. 649–53; Cushing, December 27, 1842, to Tyler, Cushing MSS, Library of Congress; Newburyport *Herald,* October 13, 1845. Although Cushing was aware of the intense commercial rivalry between the United States and Great Britain in many parts of the world—including the Far East—he acknowledged the excellent treatment he received from British officials throughout his voyage. Everett, May 14, 1844, to Calhoun, *Calhoun Papers* vol. 18, pp. 505–508; Calhoun, August 9, 1844, to Everett, ibid., XIX, p. 548; Hietala, *Manifest Design,* p. 93.

29. Boston *Journal,* October 18, 1845; Fuess, *Cushing,* vol. 2, pp. 23–26.

30. Cushing remarks, May 16, 1836, *Congressional Globe,* 24th Congress, 1st Session, vol. 12, pp. 3726–27; J. W. Stuart, July 26, August 1, 1837, to Cushing; Cushing, July 28, 1837, to J. W. Stuart; Cushing, July 28, 1837, to Rev. H. Wright; Rev. H. Wright, August 1, 1837, to Cushing; D. Bagley, August 1, 1837, to Cushing; Cushing, August 7, 1837, to D. Bagley; New Bedford Citizens, August 30, 1837, to Cushing; Cushing, August 7, 1837, to William Balch, Cushing MSS, Library of Congress.

31. Cushing remarks, December 31, 1838, *Congressional Globe,* 25th Congress, 3rd Session, vol. 7, pp. 81–82; *Memoirs of John Quincy Adams,* vol. 10, entry for June 14, 1838, p. 18; vol. 11, entry for February 23, 1843, p. 330. The Massachusetts legislature passed resolutions opposing Texas annexation on March 16, 1838. Cushing, "Material Growth and Progress"; I. VanZandt, March 15, 1843, to A. Jones, in L. G. Tyler, ed., *Letters and Times of the Tylers,* vol. 3 (New York: Da Capo Press, 1970), p. 129; Cushing, February 5, 1845, to P. George, Cushing MSS, Library of Congress.

32. *Niles National Register,* November 8, 1845, from the New York *Courier.* Cushing's father also pushed for the acquisition of San Francisco or other Pacific ports. J. N. Cushing, February 27, 1845, to Cushing, Cushing MSS, Library of Congress.

33. Cushing speech to the Massachusetts legislature, January 8, 1847, in the Washington *Daily Union,* January 22, January 29, 1847; Newburyport *Daily Advertiser,* July 28, 1848; New York *Tribune,* November 11, 1853. James Russell Lowell also laughingly commented, "Caleb haint [got] not monopoly to court the seenoreetas," *Poetical Works,* p. 176.

34. Memoir on the Mexican Republic, Cushing, March 22, 1845, to J. Buchanan, Dispatches, China, #108, p. 21; Cushing, April 20, 1846, to J. Buchanan; Cushing, October 18, 1847, to Democratic Nominating Committee, Cushing MSS, Library of Congress.

35. W. Prescott, April 7, 1848, to Cushing; C. Palmer, August 14, 1845, to Cushing; H. Wilde, February 25, 1848, to Cushing; M. J. Smith, December 5, 1847, to Cushing; Cushing, December, 1850, to the *National Intelligencer;* Cushing, thoughts on Mexico, undated, Box 381, Cushing MSS, Library of Congress.

36. Cushing, April 9, 1858, to F. Pierce, Cushing MSS, Library of Congress; *New York Times,* November 1, 1858.

37. Cushing, June 15, 1850, to G. Madan; G. Madan, July 10, August 13, 1850, to

Cushing; R. Stewart, February 15, 1854, to Cushing; A. Harris, September 2, 1854, to Cushing; M. H. Grinnell, October 23, 1854, to Cushing; A. J. Gonzalez, June 20, 1854, to Cushing; C. A. Stetsin, December 13, 1854, to Cushing, Cushing MSS, Library of Congress. E. Everett Diary, November 3, 1852, quoted in Alan Dowty, *"The Limits of Isolation": The United States and the Crimean War* (New York: New York University Press, 1971), pp. 51–52.

38. Gara, *Pierce,* 151; Nichols, *Pierce,* 353; Declaration of the Worcester, Massachusetts, Convention, July 20, 1854, Cushing MSS, Library of Congress.

39. See endnote 1 of this chapter; Stampp, *1857,* p. 194; Blassingame, ed., *Frederick Douglass Papers,* vol. 4, p. 231. Cushing, July 5, 1858, to Tammany Society, Cushing MSS, Library of Congress; Nichols, *Pierce,* p. 248; B. F. Butler, "Cushing eulogy."

"This Splendid Juggernaut"

WESTWARD A NATION

AND ITS PEOPLE

Thomas R. Hietala

Many prominent politicians in the United States during the 1840s envisioned a magnificent destiny for their country and its people. They viewed the unprecedented territorial acquisitions of that time as a clear manifestation of both national and racial superiority. Though they stressed noble democratic ideals in their quest for more land, markets, and ports while urging the annexation of Texas, the acquisition of Oregon, the conquest of Mexico, and the ongoing removal of Native Americans, their pleas contained rank prejudice as well as lofty principle. Fiercely self-righteous and nationalistic, they seldom doubted the purity of their motives or methods.

Not all voices, however, sang in unison or harmony. Some who observed the dramatic events of the Jacksonian era offered a more nuanced interpretation of westward expansion and its consequences. Among them was George Catlin, a painter who traveled and dwelled extensively among Native Americans during the decade preceding the expansionist surge of the mid-1840s. Like many contemporaries who served in Congress or penned editorials, Catlin believed that the rise and fall of nations and peoples in North America was unfolding in accordance with a divine plan, a destiny made manifest in the relentless dispersion of restless pioneers and the cumulative record of expansionist leaders. Yet Catlin realized that this process looked radically different from opposite sides of the frontier. He condemned Indian removal and rejected the expansionists' smug assumption of Anglo-Saxon superiority and Native American inferiority.

To Catlin the clash of cultures and peoples was complicated and ambiguous, hardly reducible to a catchphrase like *Manifest Destiny*. He lamented the onslaught that had confined the Native American to a rapidly diminishing refuge between the expanding Anglo American frontier and the Pacific coast. "I have seen him shrinking from civilized approach, which came with all its vices, like the dead of night, upon him," Catlin observed in 1842. "I have seen him raised, too, in that darkness, religion's torch, and seen him gaze and then retreat like the frightened deer that are blinded by the light." Aware of many virtues in the whites' way of life, Catlin nevertheless stressed how "all its vices" had nearly destroyed the Native. "I have seen him set fire to his wigwam, and smooth over the graves of his fathers," the artist recalled. "I have seen him . . . with tears of grief sliding over his cheeks, clap his hand in silence over his mouth, and take the last look over his fair hunting grounds, and turn his face in sadness to the setting sun."

Who, then, were these trappers, traders, soldiers, and settlers who drove the Natives toward "the setting sun" in their ambitions to tame and transform the West? Unlike the proponents of Manifest Destiny, Catlin saw an unsavory side in the politicians and pioneers who sought dominion over the land and its peoples. "I have seen as often, the approach of the bustling, busy, talking, whistling, hopping, elated and exulting white man, with the first dip of the ploughshare, making sacrilegious trespass on the bones of the valiant dead," Catlin reflected. "I have seen the skull, the pipe, and the tomahawk rise from the ground together, in interrogations which the sophistry of the world can never answer." He expected the onslaught to continue. Soon, he predicted, the red race would survive only on canvas and paper. "I have seen thus, in all its forms and features, the grand and irresistible march of civilization," Catlin noted. "I have seen this splendid juggernaut rolling on, and beheld its sweeping desolation."[1]

Whatever his limitations as an artist and ethnographer, Catlin recognized that one nation's glorious destiny necessitated other people's decline and demise. Moreover, he realized that the harsh realities of cultural contact, violence, and removal of natives often belied the grand principles of those who excused the actions of the United States and its people. He doubted the Jacksonians' argument that removal best served the needs of tribes relocated to the West. "I believe the system one well calculated to benefit . . . the voracious land-speculators and Indian traders; the first of whom are ready to grasp at their lands, as soon as they are vacated—and the others, at the annuities of one hundred and twenty thousand extravagant customers," Catlin objected. "I believe the system is calculated to aid these, and perhaps to facilitate the growth and the wealth of the civilized border; but I believe, like everything else that tends to white man's aggrandizement, and the increase of his wealth, it will have as rapid a tendency to the poverty and destruction of the poor red men; who, unfortunately, almost seem doomed, never in any way to be associated in interest with their pale-faced neighbours." While defenders of removal emphasized the government's desire to protect and improve the Natives, Catlin detected other, more sordid, motives at work. Traders and diseases had ravaged the Natives for two centuries. "And no one but God," Catlin lamented, "knows where the voracity of the one is to stop, short of the acquisition of everything that is desirable to money-making man in the Indian's country, or when the mortal destruction of the other is to be arrested, whilst there is untried flesh for it to act upon, either within or beyond the Rocky Mountains." Though powerless to stop the juggernaut with his pen and brush, Catlin at least reminded his readers that their country had compiled "an unrequited account of sin and injustice" in dealing with Indians. U.S. citizens, "everywhere proud of their growing wealth and their luxuries," had, Catlin concluded, become "cruel dispossessors" who would ultimately have to atone for their manifold wrongs. A rare voice in the 1840s, Catlin refused to join in the refrain of mindless racism and nationalism.[2]

If Catlin has not been heard by later generations, perhaps his cry has been drowned out by journalist John L. O'Sullivan, who coined the phrase *Manifest Destiny* in mid-1845. Historians often pay homage to O'Sullivan by referring to the 1840s as "the decade of manifest destiny." This label, however, tells us little about the actual dynamics of expansion at the time. Nor does it capture the complexity of O'Sullivan's own arguments for new lands and markets. Like other antebellum Americans, O'Sullivan contended that God sanctioned the ambitions of politicians, publicists, merchants, and adventurers who hoped to secure the continent, exploit its resources, accrue wealth, and enhance national security. Where true believers saw the hand of the almighty, however, skeptics detected the grasping fingers of mere mortals such as James K. Polk, Robert J. Walker, Lewis Cass, Stephen Douglas, and O'Sullivan himself.

That fate favors some nations and peoples over others might comfort the consciences of the winners, but leaders in the 1840s were too impatient to allow fate to run its course. O'Sullivan, for example, predicted in 1845 that the United States would soon acquire California in the same way it had just garnered Texas. American pioneers would venture to California, shed the yoke of Mexican rule, then seek annexation. "Texas has been absorbed into the Union in the inevitable fulfilment of the general law which is rolling our population westward," O'Sullivan wrote in July, "in . . . connexion . . . with that ratio of growth in population which is destined within a hundred years to swell our numbers to the enormous population of *two hundred and fifty millions* (if not more), is too evident to leave us in doubt of the manifest design of Providence in regard to the occupation of this continent." O'Sullivan offered a more sweeping vision of empire three months later. "We . . . prophecy the rebellion, revolution, and independence of New Mexico, Chihuahua, California, and Yucatan, at no very distant period," he predicted in October. "Such a result is certainly more probable than was the ascertained destiny of Texas ten years ago."[3]

O'Sullivan proved too impatient, however, to allow pioneers to wrest the borderlands from Mexico. When soldiers from the United States and Mexico clashed in the disputed territory north of the Rio Grande River in the spring of 1846, he initially deplored the bloodshed. "We are," he warned on May 26, "in all probability, on the threshold of a long, troublesome, destructive, and expensive war." But O'Sullivan realized the potential advantages in this conflict. He advised that U.S. strategy not be "confined to the defense of our own territory." The aim, he counseled, should be "the immediate acquisition of California."[4]

To attribute the unprecedented expansion of the United States to Manifest Destiny obscures more than it clarifies. It fails to convey the impatience and anxiety of U.S. leaders. Nor does it explain their willingness to resort to war to enlarge the union. Their concerns were commercial as well as territorial, their ambitions global, not just continental or hemispheric. The means became secondary to the ends; negotiation, bluster, intrigue, and conquest all served to extend the empire. With considerable haste the expansionists largely attained their goals. Yet they struggled to reconcile rapid aggrandizement with their belief in American innocence. In many ways they reflected the nation as a whole—optimistic yet anxious; brash but insecure; generous while also petty and vindictive; progressive but nostalgic for a romanticized past. These seemingly contradictory strains in American thought and life defined the 1840s and helped precipitate the hasty acquisition of a continental empire.[5]

George Catlin recognized two of the principal factors that drove this juggernaut to the Rio Grande River and the Pacific Ocean. He emphasized racial and economic considerations in his writings on the clash of cultures: white Americans regarded themselves as racially superior to Native Americans, and they believed that they could utilize the rich resources of the continent better than the Indians did. Whites represented civilization, but Native Americans symbolized savagery. Catlin wrote mainly about the encounter between Native Americans and newcomers, but his insights also help explain the tension with Mexico, the conquest of the borderlands, the march to Mexico City, the occupation of the capital, and the extensive territorial demands included in the peace treaty.

Two additional factors complemented the racial and economic elements stressed by Catlin. By the mid-1840s, many politicians and publicists regarded the U.S. system of distinct and diverse states joined together to form an effective but limited national government as the ideal blueprint for a vast empire. They went further, arguing that previous acquisitions had greatly strengthened the union and aided its people. New states and a diffuse population protected rather than imperiled liberty. In addition, they hailed technological innovations in travel and communication as ideal servants of empire. The steamship, the rotary press, the railroad, and the telegraph would bind the disparate parts of the expansive republic into a greater Britain destined to surpass and defy rival empires. Yankee ingenuity could make a continental empire more compact and cohesive than the original thirteen states had been at the time of George Washington's inauguration.[6]

As Catlin knew, Americans of West European ancestry in the 1840s were an extremely race-conscious people. Anglo-Saxons stood at the top of the great chain of being; Africans, Native Americans, and any nation that had mixed the races—Mexico, for instance—were clustered at the bottom. From president to army private, from senator to settler, white Americans regarded peoples of African and Asian origin with distaste, even disdain. This rampant bias made Indian removal palatable to most Americans. It provided a sanction for the explosive growth of the slave population during this period. Such prejudice (along with an appetite for expanded markets) lay behind Cushing's "opening" of China in 1844. Last but not least, the repugnance toward Mexicans helped Americans justify the conquest of the borderlands and the campaign that brought Winfield Scott's army to Vera Cruz, then on to Chapultepec and Mexico City.

Journalists and political leaders savaged the Mexicans during the war, attributing U.S. military successes to the corruption of the enemy's church and state, the cowardice of its soldiers, and the degeneracy of its people. A month after Congress declared war, editor James Gordon Bennett of the

New York Herald absolved the United States of blame for the bloodshed while also linking critics of President Polk's policies to the abolitionists. "It is absurd to refer the imbecility and degradation of the Mexican people to any other cause than the amalgamation of races, and there is no doubt that this same deterioration of national character would follow the success of abolition doctrines in this country," Bennett contended. "The idea of amalgamation has been always abhorrent to the Anglo-Saxon race on this continent. Wherever they have spread themselves, they have kept aloof from the inferior races, and the result is . . . that barbarism has receded before the face of civilization. It is the manifest destiny of the Anglo-Saxon race to people this vast continent."[7]

Democrats who supported the war echoed Bennett's views on Mexico and its people. "The truth is," Senator John Fairfield of Maine complained, "the Mexicans are a rascally, perfidious race. No reliance can be placed in their most solemn compacts. They are little better than a band of pirates and robbers." The halls of Congress echoed with such denunciations. "Rapine, plunder, and the spoils of conquest seem to be the only sentiment that animates the bosom of her people," Orlando Ficklin of Illinois told the House when urging the annexation of Texas. "They are most emphatically a sordid and treacherous people." The passions of war inspired further attacks. "The masses are inert, idle, ignorant, degraded, and superstitious," Ficklin declared in early 1848, "and have for centuries been the dupes and timid slaves of an army of cunning priests."[8]

An article in the *Democratic Review* suggested that the Mexicans' future could be read in the history of Native Americans who had once occupied all of North America. "The Mexican race now see, in the fate of the aborigines of the north, their own inevitable destiny," a writer noted in 1847. "They must amalgamate and be lost, in the superior vigor of the Anglo-Saxon race, or they must utterly perish. They may postpone the hour for a time, but it will come, when their nationality shall cease." Other expansionists repeated this refrain. "The aboriginal races, which occupy and overrun a portion of California and New Mexico," Senator John Dix of New York predicted in early 1848, "must there, as everywhere else, give way before the advancing wave of civilization, either to be overwhelmed by it, or be driven upon perpetually contracting areas, where, from a diminution of their accustomed sources of subsistence, they must ultimately become extinct by force of an invincible law."[9]

Congressman Thomas Turner of Indiana drew a parallel between Indian removal in the Ohio Valley and his country's acquisition of Mexican land.

"It is probably true that the Mexican people would prefer to keep their territory," Turner conceded in 1848, "but is it not equally true that the Indian tribes would have preferred to keep their territory?" Turner recalled "with what reluctance" Native Americans had ceded their lands. "I witnessed myself the removal of the Pottawatomies, the Winnebagoes, and the Sioux," he explained, "and however it may wound the pride of Mexico to yield to us California and New Mexico, it will not wring their hearts as it did the hearts of those savages when they turned their eyes for the last time upon their council fires and the graves of their fathers." Like other expansionist Democrats, Turner demanded a vast territorial indemnity from Mexico.[10]

Soldiers in Mexico serving under Generals Zachary Taylor and Winfield Scott expressed similar views. They at least could rely on personal observation. But often they rushed to judgment, an indication that they carried preconceptions and racial prejudices with them to Mexico. George McClellan, an 1846 graduate of West Point and a second lieutenant in a company of engineers, arrived at the Rio Grande in November. Near Matamoros McClellan offered his first impressions of the land and its people. "Cotton appears to grow quite plentifully on the banks, but is not cultivated at all," he recorded in his diary. "The Mexicans appear to cultivate nothing whatever but a little Indian corn (maize). They are certainly the laziest people in existence—living in a rich and fertile country . . . they are content to roll in the mud, eat their horrible beef and tortillas, and dance all night at fandangos."[11]

From Puebla, Lieutenant Ralph Kirkham, a New England native, conveyed his impressions of the local inhabitants to his wife, Kate. "Nine-tenths of the people resemble the Cherokee Indians as much as possible," he wrote in 1847. "The lower classes, which embrace at least nineteen-twentieths of the whole population, are poor, miserable beings who are as ignorant and superstitious as it is possible to be." Women worked hard, but their idle husbands quickly spent whatever money they had. "The majority of the Mexicans seem rather to vegetate than otherwise," Kirkham concluded. "The rascally priests live well enough. . . . They are a grand set of rogues." Additional time in Mexico merely hardened his opinions. "But I suppose there is no nation on earth where there is so much wickedness and vice of all kinds," Kirkham wrote from Mexico City in November. "There is little incentive to virtue here. How little of that pure and holy religion which our blessed Savior taught is to be found in this country. No one could believe how low and depraved these people are, and instances are common of men selling their wives and sisters, and often their mothers and daughters. The clergy, generally, are very immoral and ready to stoop to the very lowest acts of villainy and wickedness."[12]

Often at odds with officers and recruits in the standing army, the volunteers from around the country found little to dispute in the regulars' harsh views of Mexican race, character, and religion. Thomas Barclay, a volunteer from Western Pennsylvania, pondered the significance of his country's rapid advance through Mexico and the conquest of its capital. Mexico's "downfall is inevitable," he predicted shortly after the sounds of "Yankee Doodle" heralded that *los norteamericanos* had occupied the halls of Montezuma:

> It will not take place at present but the time is approaching and the young of the present generation may see the day when the "Stars and Stripes" which now float in triumph over the City will be the banner under whose folds the inhabitants of all Mexico will find shelter and protection. The Anglo Saxon race, that land-loving people, are on the move. In an incredible short time they have overrun an immense territory in the north. Long since have wishful eyes been cast towards the fertile plains of Mexico. And the same people who have driven before them the various Indian tribes and have in Texas come in contact with the Spanish race will soon hang like a wave over the province of Mexico. No embankments, no treaties can prevent the inundation. A contest between the races will follow and the Anglo Saxons have never been conquered. If they once obtain a footing, entire possession will be the result.

Barclay hoped that the victory of the United States would hasten the demise of "the Church and the Army" in Mexico, two institutions that allowed "neither commerce, manufactures, or agriculture [to] flourish."[13]

Franklin Smith, a captain of Mississippi volunteers, also predicted that enterprising pioneers from the north would transform the Rio Grande Valley. "The land from Matomoras [*sic*] to Camargo all along both sides lies high [and] is well adapted to cultivation, and when the Anglo Saxons get to work on it will lay the region of the lower Mississippi in the shade," he wrote in August, 1846, while sailing the river. "Let the government do as it may, the Americans will in a few years occupy both banks of this River along the whole levee. The darkness flies before the sun; Laziness, cowardice, and ignorance must give way before industry, courage, and intelligence." Further exposure to the country and its people bred more contempt. "Everything proves that the Mexicans as a people are capable of any treachery, bribery, corruption, fraud, and robbery," Smith noted in October. "There is and must be in every country . . . [a] civilized class that has pride of character—the men honourable—the women virtuous, but in Mexico this class must be smaller than in any other country called *civilized*."[14]

Many U.S. soldiers anticipated scant resistance from Mexican troops and predicted a quick victory once the war began. En route to join Taylor's forces near Matamoros, Lieutenant Napoleon Dana expressed this bravado to his wife, Sue. "If we come to the fight our men will fight well and no mistake, and when we commence we expect to see some tall walking on the other side," Dana wrote. "We will make them run to the tune of 'Yankee Doodle,' the black rascals. The best of them are robbers and murderers, I believe." Four months into the war Dana longed to be with his wife again, but he advised her not to venture south of the Rio Grande. "Mexico is about the last place I want you to travel to," he counseled. "It is a mean, miserable, dirty, good-for-nothing place, at least so much of it as we have seen." From Tampico in early 1847, Dana contradicted *New Orleans Picayune* reporters who had written of the beauty of Mexican women. "It is all a lie, or else these people have very strange tastes," he assured his wife. "Indeed I believe I have seen mulatto girls in the United States as good looking . . . as any I have seen in Mexico. And as for ugliness, I have never seen any old Negro half so hideous and disgusting in appearance as very many of the wretched hags of this ill-famed race. . . . [T]he brown order of Mexican women as a race . . . are without exception the most revolting, forbidding, disgusting creatures in the world, not even excepting our own Indians."[15]

Two weeks before the skirmish that sparked the war, Lieutenant William S. Henry heard rumors that Mexican troops had crossed the Rio Grande to attack Taylor's army. "That is all we ask of them," Henry declared. "Cross and fight us, and we will exterminate them." After Taylor's outnumbered forces won stunning victories at Palo Alto and Resaca de la Palma, Henry predicted that his fellow Americans would inevitably occupy Northern Mexico. "It certainly never was intended this lovely land, rich in every production, with a climate that exceeds any thing the imagination can conceive of, should remain in the hands of an ignorant and degenerate race," he observed. "The finger of Fate points, if not to their eventual extinction, to the time when they will cease to be the owners, and when the Anglo-American race will rule with republican simplicity and justice . . . and populate the country with a race of men who will prove the infinite goodness of our Maker in creating nothing but what is for use and some good purpose." Critical of the local people, Henry nevertheless praised the area's soil and climate. "Young people should come here to make love," he advised, "and the old should emigrate and rejuvenate themselves."[16]

Politicians, scribes, and soldiers seemed to read from the same script. They repeated similar views, often using the very same adjectives to describe Native Americans and Mexicans. Whether "savages" or "greasers," the lesser breeds appeared lazy, treacherous, dull, and backward. They occupied valuable lands they neither appreciated nor developed. They had no concept of good government, no grasp of science and technology, no work ethic, no respect for real religion. Because of their weakness, Native Americans and Mexicans could not halt the juggernaut of progress. Not even the U.S. government could control its citizens. The volunteer soldiers who invaded Mexico would form the vanguard of settlement, then civilian pioneers from the states would follow. Federal negotiators might temporarily define new borders between antagonistic races, but enterprising Americans would defy those boundaries and wrest land and resources from those with a tenuous hold on them.

Racism and ethnocentrism alone did not precipitate Indian removal, the acquisition of Texas and Oregon, and the war against Mexico. Peoples deemed inferior held valuable lands, and Catlin's "avaricious" Americans coveted them. Catlin's contemporaries worried as much about economics as they did about race. Anxieties and ambitions drove them to seek economic advantages by adding territory, opening markets, acquiring ports, and attaining a monopoly over cotton and grains. Expansionists feared that industrialization might fasten "white slavery" upon the nation's landless workers. Hoping to avoid sharp class stratification and labor unrest, the neo-Jeffersonians of the 1840s viewed expansion as a panacea for the ills of modernization.

Editor John Jones, the voice of the Tyler administration in the capital, warned in 1843 that wage slaves in industry posed a greater danger to the country than slaves on Southern plantations. "In the thickly settled parts of our non-slaveholding states, the condition of the poorer class of population is fast assimilating itself to that of the servile class in Europe," Jones wrote in the *Daily Madisonian*. "Already they are but hewers of wood and drawers of water to their wealthier brethren." John O'Sullivan shared this anxiety. "Already is the corporate factory system beginning to produce in the United States that depth of distress which has long excited the horror of every observer of the condition of Lancashire," O'Sullivan observed in 1845. Mill owners ruled "with an iron hand" and "cut down wages at their pleasure, until the miseries of Lancashire are reproduced in New England."[17]

Fearful of manufacturing and urbanization, the expansionists supported aggressive policies to extend the national domain. Senator Lewis Cass of Michigan, an ardent proponent of Indian removal, the acquisition of Texas and all Oregon up to 54°40′, and the seizure of all Mexican territory north of the Sierra Madre mountains, defended Polk's war and urged a large territorial indemnity from Mexico. "In Europe, one of the social evils is concentration," Cass told fellow senators in 1847. "Men are brought too much and kept too much in contact. There is no room for expansion. Minds of the highest order are pressed down by adverse circumstances, without the power of free exertion." Cass had ventured to Paris in 1836 and had traveled to Britain as Jackson's minister to France, and he deplored what he had seen. "I trust we are far removed from all this, but to remove us further yet, we want almost unlimited power of expansion," he advised. "That is our safety valve." Abundant land, Cass concluded, had created a new people and a new nation in North America, and so long as cheap land existed, "whatever other evils betide us, we shall be free from the evils of a dense population, with scanty means of subsistence, and with no hope of advancement."[18]

Congressman Thomas Turner reached the same conclusion in 1848. "Extension and expansion are preeminently democratic, but the anti-war Whigs prefer the government of corporations," he complained. "The great West has found an outlet for our people and thus has frustrated their designs. But circumscribe our limits, give corporations the controlling influence, and white slavery will be substituted for black."[19]

New territory could shield Americans from these social ills. With ample and affordable land, most poor Americans would choose farming over industrial labor. Their desire to own property would disperse them over great distances and quell dissent. By drawing the masses westward out of major cities, abundant land would guarantee a shortage of labor and thereby ensure decent pay for wage workers. As Americans settled the continent, the nation would become more secure against foreign attack. Acquisitions, then, offered preferable alternatives to unionization, strikes and lockouts, urban congestion, an onerous tariff, and a large standing army. In terms of the benefits promised, the price for Indian removal and the conquest of California was negligible, not worthy of debate.

Expansionists looked for commercial opportunities far beyond the continent. They wanted new land, but for maritime as well as territorial advantages.[20] "We want Texas to protect our commerce in the Gulf," Congressman Stephen A. Douglas observed in early 1845, "and we want Oregon to protect our fisheries and our trade with China, and to put a stop to the unscrupulous aims of Great Britain at universal dominion." Douglas repeated his plea a year later. "The great point at issue, the great struggle between us and Great Britain, is for the freedom of the Pacific Ocean, for the trade of China and of Japan, of the East Indies, and for the maritime ascendancy on all these waters," he declared during the Oregon crisis. "In order to maintain these interests, and secure all the benefits resulting from them, we must not only go to 54°40′, but we have got to exclude Great Britain from the coast in toto."[21]

Other expansionists shared Douglas's desire to oust Britain from the Pacific coast of North America in order to monopolize East Asian commerce. But they considered California, not Oregon, the key to attaining that ascendancy. Thomas Larkin, a consul in Monterey and a confidential agent of the Polk administration to watch political developments in California, advised that the United States bring the province under the stars and stripes. "We must have it," Larkin informed James Gordon Bennett on May 20, 1846. "Others must not." Larkin wrote again to Bennett several days later. "Be it for fame, profit, or sport, the Anglo Saxon is ever the same," he explained. "Born in Maine or Missorio, he is ever going ahead, ever seeking and g[r]asping something he has not." After United States naval and land forces occupied California and proclaimed it a part of the union, Larkin urged Bennett and editor Moses Beach of the *New York Sun* to defend the administration's move. "The flag of our country now protects California," Larkin wrote in August. "California is free. Revolutions within the Territory are ended. Agriculture revives. Commerce will flourish; and the country proves to the world its resources."[22]

With Texas, Oregon south of 49°, and California won by mid-1848, political leaders pondered the likely rewards from their policies. In July President Polk stressed the many advantages he anticipated from the Mexican cession. "In this vast region, whose rich resources are soon to be developed by American energy and enterprise," Polk advised Congress, "great must be the augmentation of our commerce, and with it new and profitable demands for mechanic labor in all its branches and new and valuable markets for our manufactures and agricultural products." Robert Walker, secretary of the Treasury and Polk's most influential adviser, expressed similar views in his annual report in December. "Our maritime frontier upon the Pacific is now nearly equal to our Atlantic coast," Walker noted, "with many excellent bays and harbors, admirably situated to command the trade of Asia and of the whole western coast of America, whilst our coastwise trade between the Atlantic, the Gulf, and Pacific must soon become of great value."[23]

Soldiers in the field agreed that new territories would provide opportunity and mobility for enterprising Americans. Headed to Camargo with Taylor's army in 1846, Lieutenant William Henry looked over the land and predicted that "the Anglo-American race" would soon "by their energy and *go-ahead-a-tiveness* . . . render available the surprising fertility of the soil [and] its immense mineral wealth." Though numerically inferior, U.S. troops still defeated the Mexican forces and watched them flee for their lives. "Our victories are almost incredible," Napoleon Dana bragged after two initial triumphs. "It is seldom that an army can whip three-and-a-half times its numbers, still more seldom that it can rout and disperse them, and almost unparalleled that the beaten force should lose all its artillery and baggage." After the two nations agreed to peace terms in 1848, Private Richard Coulter of Pennsylvania returned to the Gulf Coast to embark for home. "Vera Cruz is much altered and for the better," he observed prior to departure. "It is now decidedly a handsome business place, almost completely Americanized."[24]

When expansionists speculated about how new territories would become "completely Americanized," they emphasized three major advantages the United States and its dominant white population enjoyed. Because of race superiority, Anglo-Saxon migrants would eclipse lesser races and gain predominant political power. The pioneers would then join the federal compact, made possible by the enviable elasticity of American republicanism. Finally, technological marvels would shrink the continent and facilitate the rapid transit of people, products, and information over vast distances. In his inaugural address in early 1845, President Polk had reviewed the nation's progress since its birth. "The title of numerous Indian tribes to vast tracts of country has been extinguished," he recalled, "new states have been admitted into the Union; new Territories have been created and our jurisdiction and laws extended over them." Rather than imperil the republic, this growth had safeguarded it:

As our population has expanded, the Union has been cemented and strengthened. As our boundaries have been enlarged and our agricultural population has been spread over a large surface, our federative system has acquired additional strength and security. It may well be doubted whether it would not be in greater danger of overthrow if our present population were confined to the comparatively narrow limits of the original thirteen States than it is now that they are sparsely settled over a more expanded territory. It is confidently believed that our system may be safely extended to the utmost bounds of our territorial limits, and that as it shall be extended the bonds of our Union, so far from being weakened, will become stronger.

Polk demonstrated the courage of his convictions. Not only had he bluffed Britain and bullied Mexico to acquire Oregon and California in 1846, but by the fall of 1847 he had decided to try to obtain all Mexican territory north of the Sierra Madres as indemnity for the war. With peace restored early in 1848, he considered a show of force in the Yucatan peninsula and the purchase or seizure of Cuba, a colony of Spain. Among those who coveted Cuba was none other than John O'Sullivan, whose notion of manifest destiny now included wresting Caribbean colonies from European empires.[25]

After adding countless acres of Indian land, half of Oregon, and California and New Mexico to the national domain, Polk in late 1848 reflected on the value of expansion. Had "our present population . . . been confined within the limits of the original thirteen States," Polk argued, "the tendencies to centralization and consolidation would . . . have been such as to have encroached upon the essential rights of the States, and thus to have made the Federal Government a widely different one, practically, from what it is in theory, and was intended to be by its framers." An overweening federal government, not a vast empire, most jeopardized American concord. "So far from entertaining apprehensions of the safety of our system by the extension of our territory," the president concluded, "the belief is confidently entertained that each new State gives strength and an additional guaranty for the preservation of the Union itself."[26]

Senator Sidney Breese of Illinois recalled that previous expansionists had been rebuked for seeking new territory, yet they had persisted in their course. "I think our system is most admirably adapted to almost any degree of extension," Breese declared at the height of the war. "This objection was urged in 1787 and a preference manifested in some quarters for a division of the states into three or more small confederacies." The founders, however, had wisely forged a single union from the separate states. "So when Louisiana was acquired," Breese continued, "the same objections were urged, but time has shown their groundlessness." Jefferson had secured the Mississippi Valley, removed Native Americans further west, and gained undisputed control over the vital port of New Orleans. "Since the adoption of the Constitution," Breese reflected, "fifteen states have been added to the confederacy, six of them out of foreign territory, and against the same objections now urged, and all of them contributing new vigor to the system, and increased strength to the circle."[27]

Senator Daniel Dickinson of New York agreed. "Our form of government," he argued in early 1848, "is admirably adapted to extended empire." Senator Cass concurred. "Our government has a wonderful power of accommodating itself to the extension of the country," he assured skeptics when hailing the Mexican cession. "Its double formation . . . of external and internal sovereignties, enables it to spread without weakness, and to preserve its power of cohesion with its process of enlargement." Some of this rhetoric had the clear ring of partisan bombast to it, but Polk, Cass, and others correctly discerned a crucial difference between previous empires and their own. The United States did not expand to obtain subservient colonies; it transformed acquisitions into new states with the same privileges and immunities of the original thirteen. To that end expansionists supported measures to reduce public land prices to hasten settlement in the territories, hoping to admit them to the union as quickly as possible. Rebellious subjects menaced other empires, but equal citizens—however distant from the seat of government—added strength to the nation.[28]

Blessed with a novel notion of government, Americans also seemed to have a genius for invention. Not only could the country conquer Indians and Mexicans, it could conquer time and space. Urging the annexation of Texas in early 1845, Stephen Douglas dismissed concerns about its distance from Washington. "The application of steam power to transportation and travel has brought the remotest limits of the confederacy, now comprising twenty-six states . . . much nearer to the centre than when there were but thirteen," he observed. "The revolution is progressing, and the facilities and rapidity of communication are increasing in a much greater ratio than our territory or population." Lewis Cass offered similar assurances. "As we increase in numbers and extend in space, our power of communication is still more augmented," he told the Senate in 1847. "The telegraph has come with its wonderful process to bind still closer the portions of this empire, as these recede from its capital." Sidney Breese agreed with his fellow Democrats. "By the agency of steam operating upon the boat, the railroad car, and the press, combined with that great American intervention—the greatest of the age and of the world—the magnetic telegraph," Breese proclaimed in early 1848, "we will be more compact, and in more constant and harmonious intercourse than the old thirteen states at . . . the adoption of our Constitution."[29]

Even before Mexico ceded California to the United States, Asa Whitney, promoter of a transcontinental railroad, tried to win Robert Walker's support for his project. Such a railway, Whitney maintained, would foster an integrated, self-reliant domestic economy, "an internal system placing us entirely independent of *all* the nations of the earth, and at the same time forcing tribute from them." Federal land grants would facilitate construction. "Now is the time for this great work," Whitney urged Walker, "which would place us in a position to defy and if we please dictate to all the world." Defiance and dictation—these were the prerogatives of an impregnable empire.[30]

Contrary to the expansionists' high hopes and promises, the acquisitions of the mid-1840s increased domestic rancor, fostered sectionalism, and eventually helped provoke secession and the outbreak of the Civil War. The fragmentation of the Union proved the expansionists false prophets. "Politicians could not dissolve it if they would," Senator Dickinson had declared in 1847, "and would not if they could."[31] But they could, and they did. Obsessed with a supposedly rapacious Britain, offended by a weak yet proud Mexico, and wary toward Indians and black slaves, white Americans ironically found themselves to be their own worst enemy. Skeptics had sounded the alarm. Henry David Thoreau, for example, condemned the war of conquest against Mexico. "How does it become a man to behave toward this American government today?" Thoreau queried. "I answer, that he cannot without disgrace be associated with it." A land of peace and freedom had become a land of war and slavery. "When a sixth of the population of a nation which has undertaken to be the refuge of liberty are slaves, and a whole country is unjustly overrun and conquered by a foreign army, and subjected to military law," he warned, "I think that it is not too soon for honest men to rebel and revolutionize. What makes this duty the more urgent is the fact that the country so overrun is not our own but ours is the invading army." Nor did Thoreau share the expansionists' faith in iron rails and talking wires. "Our inventions are wont to be pretty toys, which distract our attention from serious things," he protested. "They are but improved means to an unimproved end, an end which it was already but too easy to arrive at; as railroads lead to Boston or New York. We are in great haste to construct a magnetic telegraph from Maine to Texas; but Maine and Texas, it may be, have nothing important to communicate." Indeed, by the time of Lincoln's election in 1860, perhaps earlier, Maine and Texas had precious little to say to one another. Railways symbolized progress for many of Thoreau's contemporaries, but he differed. "We do not ride on the railroad," he objected. "It rides upon us."[32]

Critics of Manifest Destiny were not confined to the world of arts and letters. Philip Hone, a New York banker and insurance broker, feared the consequences of annexing Texas. "If the Union can stand the shock," he mused, "it will only be another evidence that Divine Providence takes better care of us than we deserve." During the Mexican War Hone described his nation as one "of rapid progress and reckless management." He blamed U.S. leaders for the resort to arms. "The war," he grumbled, "originated in the vilest cabal that ever was set on foot by corrupt demagogues." Whigs in Congress denounced Polk and his advisers for their conduct toward Mexico. "I consider this war a great calamity," Columbus Delano of Ohio complained. "It is wicked and inhuman; its object is national robbery, consummated, if carried on, by a sacrifice of human life that falls but little short of murder." Daniel King of Massachusetts, who, like Delano, voted against the declaration of war in 1846, suggested that "the true history of the war" would become "the blackest page in the annals of our country." He rejected Polk's pleas of innocence. "The object desired was not peace with Mexico," King gibed, "but a piece of Mexico." Abraham McIlvaine of Pennsylvania opposed any addition of slave territory to the union. The war, McIlvaine told the House in 1847, was "wrong from beginning to end: wrong in its inception; wrong in its prosecution; wrong in its designs and ends."[33]

Years of close observation convinced George Catlin that neither federal officials nor the nation's "money-making individuals" could avoid "the sin of injustice" in dealing with Native Americans. "But the humble biographer or historian, who goes amongst them from a different motive," he added, "*may* come out of their country with his hands and his conscience clean."[34] Catlin conceded good intentions in those who sought to "civilize" and "uplift" the Native Americans, but he also realized that the whites' contact with Indians had been disastrous, with utter annihilation a real possibility. The expansionists also professed occasional benevolence toward the Mexicans. But by 1848 *la invasión norteamericana* had convinced those beyond the Rio Grande that Anglo Americans expected, even welcomed, the eclipse, if not the extinction, of the mixed races in the borderlands.

Catlin witnessed "the grand and irresistible march of civilization" westward, the "splendid juggernaut" that rolled inexorably across the continent. Unlike most antebellum Americans, however, Catlin viewed the process from both sides of the frontier. That dual perspective left him uneasy, angry, and remorseful. The stunning triumph of the United States over Indians and Mexicans validated Catlin's prophecy that the march to the Pacific was "irresistible." How "grand" it was remains subject to debate, a topic as controversial and divisive today as it was in the 1840s.

NOTES

1. George Catlin, *Letters and Notes on the Manners, Customs, and Condition of the North American Indians*, 3rd edition, vol. 2 (London: Tilt and Bogue, 1842), p. 156. On Catlin see the following: Marjorie Catlin Roehm, *The Letters of George Catlin and His Family: A Chronicle of the American West* (Berkeley: University of California Press, 1966); Marvin C. Ross, ed. , *George Catlin, Episodes from Life among the Indians, and Last Rambles* (Norman: University of Oklahoma Press, 1959); Harold McCracken, *George Catlin and the Old Frontier* (New York: Dial Press, 1959); Mark Sufrin, *George Catlin: Painter of the Indian West* (New York: Atheneum, 1991); Brian Dippie, *Catlin and His Contemporaries: The Politics of Patronage* (Lincoln: University of Nebraska Press, 1990).
2. Catlin, *Letters and Notes*, vol. II, pp. 249–50, 255–56.
3. "Annexation," *Democratic Review*, July, 1845, p. 7; "Territorial Aggrandizement," *Democratic Review*, October, 1845, p. 244.
4. *New York Morning News*, May 18 and 26, 1846.
5. For a detailed analysis of these ambitions, ideals, and fears, see Thomas R. Hietala, *Manifest Design: Anxious Aggrandizement in Late Jacksonian America* (Ithaca and London: Cornell University Press, 1985).
6. See Hietala, *Manifest Design*, 173–203.
7. *New York Herald*, June 5, 1846.
8. John Fairfield to Anna Fairfield, January 10, 1847, in *The Letters of John Fairfield*, ed. Arthur G. Staples (Lewiston, Maine: Lewiston Journal Publishing Co., 1922), p. 437; *Congressional Globe*, 28th Cong., 2nd Sess., p. 183 (January 23, 1845) (hereafter abbreviated *CG*]; *CG*, 30th Congress, 1st Sess., App. 355 (March 2, 1848).
9. "The War," *Democratic Review*, February, 1847, p. 100.
10. *CG*, 30th Cong., 1st Sess., App. 181 (January 26, 1848); ibid., App. 511 (April 6, 1848). Several recent interpretive studies note the extreme race consciousness of the 1840s and emphasize its role in the push to the Pacific. See, for example, Robert F. Berkhofer, Jr., *The White Man's Indian: Images of the American Indian from Columbus to the Present* (New York: Alfred A. Knopf, 1978); Richard Drinnon, *Facing West: The Metaphysics of Indian-Hating and Empire-Building* (Minneapolis: University of Minnesota Press, 1980); Reginald Horsman, *Race and Manifest Destiny: The Origins of American Racial Anglo-Saxonism* (Cambridge and London: Harvard University Press, 1981); Gene M. Brack, *Mexico Views Manifest Destiny, 1821–1846* (Albuquerque: University of New Mexico Press, 1975); Hietala, *Manifest Design*, pp. 10–54, 132–72, 193–95, 261–62, 267–70.
11. *The Mexican War Diary of George B. McClellan*, ed. William Starr Myers (Princeton, N.J.: Princeton University Press, 1917), pp. 11–12.
12. *The Mexican War Journal and Letters of Ralph W. Kirkham*, ed. Robert Ryal Miller (College Station: Texas A&M University Press, 1991), pp. 21, 78.
13. *Volunteers: The Mexican War Journals of Private Richard Coulter and Sergeant*

Thomas Barclay, Company E, Second Pennsylvania Infantry, ed. Allan Peskin (Kent, Ohio, and London: Kent State University Press, 1991), 180–81.

14. *The Mexican War Journal of Captain Franklin Smith,* ed. Joseph E. Chance (Jackson and London: University Press of Mississippi, 1991), 11, 89.

15. *Monterrey Is Ours! The Mexican War Letters of Lieutenant Dana, 1845–1847,* ed. Robert H. Farrell (Lexington: University Press of Kentucky, 1990), pp. 46, 108, 180–81.

16. Lieutenant William S. Henry, *Campaign Sketches of the War with Mexico* (New York: Harper & Brothers, 1847), in *To Mexico with Taylor and Scott, 1845–1847,* ed. Grady McWhiney and Sue McWhiney (Waltham, Mass.: Blaisdell Publishing, 1969), pp. 21, 44, 45. For scholarly assessments of the attitudes and observations of U.S. soldiers during the war, see James M. McCaffrey, *Army of Manifest Destiny: The American Soldier in the Mexican War, 1846–1848* (New York and London: New York University Press, 1992); Robert W. Johannsen, *To the Halls of the Montezumas: The Mexican War in the American Imagination* (New York and Oxford: Oxford University Press, 1985).

17. *Daily Madisonian,* October 30, 1843; *New York Morning News,* October 24, 1845. O'Sullivan frequently denounced the protective tariff, the growth of manufacturing, abolitionists, and antiexpansion Whigs. See "White Slavery," *Democratic Review,* September, 1842, p. 270; "One of the Problems of the Age," *Democratic Review,* February, 1844, p. 167; "Free Trade," *Democratic Review,* March, 1844, 296–97; *New York Morning News,* May 30, November 28, December 22, 1845, July 6, 13, August 1, 6, 1846.

18. *CG,* 30th Cong., 1st Sess., 367–68, App. 189 (February 10, 1847).

19. Ibid., App. 512 (April 6, 1848).

20. Norman Graebner emphasized the commercial dimensions of Polk's policies in his watershed work on westward expansion in 1955. Norman A. Graebner, *Empire on the Pacific: A Study in American Continental Expansion* (New York: Ronald Press, 1955). His emphasis, however, might have been overdone. The expansionists did not separate territorial from maritime goals; they saw them as complementary. New lands often contained new ports. New ports enhanced the value of new lands. Americans in the 1840s produced significant surpluses of several agricultural commodities, from hemp to corn, cotton to tobacco. New lands would increase that output, so the United States would need additional ports and markets to unload the excess production.

21. *CG,* 28th Cong., 2nd Sess., p. 226 (January 31, 1845); *CG,* 29th Cong., 1st Sess., p. 259 (January 27, 1846).

22. Thomas O. Larkin to James Gordon Bennett, May 20, 30, July 26, 1846; Larkin to Moses Y. Beach, July 29, 1846, Larkin to William M. Rogers, August 26, 1846, in *The Larkin Papers—Personal, Business, and Official Correspondence of Thomas Oliver Larkin,* ed. George P. Hammond, vol. 4 (Berkeley and Los Angeles: University of California Press, 1953), pp. 383, 403; vol. 5 (1955), pp. 169, 172, 220.

23. James D. Richardson, ed., *A Compilation of the Messages and Papers of the Presidents,* vol. 6 (New York: Bureau of National Literature, 1897), p. 2439; "Report of the Secretary of the Treasury," *House Documents,* 30th Cong., 2nd Sess. vol. 538,

no. 7, 14 (December 11, 1848). Polk in his final annual message on December 5, 1848, reminded legislators of the value of California. "From its position it must command the rich commerce of China, of Asia, of the islands of the Pacific, of Western Mexico, of Central America, the South American states, and of the Russian possessions bordering on that ocean," Polk predicted. "A great emporium will doubtless speedily arise on the California coast which may be destined to rival in importance New Orleans itself." Richardson, *Messages and Papers*, vol. 6, p. 2485.

24. *To Mexico with Taylor and Scott*, p. 45; *Monterrey Is Ours!*, p. 78–79; *Volunteers*, p. 313.

25. Polk's Inaugural Address, March 4, 1845, in Richardson, *Messages and Papers*, vol. 5, p. 2230; *The Diary of James K. Polk*, ed. Milo Milton Quaife (Chicago: A. C. McClurg & Co., 1910), May 30, June 30, 1846, vol. 1, 438, 495–97; July 7, 1846, vol. 2, p. 15–16; September 4, 1847, vol. 3, p. 161; January 2, 1848, pp. 281–82, February 21, 1848, pp. 347–48, April 25, 1848, p. 433, May 6, 10, 30, 1848, pp. 444–45, 446, 469, June 1, 2, 3, 17, 1848, 475, 476, 478–79, 493; James K. Polk to William H. Polk, "Private," October 2, 1846, Polk Papers, Library of Congress; O'Sullivan to Buchanan, March 19, 1848, James Buchanan Papers, Library of Congress.

26. "Polk's Fourth Annual Message to Congress, December 5, 1848, in Richardson, *Messages and Papers*, vol. 6, 2493–94.

27. *CG*, 29th Cong., 2nd Sess., App. 210 (February 23, 1847).

28. *CG*, 30th Cong., 1st Sess., p. 157 (January 12, 1848); *CG*, 30th Cong., 1st Sess., App. 428 (March 17, 1848).

29. *CG*, 28th Cong., 2nd Sess., App. 68 (January 1, 1845); *CG*, 29th Cong., 2nd Sess., App. 189–90 (February 10, 1847); *CG*, 30th Cong., 1st Sess., App. 350 (February 14, 1848).

30. Asa Whitney to Robert J. Walker, April 7, 1847, Walker Papers, Library of Congress.

31. *CG*, 29th Cong., 2nd Sess., App. 445 (March 1, 1847).

32. Henry David Thoreau, *Walden and "Resistance to Civil Government,"* 2nd edition, ed. William Rossi (New York and London: W. W. Norton, 1992), pp. 35, 228–29.

33. *The Diary of Philip Hone, 1828–1851*, ed. Bayard Tuckerman, vol. 2 (March 1, 1845), p. 243, (July 31, 1847), p. 321, (March 13, 1848), p. 347; *CG*, 29th Cong., 2nd Sess., App. 316–17 (February 2, 1847); *CG*, 29th Cong., 2nd Sess., App. 331 (February 4, 1847); *CG*, 29th Cong., 2nd Sess., App. 176 (February 4, 1847). Delano heralded the birth of the free-soil movement and also declared war on those who would extend slavery. "Go on if you will; conquer Mexico and add the territory," he challenged. "But we will make it free: if not with the politicians we have now, the people of the North will bury them and send honest men in their places."

34. Catlin, *Letters and Notes*, vol. 2, p. 225.

The Uncertain Road to Manifest Destiny

ARMY OFFICERS AND THE COURSE OF AMERICAN TERRITORIAL EXPANSIONISM, 1815–1846

Samuel J. Watson

Is occupation (or more bluntly put, interest) destiny? Tasked with acting as the nation's leading "Agents of Empire"[1] during an era of exuberant nationalism and territorial expansion, U.S. Army officers have naturally appeared to historians as ardent expansionists themselves. Beyond the influence of mid-nineteenth-century American society's boisterous national and ideological chauvinism, participation in expansionist wars provided army officers with rare chances for command responsibility and martial glory against "civilized" opponents—one of their primary psychological compensations for the boredom of peacetime routine on isolated posts along the frontiers. Materially, a larger army and the casualties of war promised promotion (and thus higher pay) for ambitious young regulars. With few exceptions, historians have logically taken it for granted that these men welcomed the annexation of Texas and looked forward to further expansion, but officers policing the borderlands were forced to play multifaceted diplomatic roles that posed dilemmas as well as opportunities, and their responses to the possibilities associated with territorial aggrandizement were far more nuanced than the existing explanatory models of self-interest and romantic nationalism suggest. Indeed, these responses changed significantly between 1815 and 1846, and no single factor can explain officers' diverse reactions to the contingencies of territorial expansion and war. Instead, military enthusiasm for expansion clearly varied from crisis to crisis and from officer to officer depending on the specific circumstances and individuals in question. This essay pursues the sometimes paradoxical motives, trends, and meanings of officers' reactions to the crises they encountered along the borders of the United States during the 1830s and '40s and discovers a growing sense of accountability to the national government that often restrained expansionist sentiments and bellicosity. In addition, the army's efforts had the practical impact of restraining filibusters whose actions might otherwise have drawn the United States into war with Britain.

Recent historians of American foreign relations have begun to emphasize that the nation's foreign policy was not solely the creation of the state, especially under the decentralized social and political conditions which prevailed in the early republic. Under the federal territorial system the process of geographic expansion was one of nation-state formation as well as one of extending the existing pattern of local self-government; expansion therefore contained the potential for both social reproduction in the decentralized agrarian mode envisioned by Jefferson and for the institutional elaboration and political consolidation of a more powerful nation-state. During this process the central government and its agents were constantly forced to reckon with the expansive—and potentially explosive—demands and actions of a mushrooming frontier population which remained essentially unregulable and therefore capable of withholding its sanction from national policies or reshaping them in pursuit of local objectives. Indeed, viewed from the centralist (and often openly authoritarian) perspective of officers charged with enforcing federal sovereignty, the most immediate product of territorial expansion usually seemed to be social entropy and disorder. As the most visible and potent agents of national power, army officers repeatedly had to confront and constrain aggressive private initiatives along the borders, often in the face of criticism from congressmen from the frontier regions. Moreover, regular officers always had to compete (whether overtly or, more often, implicitly) with locally appointed militia and volunteer commanders for control over the direction of military force, a struggle over occupational jurisdiction (and ultimately employment) that gave focus to the officer corps' growing sense of internal cohesion, professional identity, and accountability to its patrons and paymasters, the civilian authorities of the national government.[2]

Army officers' attitudes toward territorial expansion were profoundly shaped by their experiences—usually antagonistic ones—with civilian borderers. Because they were bound to execute contested national policies, officers frequently became embroiled in conflicts with local civilian authorities and their representatives and allies in Congress. The experience of these conflicts led many officers to advocate and where possible to practice dual policies of domestic and international restraint for fear that the "disorderly" borderers would get out of hand, responses which reflected a quasi-Hamiltonian preference for the order and stability imposed by the nation-state through the rules of international law. Indeed, contrary to the beliefs held by most historians, regular officers' long-term material interests as an occupation and a class—in secure employment and social status through a political monopoly over the direction of military force by the nation-state—increasingly dictated caution in the pace and process of expansion, and on the whole the officer corps was substantially less enthusiastic about expansion in 1846 than it had been thirty years before.[3]

This essay explores the officer corps' experiences along the nation's borders to show how officers came to serve the nation-state not as individual free agents and loose cannons like Andrew Jackson, nor as ad hoc law enforcement officers and diplomats like Winfield Scott and his subordinate William Worth on the Canadian border in 1838, but ultimately as the politically accountable military agents of an empire that many of them (like Zachary Taylor, commander of the Army of Occupation in Texas) were privately reluctant to see absorbed into the United States. In the process of exploring this transition I also survey General Edmund Gaines's career on the borders of Texas between 1823 and 1846, where he attempted to practice the bellicose expansionism he had learned at Jackson's knee but was repeatedly disavowed by the national government, including expansionist presidents Jackson and Polk. By moving from Jackson through Scott and Worth to Gaines and Taylor and the junior officers who served under them, we can follow the officer corps' gradual evolution into a socially, politically, and professionally accountable instrument of U.S. foreign and national security policy. Army officers served the cause of national expansion in 1846, but they did so as members of a bureaucratically structured and constitutionally accountable organization under national control, not as individuals or representatives of a single sectional and economic interest (slaveholding Southerners or land-hungry yeoman farmers), and they did so without the ardent enthusiasm that characterized the officers of the 1810s or the civilian expansionists of the 1840s. In the final analysis, the personal material security guaranteed by stable careers in large-scale organizations led army officers to restraint rather than belligerence in their responses to foreign policy crises.

As we should expect, officers of different backgrounds and rank responded in distinct ways to the complex situations that confronted them along the nation's borders, and the social, political, and institutional factors behind these responses were usually closely connected to each another. Officers' views varied according to office and rank, posting and duties, and individual temperament and political affinity. Their attitudes also changed according to the nation's strength, the specific strategic situation and balance of military power in question during a given crisis, and the army's public stature and evolution as an institution. The social and sectional composition and attitudes of the officer corps changed as American society became more economically and occupationally specialized, forcing part-time soldiers to make a choice of career and leading the remaining officers to serve for significantly longer periods of time than their early national predecessors. This process was especially significant in the South among the planter class that led the nation's expansion prior to 1820, for graduates of West Point held a virtual monopoly on commissions issued between 1821 and 1837 (when large-scale resignations led to a wave of appointments directly from civilian life). The rigid system of promotion by seniority and the de facto requirement that officer candidates pass through four years at the academy excluded established gentlemen-planters of the sort who had been appointed to field and general command directly from civilian life under the less rigid conditions prevailing before 1821, while inadequate academic preparation meant that fewer Southerners were able to enter the corps through the academy than had done so between 1802 (when the academy was founded) and 1821. Besides fewer opportunities for high rank and command, the attractiveness of military careers declined for these men as they concentrated their energies on territorial and economic opportunities in the Old Southwest that they had helped to conquer. With the growth of settlement and export markets after the War of 1812, the southwestern planter class turned from part-time activities like land speculation (and military leadership) toward the full-time cultivation of cotton as the primary basis of its wealth.[4]

A similar process occurred in the political realm: as population densities grew and communications improved, territories became states with elected civilian officeholders, while the federal government turned to prominent local civilians or ex-officers rather than serving commanders for its agents, which meant fewer opportunities for civilian officeholding among army officers, whose roles became less overtly political than they had been prior to 1820. These developments gradually contributed to creating an officer corps whose primary political loyalties and identity were national rather than sectional or local. Many socially or politically well-connected men left the corps in pursuit of civilian political and economic opportunities during the years surrounding the reduction in force of 1821, and those who remained increasingly saw themselves as career employees dedicated to the full-time service of an established national institution with distinctive objectives as an occupational interest group rather than simply gentlemen free to pursue personal or sectional interests like civilians or their predecessors before 1820. Reflecting these changes, officers began to respond to threats to slavery and policies and conflicts promoting its expansion as practical military questions (as in the Second Seminole War) or personal ones (as on the Rio Grande in 1846) rather than those of sectional defense and expansion (as in the first Seminole conflict, or among southern civilians during the second). In significant contrast to many civilians, few if any officers of the 1830s and '40s advocated territorial aggrandizement in order to spread or defend the socioeconomic system of plantation slavery, a reluctance that led officers of the Jacksonian era into conflict with settlers in Florida, where their predecessors had worked together in pursuit of the same goals.

Changing attitudes toward foreign affairs were also connected to developments in the army's structure and the *mentalité* of the officer corps. Institutionally, the army's internal chain of command and accountability was somewhat clearer by 1830 than it had been a decade before, leaving fewer opportunities for officers to engage in foreign adventurism, premeditated or otherwise. As the nation's borders were clarified and civilian officials took the place of military ones in their government, efforts to alter them became the province of national political decision-makers or private filibusters rather than army officers forced or given the opportunity to decide the course of U.S. policy on the spot. Historian Robert May has recently argued that filibustering held some of the same material and psychological attractions for young American men as service in the military, while presenting greater opportunities for individuals that often drew them away from the hierarchically structured army. Psychologically, filibustering also appears to have served an alternative outlet for the more bellicose or opportunistic officers who were unwilling to accept the constraints of the army's rigid rank and promotion hierarchy. In this sense filibustering complemented the army's institutional appeal of personal and occupational security by siphoning off the excessively ambitious, whose actions might otherwise have posed a threat to the army's political neutrality and its support in Congress, perhaps leading to attacks on the officer corps' monopoly over the direction of organized military force.[5]

Army officers were directly accountable to the central government for their jobs and budgets, and they generally considered the filibusters who challenged national sovereignty over foreign policy and military force to be disruptive criminals who posed a greater threat to domestic and international order and stability (and hence national security) than the weak forces of America's southern neighbors. The same was true even along the Canadian border, where officers felt certain that the dramatic growth of American population and communications links would sustain successful offensives in any future war with Britain without requiring extensive preparations in peacetime. A similar process shaped officers' conceptions of national honor, which Jackson had viewed largely as an extension of his own aggressive will: in 1838 Scott and his leading subordinates on the Canadian frontier saw faithfulness to international law as a matter of personal and professional honor, which they attempted to affirm by dutifully securing the nation's border against all comers in support of federal sovereignty and the government's treaty obligations. Indeed, these men often cooperated closely with their British counterparts during the crises between 1838 and 1842, while acting as strenuously as possible to maintain American national sovereignty and neutrality by securing the borders against the private aggression of American citizens as well as British or Canadian retaliation.

Occupation, class, and culture were all linked in the evolution of the officer corps' attitudes toward foreign affairs. The growing cohesion and shared attitudes of the officer corps owed much to its quest for stability and order in all the interactions that affected it as an occupational group—within its units of working-class, increasingly foreign-born enlisted men, in the decentralized civilian social order of the borderlands where it was stationed, in federal sovereignty and army jurisdiction over the organized use of violence, and in the systematized diplomatic relations between established nation-states which ultimately gave the army its employment and the officers their careers. Like other Americans among the nation's elites and aspirants to that status, officers sought authority and prestige by identifying their values with those of the Old World and its elites, including European military officers. In American domestic society this meant a growing emphasis on refinement and gentility; in foreign relations U.S. soldiers and diplomats sought respectability in the eyes of their European counterparts by adhering to the customs and formalities of international law, which many of their revolutionary forebears had once denounced as tools of monarchy. Following these norms and enforcing them along the nation's borders also provided the sanction of European precedent and practical utility for the army's monopoly over the direction of organized armed force in the eyes of its employers. Class, state, and occupational formation were closely linked phenomena in the army officer corps' actions in the American borderlands, a pattern which encouraged military accountability to the authority of civilian political structures dominated by national elites.[6]

The officer corps as a whole grew more patient and less bellicose— though no less self-interested—as a result of these social and occupational developments, and a spirit of conservative legalism gradually replaced the aggressive republican internationalism of the 1810s as the basis of the officer corps' approach to foreign policy issues. Commanders seeking order and stability constantly reaffirmed the principles of international law, the inviolability of national borders, and the sovereignty of the federal nation-state over the application of organized violence, and their activities on the frontiers gave these abstractions a concrete reality they had lacked in the turbulent southern borderlands before 1820. This process of attitudinal and behavioral change accelerated with experience as the dangers of a decentralized foreign policy and the demands and consequences of adherence to international law became more real to officers during the border crises of the 1830s and '40s. Indeed, the officer corps came to feel as much of an interest in stability along the borders as in military preparedness per se, because both were equally essential to its employment and jurisdiction as a discrete occupation and an internally self-governing organization facing politically potent competition from the militia and volunteers. In this sense, the officer corps' quest for military preparedness was only the specifically military manifestation of a more general search for individual, organizational, and social security and stability, which encompassed personal, occupational, and ultimately class concerns.

By the late 1830s commanders along the borders of Texas and Canada took much less belligerent and expansionist stances than their predecessors two decades before, while Oregon and California went virtually unmentioned in officers' papers before the mid-1840s. Indeed, diplomatic historians have often characterized the Mexican War as a "war for California, rather than a war over Texas," but (however true of the Polk administration and U.S. intentions in general) this statement simply does not hold up when applied to the army officer corps, whose members were concentrated in Texas and wrote virtually nothing about California prior to the outbreak of the war.[7] Whatever his own intentions might have been, General Edmund Gaines was as clearly Andrew Jackson's subordinate on the Texan frontier in 1836 as he had been on the Floridian one in 1818, and he obeyed the president's demand for restraint just as he had obeyed the general's demand for action. Two years later Winfield Scott was instrumental in breaking up private efforts to invade Canada and plunge the United States into war with Britain. Though Scott and some of his key subordinates initially welcomed the "Patriot" risings, they quickly reverted to a dutiful stance that stressed the sovereignty of the nation-state and the inviolability of international borders rather than the possibility of American territorial or ideological expansion. Although Gaines continued to exhibit the aggressiveness he learned under Jackson, Zachary Taylor and his subordinates in the Army of Occupation demonstrated less eagerness and belligerence toward Mexico than a practical (albeit equally self-interested) desire to end the uncertainty of their prolonged tenure on the border distant from their families and the amenities of their peacetime stations.

The officer corps, which can fairly be said to have directed and led the U.S. conquest of Spanish Florida during the 1810s (albeit in general agreement, and often cooperation, with those civilians, mostly southerners and filibusters, who took a strong interest in the subject), proved content to follow the gradual trajectory of American public opinion in coming to imagine and accept that of the Mexican Southwest. Taylor himself was rumored to oppose annexation "in toto,"[8] and if he had any personal cause for aggressiveness it was to win laurels for the regular army before the volunteers arrived, an occupational rather than an ideologically expansionist motive that was not in any way the source of the army's presence opposite Matamoros. Indeed, it is both remarkable and highly significant that in the highly partisan context of Jacksonian America a Democratic president elected on a platform of aggressive expansionism should have chosen to entrust the command of the force he intended to occupy Texas (if not to precipitate war with Mexico) to a known Whig, and to leave it under his command even after Taylor's opposition to expansion became widely known. (Political pressures obviously played a complex but powerful role in these decisions.) Indeed, Polk reprimanded Gaines for making a premature call for volunteers in the spring of 1845, and that fall Gaines was court-martialed and transferred to a quiet post in New York City because the administration doubted his ability to restrain his belligerence. Jackson's impact on the nation's foreign policy was independent and strategic, Gaines's disruptive but controllable, and Taylor's subordinate and tactical, and there in a nutshell lies the difference in foreign policy activism, bellicosity, and accountability to national civilian political authority between the officer corps of 1818 and that of 1846.

The army was small enough that the officer corps' impact on the practice of foreign relations was largely made by the actions of individual commanders, and much of the aggressiveness of the officers of 1815–20 can be traced to the influence of Andrew Jackson, major general in command of the army's Southern Division. Jackson's national political standing and inhuman willfulness notwithstanding, his lust for territorial aggrandizement was not exceptional among the army officer corps of these years, given the personal and sectional economic interests of planter-officers and junior military aspirants to that status. Indeed, the expansionist officers of the immediate postwar years were following a pattern of adventurism that went back to General James Wilkinson (the army's commanding general from 1796 to 1812) and the Burr Conspiracy. Following in the footsteps of the Gutiérrez-Magee expedition, which had plunged Spanish Texas into a devastating civil war in 1812, General Eleazar Wheelock Ripley, a New Englander who reacted to filibustering proposals with republican rhetoric but practical caution while the departmental commander of West Florida in 1816, resigned in 1820 to help lead a new wave of filibusters (James Long's second attempt) against Texas. (Texas was otherwise not much of a consideration in even the most expansionist officers' minds during the 1810s and '20s, and Jackson repeatedly downplayed reports of Spanish activity along the Sabine.) Similarly, a number of officers, including Ripley, Jackson, and Major Thomas Sidney Jesup (Ripley's predecessor in command and the quartermaster general from 1818 until 1860), proposed seizing Cuba between 1816 and 1819, but none were so reckless (or capable of gaining the necessary naval support independent of civilian authorization) as to attempt it.[9]

Officers advocated and led the campaigns that secured Florida for the United States during the half-decade of nationalism that followed the War of 1812, but Jackson resigned in 1821 to take up the governorship of Florida and was followed by a number of other well-connected officers (especially Southerners, who sought positions from which to pursue their interests in the expansion of white settlement and commercial cotton production into Florida and the Old Southwest) over the next few years. The army officer corps had fairly little to do or say about territorial aggrandizement during the two decades thereafter, as nation and army alike concentrated on consolidating their internal affairs in the absence of foreign threats or immediate opportunities for expansion. Officers thus said very little about the possibility of expansion in Cuba or other regions of Latin America and the Caribbean during the 1820s and '30s; American military attention to Cuba did pick up toward the end of the 1830s as British and American relations soured during the Canadian border crises and officers became concerned over the growing commercial rivalry between the two nations, but few of them expressed the heady enthusiasm of the 1810s again prior to the onset of hostilities with Mexico.

Indeed, aside from their attention to Florida and coastal fortifications, officers like most civilian Americans increasingly turned their attention inward after 1815. Many senior officers gave rhetorical support to democratic revolutions in Europe and Latin America during the years before 1823, but like most civilians they came to see the nation's political role overseas primarily as a matter of setting an example to the world rather than one of acting as an aggressive agent of international republicanism or liberal revolution. Like civilians, officers came to use the language of revolution as a rhetorical trope for application to distant lands; when applied to Florida or Texas it served as a cover for American expansionism rather than the liberation of indigenous peoples from colonial oppression. Consequently, though officers often sought a larger military establishment, their realistic assessment of the nation's ideological and fiscal aversion to large peacetime establishments led the majority of experienced commanders to caution in advocating war or territorial expansion against opponents—like Britain—more powerful than Spain. This sense of restraint was acceptable to experienced officers because of their confidence in the latent power and future prospects of the United States: although they constantly called for larger budgets and measures to improve the nation's military capability, officers ultimately shared the confidence of civilian policy makers that the nation would be able to defend itself in case of attack and expand in case of opportunity regardless of the limited effort put into military preparations. In the meantime, the tumultuous conditions which had encouraged American interventionism along the southern borders before 1821 declined into relative insignificance after the United States successfully asserted its sovereignty through the annexation of Florida and the delineation of the Sabine boundary, while Anglo-American tensions calmed and the danger of a European alliance against the American republics virtually disappeared after the proclamation of the Monroe Doctrine and its British analogue. Aside from the Yellowstone Expedition of 1824 and operations connected with Indian removal within the supposed boundaries of the United States, American expansionism proceeded largely through the private paths of commerce and settlement during the 1820s and '30s, and the thinking of army officers followed suit: of the officers asked to submit reports on the 1821 reduction, only Winfield Scott referred directly to the potential for "another offensive war against Canada" in his projections, and expansionist statements are difficult to find among officers' papers from the years between 1821 and 1836.[10]

Aside from some expressions of interest and sympathy for the Polish rebellion of 1830, the evidence that army officers remained conscious of the struggles of European liberals is almost equally sparse, and the Greek struggle for independence did not cause nearly the excitement among officers that it did among civilians. Similarly, the proclamation of the Monroe Doctrine had little impact on officers' lives or presence in their letters before the 1840s. Early in 1824 Lieutenant Colonel Zachary Taylor addressed an extensive commentary on the subject to his friend General Jesup, flatly asserting that "the nation will be prepared to go any lengths" to prevent the reimposition of Spanish rule in Latin America, but as a corollary Taylor believed that the United States should avoid entanglement in European conflicts (specifically the Greek revolt). Writing several weeks after Monroe's proclamation, Taylor's views effectively aligned him with the Jacksonians who emphasized the defense of U.S. national interests rather than pan-American cooperation or the extension of support to European revolutionaries. Indeed, Taylor provides a personal example of the transition reflected in the Monroe Doctrine, from the expansive revolutionary ideology and internationalism of early republican politicians and officers like Thomas Jefferson and Winfield Scott to the more narrowly defined realism and national self-interest that characterized Jacksonian diplomacy. On the whole, the isolationist aspects of Jefferson's "doctrine of the hemispheres" were echoed by the silence of officers on the internal affairs of Europe, while its expansionist implications received little comment among army officers during the quiet of the late 1820s and the Indian-fighting of the 1830s.[11]

The army's law enforcement duties along the nation's borders and frontiers also contributed to the decline of military belligerence during the 1820s and '30s. Indeed, service along the western frontier engendered as much disdain for white settlers as for the Indians, resentment that turned to outright disgust and near alienation as the army became bogged down executing the removal policy in Florida after 1835. The distaste officers felt for this dangerous yet thankless work multiplied their distrust for expansion, especially as social and cultural distinctions grew between West Pointers socialized in the allied values of nationalism and gentility (especially in the form of disinterested service) and rough-hewn local settlers pursuing material self-interest at the expense of social hierarchy and federal sovereignty. Indeed, by the late 1830s many officers had come to see themselves as the nation's policemen, whose duties involved preserving law and order among unruly whites as much as facilitating the westward movement. On the other hand, resignations by officers who entered the burgeoning field of civil engineering during the boom of the mid-1830s combined with the difficult experiences of the Seminole War and the economic depression of the late 1830s and early 1840s to temper the loyalties of the officer corps in the forge of adversity. Over a hundred and fifty resignations between 1835 and 1837 left behind a group that was willing to give political accountability in return for secure careers regardless of the nature of the service, and although some officers resigned when sent to Texas, their numbers were far fewer than those a decade earlier.

The officer corps' heightened sense of the connections between foreign policy, domestic order, and occupational monopoly was perhaps best illustrated by its responses to the border unrest precipitated by the Canadian rebellions of 1837. Following the *Caroline* incident that December, President Van Buren immediately sent Winfield Scott and other officers to reassure the frightened borderers and to maintain peace by securing the boundary against violation from either side, "manifesting to friends and foes," as then-major William Worth put it, "the continued disposition of the Government to put forth every energy in maintenance of the laws and the National Faith." For the next four years experienced but by today's inflated standards relatively junior officers—regimental colonels like Worth and Hugh Brady, and the army's inspector general, John Wool (the principal commanders along the Buffalo, Detroit, and Vermont frontiers)—were the chief agents of federal policy along the border, battling a series of private attempts to precipitate a war between the United States and Britain by invading Canada. Doing so was a complex task: given the delicate balance of U.S. public opinion and the inadequacy of federal neutrality law, peacekeeping in the borderlands was as much a job for civil-military diplomacy as for the overt display of force, because the Patriot sympathies of many local civil officials and militiamen frequently deprived army officers of the legal authority and manpower they needed to act as an effective barrier to Patriot expeditions.[12]

Many American civilians supported the "Patriot" filibusters on ideological grounds as inheritors of the Revolutionary tradition, or on nationalistic ones of Anglophobia, and the crisis was exacerbated by high unemployment during the Panic of 1837. Army officers were caught in the middle between the filibusters and their civilian supporters and the British authorities and loyal Canadians who wanted to pursue the Patriots into the United States to avenge their raids. Regular officers believed that the most ethical and efficient way to defend American national sovereignty was to preempt conflict by preventing Patriot incursions against Canada, rather than trying to stop British forces pursuing the Patriots across the border after the fact, but the actions of the military commanders were tightly constrained by their belief that any substantive action required the legal sanction of civilian authority, and they felt overwhelmed by the problems of policing a long, wooded frontier with a mere handful of men. The army received little assistance from local civilian officials, but U.S. commanders acted energetically against the Patriots, successfully maintaining federal authority and containing incidents that might otherwise have led to war with Britain.[13]

The international context for officers' actions along the Canadian border was substantially different from that in 1815. Early republican fears that Canada would provide Britain with a base for aggression against the Unites States were in seeming decline by the 1830s, though U.S. policy makers (including army officers) still feared geostrategic encirclement. These fears were strongest among the Democrats, who sought a decentralized national future founded on territorial expansion and social replication, but the officer corps was at least evenly split between Whigs and Democrats, and even Democratic officers expressed little sympathy for the small farmers they encountered while policing the nation's frontiers. The boom in Anglo-American trade and investment, the rise of Anglo-Saxon racialism, the growth of American power and self-confidence, and the successful conclusion of a number of agreements with England during the 1810s led to a faith in negotiation and coexistence with Britain among most American policy makers and military officers during the 1820s and early 1830s, and they gave little attention to military preparations along the Canadian border until 1838. On the whole, officers, like most Americans, assumed that Canada would gradually but inevitably move toward independence and possible union with the United States as the influence of U.S. economic ties and political institutions increased.[14]

In this context, moderate and conservative Americans (including most army officers) viewed the Patriot filibusters as threats to international law and domestic order—Jacksonian democrats gone mad—at a time when the nation was caught in the throes of depression and in no shape to fight. Confident in the example of their free economy and republican institutions, most Americans were willing to bide their time rather than risking war and economic devastation by subverting British rule directly, and the Van Buren administration refused to use the Patriot crises as grounds to do so. War with Britain and the Royal Navy was a dangerous gamble when American entrepreneurs expected to outpace their competition peacefully, and officers' references to the possibility of American expansion against Canada are notable only by their extreme rarity. More characteristically, Captain Robert Anderson wrote to New York congressman Gouverneur Kemble that "instead of allowing the Canadians to work at the Altar of Liberty, forming and fashioning it to suit themselves—we have attempted to force our plan upon them . . . That many Canadians desire some change—there can be no doubt . . . but they desire reform not revolution—a reform brought about by the quiet, steady action of public sentiment and virtue—not revolution bathed in blood." Major William Worth echoed Anderson's assessment of the Canadian political climate almost to the letter. Like Worth, all of the senior commanders on the frontier in 1838 had fought the British there during the War of 1812, while Worth later showed an interest in filibustering against Yucatan and Cuba, but any sympathy these men felt for the rebels was curbed by the officer corps' pervasive fear of lawlessness and social disorder, mixed with practical considerations about the disadvantageous balance of military forces and a vague Anglophilia born of class and occupation.[15]

Indeed, the regulars' sympathies were usually with the British rather than their fellow countrymen, and the officer corps' search for social, institutional, and international stability restrained whatever enthusiasm its members may have had for territorial expansion against Canada or war with Britain. The importance of national sovereignty and the corollary demand for centralized control over the direction of armed force emerge as the keys to understanding the value that regular officers put on domestic and international law, for officers feared, should these restraints fail, social chaos and a war the United States was unprepared for and had no need to fight. Territorial expansion only became acceptable to the officer corps when it followed the orderly processes provided for by national and international law and the direction of officers acting as agents of the American nation-state, so officers who would soon be eager for war over Oregon or Texas withheld their support from a Manifest Destiny of private individuals acting beyond the restraints of congressional sanction and professional military command.

Worth's largely class-based antagonism against the Patriot "Brigands" was almost uniformly shared by his fellow commanders along the border, and their language was without exception one which contrasted stability with disorder. General Winfield Scott responded to borderers outraged by the destruction of the *Caroline* in terms resonant with deeper cultural meaning, maintaining that "at no time, could any portion of our people usurp the right of retaliation and revenge; that such would not be in the manner and forms of a civilized people, but according to the practice of savage tribes." "Usurpation"—the use of force outside the control of federal law and professional direction—was also a prominent theme in Worth's dispatches on the Patriots and their American sympathizers: he warned one subordinate that "the view some of your [civilian] neighbors take of the neutrality law is the very ultraism of nullification." Worth and Scott were echoed by Colonel Hugh Brady on the Detroit frontier, who spoke of "these violators of our Laws" as "marauders" and "desperadoes."[16] These strictures reflected the officer corps' fear of instability in any guise, and commanders routinely characterized the rebels in socially loaded terms as "disorganizers," "agitators," and "miserable" and "unprincipled" "adventurers."[17] Brady labeled these "disturbers of peace and good order" "the rabble," and Worth blamed "the floating population that infests the border (of every country)" for the unrest.[18] Disorder and dishonesty went hand-in-hand in the language of character, and officers commonly denounced the insurgents as both "reckless and unscrupulous." Indeed, their rhetoric sometimes verged on the dehumanizing, suggesting mental illness or psychological instability among the Patriots, whom Worth once demonized as "lawless and insane." Brady also spoke of the "feverish state" of "desperate and uneasy spirits" along the frontier; the filibusters were "misguided" and "deluded" men, deceived by their leaders' "vile and mischievous fabrications." Indeed, Worth concluded that these "miserable youths" were mere "tools," "the unfortunate dupes of designing demagogues."[19] The values of the officer corps were also evident in their recurrent portrayal of the Patriots as greedy cowards: quartermaster colonel Henry Whiting asserted that "the eyes of needy [and] unprincipled adventurers began to glisten with rabid hope" when "the Brigand fever" ensnared them in its toils, while Robert Anderson labeled the Patriot leaders "cowardly scamps," who preferred "the lights of the lecture rooms, and the sounds of silver falling into the hats passed around for contributions . . . to the flame of the death dealing gun, and the moans of the wounded [and] dying patriots" at the battle of Windmill Point. Indeed, Worth, who had secured a tacit understanding with the local British commander to allow an evacuation attempt there, blamed "cowardice and treachery" for the invaders' "feeble effort" to save their fellows.[20]

This language indicates that conservative senses of class and social order were closely linked in the minds and actions of army officers on the border, who made a sharp distinction between Patriot rabble-rousers and the "respectable" citizens whom commanders expected to uphold law and order. Worth and his counterparts believed strongly that social hierarchy and respect for law went hand in hand, which led the major to comment with vengeful relish that "many, too late indeed for their reputation and standing in society, are getting heartily ashamed of their part in the affair." Given this hierarchical understanding of social leadership and initiative, Worth suspected that the filibusters had initially been "nourished and urged on by persons of high standing in society," but as a corollary he expected that local elites could put a stop to the unrest. (Worth later attempted to reconcile these expectations with disaffection among his soldiers by blaming the influence of "the lower classes here.") Practically speaking, officers began the essential task of swaying public opinion by attempting to persuade local elites to support national policy, an approach evident in Worth's proclamation to the "Gentlemen of Ogdensburg" that "if the good citizens should be pleased to exercise their just influence in society I cannot doubt that very shortly the former relations of good neighborhood will be restored with the opposite border."[21]

Army officers also linked their keen senses of military duty and personal and national honor to their efforts to maintain neutrality and "national faith" (meaning adherence to international law). Worth therefore ordered Lieutenant Colonel Newman Clarke to inform a British counterpart of "our sincere desire to do all that we might be expected from the most fastidious sense of national and personal honour" to do to stop the Patriots. Indeed, with too few troops to physically patrol the long border, Worth was forced to rely primarily on the power of example and the gentry quest for reputation: although usually fruitless as police measures, he hoped that his officers' actions would have "the excellent effect to stimulate the civil authority to the assertion of its honor and dignity, and [to] convince our outraged neighbors, that . . . we [meaning the army's officers, as representatives of the federal government], at least perform our duties in good faith." Scott encapsulated these connections when he reported to Poinsett that "I have scornfully refused, & shall continue so to refuse, to receive or to salute, one of those *traitors to a special trust* . . . because I am the natural guardian of my own personal honour, & do not choose that that shall be defiled by fellowship with such men." In other words, the class characteristics of individual character and honor buttressed the officer's desire to support the authority of the nation-state and the inviolability of its borders, an authority expressed in the officer corps' occupational jurisdiction over direction of organized force.[22]

The most serious obstacle the regulars faced in their work as federal border police was the reluctance of politically appointed civil officers to enforce the neutrality laws. Winfield Scott warned the secretary of war that "in general they are either lukewarm [and] inefficient or the open [and] zealous abettors of the violators of law [and] order," and Worth suggested that "many are notoriously active members of the secret societies" (the Hunters' Lodges and other Patriot groups). Army officers frequently appealed to the War Department for support against refractory civil officials, but the federal government had little (or was unwilling to exert much) effective control over its local appointees under these delicate political circumstances, so army officers were forced to bear the burden of what was essentially a federal-local conflict over the direction of U.S. policy. (Executive officials at the state level generally supported the neutrality policy, and Worth cooperated extensively with New York governor William L. Marcy—later the secretary of state during the war with Mexico—in discouraging the filibusters.) Consequently, Worth and his fellows were often forced to mediate or choose between competing imperatives of professional responsibility and accountability to political authority, for they took the fundamental principle of civilian supremacy over the military seriously even when that adherence clearly hampered their immediate ability to sustain the sovereignty of the nation-state they served. "I have constant occasion for the advice [and] cooperation of the United States Civil Officers," Worth wrote to Scott, and he ordered his subordinates to "act in conjunction with [the] civil authorities of the United States Government, to yield them every aid and support which may be lawfully rendered," but he argued that "unsustained and deserted by the civil authorities it will be difficult for the military to render any efficient service by way of prevention, or to convince foreign governments of the sincere desire of our own to do so." Concerned for the consequences to the army's reputation as a disinterested instrument of national policy, he therefore ordered subordinates to send their correspondence with the civil authorities to headquarters for transmission to the War Department and Congress "as ample evidence that the Military has not been remiss in the performance of its duties."[23]

Regular commanders encountered similar disaffection and unreliability in the state militia. Worth initially referred to the militia as "the more [socially and constitutionally] appropriate aid to the civil functionaries," but army officers soon began to blame militia officers (often correctly) for allowing the filibusters to steal weapons from arsenals. In February 1838 militiamen at Plattsburgh refused to serve under federal command, and Inspector General Wool disbanded militia units called up by their commanders without proper authorization during the Patriot expedition from Vermont later that month. On the Detroit frontier Colonel Brady withdrew a requisition for militia "from want of Confidence" in their reliability after their officers lost a store of arms to the filibusters, while Winfield Scott worried that "they would almost certainly give their arms to the patriots, if not personally unite with them." On the other hand, both Worth and Brady distinguished between civilian volunteers and the militia on social grounds, much as they did between filibusters and "respectable Citizens—[the] staunch friends of Law and Order." Wool relied mostly on volunteers in his operations against the Patriots in Vermont in late February, 1838, and Brady repeatedly praised a volunteer company named after him as composed of "the most respectable young men" of Detroit. Worth not only praised a New York battalion under his direction for its "zeal, fidelity, and discipline," but reported that its members were undergoing "a course of instruction . . . which will increase their efficiency as soldiers, keep them out of idleness & send them home better citizens," no doubt after being lectured on their duty to observe the neutrality laws. Worth was clearly a strong believer in the civic and military benefits of training under professional guidance, but by early 1839 he felt certain that the pervasiveness of Patriot sympathies had rendered the militia useless, and he feared that a new move to call it to arms was driven by Patriot sympathizers who hoped to precipitate clashes with the British. Worth was able to prevent that call-up, and he asked the governor of New York to keep any arms sent for the militia under army guard, for it had quickly become clear to the regulars that without centralized control over the use of force the country would soon be plunged into war with Britain by the very militiamen so many civilians relied on to protect it.[24]

American officers expected that the British would have little difficulty rebuffing the invaders, but they could not ignore the chance that British forces would pursue the filibusters across the border onto U.S. soil. The forces that the Patriots mobilized were clearly incapable of defeating the British by themselves; they had to count on stirring up a general rebellion among the Canadians or on sucking the United States into war by provoking British retaliation, and most commanders feared that this was the filibusters' strategy for ensnaring the United States in war.[25] The abstract confidence of the 1820s and early 1830s quickly evaporated as officers came to realize that the nation's long-term ability to mobilize overwhelming forces could do little to protect the border region from British incursions. The same lack of troops that hampered their law enforcement operations left officers feeling helpless before the possibility of large-scale retaliation or war, and they hastened to absolve themselves of responsibility for the consequences. "What can a Military Commander do with a mere handful of men, when compelled to act in subordination to civil officers, a majority of whom are notoriously favorable to what is misnamed the Patriot cause?" asked Hugh Brady. "We are envired by Pirates, bold, reckless [and] unscrupulous on the one side, and by an injured people and indignant soldiery on the other with none to appreciate or ameliorate our position," Worth wrote to Scott in a moment of near panic. The British were concentrating twenty thousand regulars in Canada, while Worth and his counterparts had fewer than three thousand troops available. Worth responsibly went on to observe that "it is not for us as Soldiers to seek to penetrate the policy of the Government . . . but as a good citizen I cannot resist the belief that we are fast verging toward a contest, for which everything around us denotes total absence of decent preparation, & I can already in my mind's eye, see, for a time, the national honor, stricken to the dust." Worth was especially worried that the consequences would damage the army's credibility and prestige, for "if a contest ensues disgrace awaits us; and who amid the torrent of holy indignation will stop to inquire into our means—we may do and die but even that will not rescue our memories." Indeed, he had warned a year earlier that this disaster was inevitable without "*reliable* force to assist, and if needs be, enforce the just authority of the Government, and [the] supremacy of the Law."[26]

Army officers ultimately had to fight the Patriot war on as many as four fronts, and their methods varied according to their estimate of the most significant threat to peace at the moment in question. Consequently, Worth first deployed his troops "to inspire a sense of security in the People [and] to renew and cultivate kind and friendly feelings along the border," by reassuring frightened Americans that the federal government would protect them against any further raids like that on the *Caroline*. He then solicited the cooperation of leading citizens and the civilian authorities, in the belief that given "the impossibility on the part of the military authority of enforcing the laws while the mass of the people are so regardless of their obligations . . . the only course which remains, is to endeavour by the exertion of moral influence to bring about a more wholesome state of public opinion, and [to] stimulate the civil authorities to a more vigorous execution of their duties." When this prodding failed, Worth seized arms, set up an intelligence network, arrested Patriot leaders, and arranged his meager forces along the shore to catch filibusters retreating after their defeat by the British. He then assured the British authorities of his determination "to recall such of our own citizens as have strayed from the path of national honour and duty, and to admonish those who have sought the hospitality of our country [the Patriot exiles] of the danger of violating the laws."[7]

His efforts at civil-military diplomacy notwithstanding, the tension between accountability to the principle of civil supremacy and responsibility to enforce the neutrality policy frustrated Worth, and he ultimately initiated an independent policy of avoiding association with the local civil authorities whenever possible. Worth soon began to refuse orders from civil officers to return or auction off captured weapons, and he then went even further by directing his officers to seek evidence of negligence or criminal acts by federal, state, and local civil officials, a policy which eventually led to the arrest of a deputy U.S. marshal. In February, 1839, when a U.S. district attorney complained about an army officer's attempt to stop an assault on an official messenger, Worth bitterly responded that he would give "specific orders . . . under no circumstances to permit any interference in any brawls or civil difficulties, unless on the written request of a Magistrate." This putatively neutral approach coincided with the Patriots' turn to arsonism while recovering from their defeats at Windmill Point and Windsor the previous fall. Worth decided to classify such incidents as "civil difficulties" outside of his jurisdiction, as he had become convinced that "the Magistracy and people . . . are alone competent to the correction of such evils as now disgrace and afflict our border": "Should it please our good citizens to withdraw their countenance [and] support there is not a doubt tranquillity will be restored."[28]

Worth also began to worry that disturbances in the social order would infect the army itself, fearing that "the thoroughly corrupt character of a large portion of the frontier inhabitants is fatal to the discipline [and] fidelity of the troops, placed in garrisons in the open towns." "You will have to guard against efforts to seduce your men from their duties, and it is desirable that there should be the least practicable association between them and the citizens," he warned subordinates. As a solution Worth suggested concentrating his detachments on steamers patrolling the St. Lawrence River, which would conserve "men [and] money; keep the troops from contact with the citizens; cause by their movements less excitement, . . . [and] in a manner less obnoxious to the people . . . allow us to concentrate and mature the discipline of the men," but he first felt obligated to remove his detachments from Ogdensburg to Madison Barracks in Sackett's Harbor thirty miles to the south, as he feared that "a systematic plan to debauch and seduce them from their duty, has already been too successfully practiced."[29]

Unable to use force against the filibusters directly, Worth ultimately came to believe that only the fear of outright chaos would foster public adherence to the norms of law and order. "[T]he scandalous excesses [of the Patriots] will produce a very decisive, and fortunate, reaction in public feeling. . . . [They] have made all true men hug closer to the laws," he wrote early in 1838. This optimism proved premature, and a year later Worth instructed a subordinate that if incidents continued "you will not hesitate to withdraw the troops, and [to] try, as a last expedient, the effects of a due sense of insecurity," brought on by rumors of Canadian retaliation. In other words, not only had Worth ceased to cooperate with the civil authorities, he had decided to quell the unrest by relying on their fear—by withdrawing the very protection the army was supposed to provide. Worth reasoned that the borderers began "to look with seriousness to these matters, as the brand of the incendiary approaches their own dwellings, and there is reason to hope that in a few days they will compel the refugees [Patriots] to retire." He reported to Scott that "I am firm in the belief that perseverance in keeping the troops back from the line will in a short time bring our people to their senses [and] induce the Magistrates to do their duty." On the other hand, Worth did not resort to this extremity until he felt reasonably sure that there would be no retaliation from the Canadian side, and he admonished one critic of the new policy that "in this respect it is possible that our neighbors may have the advantage, in the point of morals."[30]

Indeed, Worth viewed regular communication with the British as his best means of deterring retaliation against U.S. soil, and (following a secret order by Winfield Scott) he frequently sent officers to confer with the British command about rumored Patriot plans and operations. Worth therefore wrote to Colonel Abraham Eustis that his talks with the British had "been characterized by high courtesy," and he believed that they would "act in a corresponding spirit" to restrain retaliation. Indeed, "the rigid discipline" of their troops and the "excellent disposition of the[ir] commanders" later led him to dismiss civilian rumors that the British had struck across the border. Senior British officials returned this praise, providing some of the best evidence of the army's success in its peacekeeping duties: despite his usually acerbic reactions to Americans, British Ambassador Henry Fox considered the regulars "so usefully employed" in restraining the Patriots that he sought and received a tacit understanding that they would be kept on the frontier to do so while the Aroostook crisis was resolved.[31]

Army commanders had not always displayed such restraint toward border crises. Indeed, Winfield Scott's first hasty reaction to the rebellions in Canada was to write to Worth that "God grant them success! My heart is with the oppressed of both Canadas," and Worth responded to his commander's enthusiasm in much more ambiguous terms than he would soon come to rely on. Nevertheless, the officers placed in crisis situations along the Canadian border ultimately exercised the greatest restraint in their words and actions of any army officers involved in borderlands crises, a delicacy derived from the intersection of their mission and values with the practical demands of international diplomacy, the adverse balance of military power, and the principles of civil-military accountability. The officer corps' calm and restraint effectively assured military subordination to national civilian authority and helped to sustain peace between Britain and the United States without substantial injury to the "free institutions" or civil rights of Americans along the Canadian border.[32]

The Maine boundary crises of these years produced little military pressure for expansion at Canada's expense, but half a decade of tensions led a number of junior officers to increasing belligerence against the British. The Anglophobia of the early and mid-1840s had militarily rational roots produced by a decade of tensions with the most powerful nation in the world, and proclamations of European decrepitude and vulnerability like those made by some civilian expansionists remained less common in the minds of military commentators during the 1840s than fears of British aggressiveness and power. Indeed, despite the army's growing engagement in the southwest, most officers stationed outside that region thought Britain a more probable enemy than Mexico until early 1846. Nevertheless, officers, like civilians, were politically divided over the desirability of annexing Oregon, particularly to the 54°40' line, and the variety of officers' reactions to the crises with Britain during the 1830s and '40s clearly suggests the difficulty of attempting to assign uniform motives and attitudes to men of varied backgrounds and careers. Belligerence and Anglophobia were much more common among inexperienced young officers, who were more eager for promotion and more frustrated by the rigid promotion hierarchy and the widespread civilian criticism of the army (largely from expansionist Democrats suspicious of the army's authoritarianism and hierarchy) during the early 1840s, than among more established senior commanders like Worth, Scott, and Wool, who though veterans of the War of 1812 felt a strong kinship with the British born of culture, ethnicity, and mutual peacekeeping service during the "Patriot War."

Indeed, the junior officers of the '40s had grown up amidst the vivid partisan conflict of Jacksonian America and felt much the same desire to assume partisan affiliations as civilians, which led many to absorb the values and attitudes of Democratic expansionism. On the other hand, their impatience still developed within the context of professional leadership under civilian political direction, and the filibustering which so many officers had engaged in before 1820 did not again become popular among officers until the experience and emotion of the war with Mexico had stirred their ardor and ambition to new heights.[33]

Aside from the implications of official reports on the protection of the Santa Fe trade, the possibility of southwestern expansion received little if any written consideration during the mid-1820s, and U.S. officers cooperated with their Mexican counterparts in pursuit of law and order along the border of Texas. Indeed, General Gaines (Jackson's chief subordinate in the invasion of Florida, who served as the commander of the army's Western Department during most of the years between 1821 and 1845) wrote in 1823 to the War Department that he believed Mexican tales of banditry in East Texas to be true, and he asked whether he might advise the Mexicans that officers "pursuing offenders to the Sabine will find [aid] at our military posts; and on application to the civil authority (with proper evidence) may recover the stolen property if found within our limits."[34] The army's concerns with Indian removal, coastal fortifications, and its internal organization seem to have diverted whatever attention officers might otherwise have devoted to Texas during the following decade, but as American settlement in Texas accelerated the concerns of army commanders on the border subtly began to shift: in 1827 Gaines called for reinforcements on the border during the Edwards rebellion and directed Zachary Taylor, then commandant at New Orleans, to "cooperate with the revenue officers and other civil authorities, to prevent violations and evasions of the law; and to suppress any disorders which may grow out of the recent or future disturbances in Texas." (Gaines did not say whether this suppression would involve crossing the international boundary into Texas.) Nevertheless, few junior officers showed much interest in the growing unrest directed at Mexican rule: two years later commissary lieutenant William Colquohoun warned his superior that the

"Spaniard" posts near Fort Towson (on the Red River) needed watching, but Colquohoun's principal worry was the "desparate and violent" whites who had threatened public officers and property to the point that he suggested abandoning the post.[35]

As departmental commander Gaines was the officer most appropriately concerned with potential scenarios involving Texas, and, having served as Andrew Jackson's protégé during the First Seminole War, it is not surprising that he favored an actively expansionist policy. In 1830 he wrote to President Jackson implying that Texas belonged to the United States as part of the Louisiana Purchase and asserting that the renunciation of U.S. claims under the terms of the Transcontinental Treaty of 1821 had been unconstitutional. The region "must and will be restored to us," Gaines proclaimed: "when the people of Texas . . . demand admission into the union . . . they cannot [and] will not be refused." Nevertheless, President Jackson was seeking annexation by purchase rather than war, and very few officers besides Gaines seem to have given much consideration to the growing unrest in Texas during the early 1830s, even as Mexico increased its garrisons and the United States bound itself to restrain the southeastern Indians it was concentrating north of the Red River boundary.[36]

The officer corps' latent interest in the southwestern border was revived by the Texas Revolution, as the emergence of open hostilities aroused civilian sentiment in favor of the Anglo Texans and threatened to unleash Indian raids along the southwestern frontier of the United States. Even then, few officers committed their thoughts on the subject to paper, but those who did so provide us with two contrasting understandings of the Texas Revolution and the issues at stake in American expansionism, both prefiguring officers' attitudes toward annexation and war a decade later. Military Academy cadet Jubal Anderson Early, then in his third year at West Point, wrote home to his father in a furor over the Mexican attempt to suppress the rebellion. Early's rhetoric of romantic nationalism exemplified the ethnocentric attitudes commonly held by American civilians toward the rulers and institutions of Mexico, as well as a republican consciousness rarely found in so explicit and thoroughly articulated a form among army officers. Indeed, Early's ardently ideological espousal of the Texan cause is a virtual study in counterpoint to those of most other officers, whether in 1836 or a decade later. Early characterized the Anglo Texans as "respectable adventurers" and took pains to warn his father that they were not "land speculators and fugitives from justice," as public opinion in the north often charged, nor did he believe that the Texans were "attempting to subvert the laws, and overturn their lawful government" as many Whigs proclaimed.[37]

More characteristic of the social and political attitudes of the officer corps as a whole, the articulately Whiggish Vermonter Captain Ethan Allen Hitchcock (who remained ethically opposed to annexation and the war with Mexico even in 1847, though he led troops in every battle on the way to Mexico City) wrote to his mother that "the Texas cause looks much better at a distance than it does upon a near approach":

> The people of Texas made no opposition to Santa Anna or the Mexican government as long as they were not required to comply with the revenue laws & were permitted to keep slaves (which the Mexican constitution prohibits). [When these conditions changed] the people saw at once an end to their dream of wealth, and accusing the Mexican government of tyranny assailed, abused, and drove off the custom house officers & prepared for defenses. . . . They were immediately joined by a large band of land speculators (who are always prowling around new countries), and this war of independence as it is called is in fact a rebellion.

Gaines sent Hitchcock (his acting inspector general) to warn Santa Anna "not to violate our neutrality" or supply the Indians, but Hitchcock's understanding of the crisis was exactly the opposite of Early's: "if [Santa Anna] abstains from enticing the Indians he . . . will deserve success." Although few if any of his fellow officers would have gone so far as to hope for the Texans' defeat, Hitchcock's suspicion of aggressive expansionism was certainly more widely expressed than Early's ardent republican expansionism among the members of the officer corps who left records of their opinions.[38]

That fall Gaines occupied Nacogdoches in accordance with War Department instructions, but he did not advance any deeper into Texas or engage in combat. Like many of the officer corps' actions on the frontiers, Gaines's measures had the potential to cause political and diplomatic embarrassment to the government but were not substantially irresponsible in and of themselves. Given the difficulty of communication and the need to grant local commanders discretion prior to the advent of the telegraph, it is hardly remarkable that this should have been the case. Indeed, if anything it is surprising that officers did not use their discretion to exceed their often (and often purposely) vague instructions and engage in unauthorized but perhaps tacitly sanctioned expansionism more frequently, as Jackson and his subordinates had in Florida between 1816 and 1818. Gaines acted aggressively in 1836, but he did not actually initiate the move to Nacogdoches or depart from basic government policy to seize pretexts or opportunities to intervene. Indeed, given his past experiences it may be said that he exercised laudable caution and responsibility, aside from his repeated calls for volunteers, a case in which the government found military preparation incompatible with political and diplomatic restraint. Neither Gaines nor Jackson acted effectively to stop the flow of American supplies and volunteers to Texas, but Gaines did not actively support the Texan forces, nor did he attack the Mexican ones, as Jackson and Ripley had done in similar situations along the Spanish frontiers two decades before. Gaines was certainly excitable, often impetuous, and occasionally petulant when he felt his pride injured by superiors, but his preparations were responsible ones given his past experiences and his sense of accountability to the citizens of the southwestern frontier, and Jackson's criticism of his former protégé concealed the reality that Gaines had acted appropriately given U.S. policy objectives and the circumstances in question.[39]

Another potential Texan crisis appeared in August 1838 when a rebellion by Mexicans and Indians near Nacogdoches led Sam Houston to call for assistance from Colonel James Many of the 3rd Infantry, a forty-year veteran. Many correctly refused this request, and that November he took a force of 165 troops and cannon to Shreveport to drive back a group of Texans who had crossed the border and attacked the Caddo Indians on U.S. soil. Orders promulgated that December gave American commanders a pretext to build up forces along the Texan border in order to prevent Indians under U.S. jurisdiction from participating in conflicts in Texas, but there was no military policy of "hot pursuit" in Texas as there had been in Florida or as was practiced from Texas against Indians raiding from Mexico after the Civil War—army officers simply did not engage in quasi-official filibusters after the conquest of Florida and the political firestorm that ensued. Indeed, the focus of the army's attention did not return to the southwest until 1842, when tensions between Texas and Mexico reached a new peak. In March of that year Ethan Allen Hitchcock reported widespread rumors of an Indian council and alliance with Mexico against Texas, and Zachary Taylor (now a brevet brigadier general by virtue of his performance in the Second Seminole War) was ordered to prevent the Indians and Texans from attacking one another across the international boundary. Taylor urged the secretary of war to ignore these rumors as self-interested exaggerations intended to precipitate American intervention on the Texans' behalf, but he received fifteen companies of reinforcements, increasing his force at Fort Towson from less than seven hundred men to about two thousand. This move represented the first large-scale commitment of forces to the southwestern border since 1836, and in some respects it can be considered the origin of Taylor's Armies of Observation and Occupation, but the overt purpose of this force was much the same as that on the Canadian border—keeping the peace and maintaining U.S. neutrality.[40]

The rumors notwithstanding, nothing beyond the usual marauding occurred, but the raids gave unscrupulous Texans and men claiming to represent that republic excuses to seek plunder by raiding into the Indian Territory. Texas also issued warrants to her citizens authorizing them to attack Mexican caravans on the Santa Fe trail, leading to protests by American businessmen and the Mexican government, and in 1843 a force of U.S. dragoons was sent to escort merchants along the trail—an expedition officers saw simply as a matter of law enforcement rather than a Trojan Horse for American expansion. That summer Captain Philip St. George Cooke met and disarmed a group of Texan privateers in U.S. territory, spurring diplomatic protests from Texas. Gaines strongly supported Cooke's decision, which was criticized in some civilian quarters as a threat to American relations with Texas, as part of the army's long-running efforts to suppress lawlessness and filibustering along the nation's borders, using language not much unlike (though characteristically more aggressive than) Worth's and Scott's along the Canadian frontier five years before: "It is our bounden duty to put down all predatory movements of this sort of land privateering, such as have too long contributed to mark the character of men calling themselves members of American Republics. . . . We must *destroy, arrest, or disarm* all such lawless combinations, whenever found within or near our *unmarked boundary.*" Indeed, Captain John Burgwin used the occasion to draw the link between officers' aspirations for personal prestige and their public services as enforcers of international law: "I hope he will get some credit for his service, which I think will be most beneficial." The State Department rebuffed Texan protests, Cooke was promptly sent out in command of a second escort, and his fellow officers cleared him of any misconduct in a court of inquiry held the following year.[41]

This restraint had definite limits, however; Gaines' support for action against "predatory bands . . . disposed to violate the known laws of war" did not represent a repudiation of expansionism, only of action unauthorized by the federal government he served. Like Jackson a quarter-century before, Gaines felt capable of interpreting the government's policy himself, assuming responsibility as the senior officer in the region to react to fluid conditions in accordance with the general trend of national policy. Doubtlessly encouraged by Polk's election, Gaines reacted aggressively to the annexation of Texas and the possibility of war with Mexico by calling for volunteers, but his proclamations were countermanded and disavowed by the War Department, and after several months of argument he was recalled to Washington, court-martialed, and sent to wait out the war in New York. Indeed, the command of the Army of Occupation was entrusted to Taylor in part because he was the senior officer on the spot when President Tyler ordered the first concentration in 1842, in part because of Winfield Scott's endless feud with Gaines, and in part because Taylor was clearly the sort of steady, unexcitable general who could and would devote his energies to the administration's policy and the mission at hand regardless of his own political beliefs.[42]

Surprisingly, Taylor was sent south from the Nueces without any guidance beyond his initial instructions to take up defensive positions opposite Matamoros, and the previously close cooperation between Taylor and American chargé d'affaires Andrew Jackson Donelson apparently ceased once the army moved south from Corpus Christi, leaving Taylor, who his most recent biographer has characterized as "one of the least [diplomatically] sensitive senior officers in the army," alone to handle the tensions exacerbated by the American advance into territory claimed by Mexico. While this decision may indicate that Polk hoped to precipitate a war through Taylor's agency, the general's responsible performance may equally suggest that his very stolidity reflected a sense of dutiful accountability to civilian political direction that calls his alleged diplomatic incapacity into question. Taylor was certainly not the diplomat Worth or Scott was, but he could be counted on to act coolly, unlike the rash Gaines or the politically active Scott. (Indeed, Gaines was probably the most "Jacksonian" of the army's experienced senior officers, for Scott was widely spoken of as a Whig presidential candidate as early as 1840. Worth was a Whig, though he came to favor expansionism to the south, while General Wool had fallen out with Jackson during his supervision of Cherokee removal in 1836. Quartermaster General Jesup was a Democrat who actively sought field command but discouraged talk of a political career, and the administration could hardly use its chief logistician when an officer of greater frontier experience was available in Taylor.) As in President Monroe's handling of Andrew Jackson in 1818, the administration's laxity was a clear prescription for war, but Taylor showed surprising patience under the circumstances and did not exceed his instructions or act to precipitate war. In contrast to the corps' record of support for aggression against Spanish Florida before 1820, the regulars of the 1840s made no effort to initiate or justify action independent of the civil government, nor did Taylor or other Whigs seek to undermine the policies their party opposed.[43]

The annexation of Texas was sanctioned by the national government, and army officers rather than private filibusters were the men who finally carried American sovereignty to the banks of the Rio Grande and beyond. Many officers enthusiastically sought posts in Texas in hopes of distinguishing themselves in combat, but their overwhelming consensus (much like Polk's expectation) was that Mexico would back down and nothing would happen. Some officers thought expansion a positive good; certainly many stressed the benefits of active professional employment and an increase in the army's size (and thus in command slots, promotions, and compensation); and a number opposed annexation, whether from principle or personal convenience. The point is not that officers were ardent Whigs morally opposed to annexation, but that they did not express expansionist sentiments ardently, articulately, or often. Self-interested careerism and the military professional's belief in the necessity for military preparation may have predisposed army officers to hope for expansion and war but did not necessarily cause them to do so, and the principal determinants of officers' reactions to being posted in Texas were personal considerations of family, health, and career opportunities rather than partisan or ideological factors. Uncertainty rather than enthusiasm dominated their emotions, for Texas was an unattractive post unless there was actually a war to be fought.

The army's most obvious mission, the role which gave its officers their strongest sense of professional purpose and identity, was war, but officers' letters and diaries expressed surprisingly little eagerness for war prior to the actual onset of combat. The papers of regular officers collected at West Point and the Library of Congress contain remarkably few references to the probability, causes, or desirability of war with Mexico, particularly in the years before 1846 itself, and those of future Civil War generals which have been collected and published show little of the ardent expansionism and belligerence one would expect from "agents of empire," Anglo-Saxon racialists, or romantic nationalists. Once they arrived in Texas, most regulars mentioned the Army of Occupation's intensified regimen of training and drills only briefly, and soon found them boring, "the dull routine of a life of military instruction," to quote Lieutenant Napoleon Dana. Most of their letters from Texas present descriptions of camp life and the climate, and their leading concern appears to have been for their health and that of their wives and families back east. Indeed, West Point cadet William Dutton hoped that Texas would choose independence rather than annexation, because he feared that "their climate will be the death of many [officers]."[44]

Indeed, even after we account for the influence of family and health considerations, officers' quietude concerning the important questions of annexation and war is nothing short of amazing unless we connect their reactions to the imperatives of employment by the nation-state and the consequent desire to maintain orderly international relations conducive to direction and monopoly by that state structure and its military agents. The officer corps reacted to the political debates surrounding the crisis with remarkable disinterest; they often mentioned the annexation question in a casual way but did not comment on it in any detail. While it seems probable that the majority of officers were pleased with the annexation of Texas and would have welcomed war with Mexico, they expressed their views quietly and nonideologically, with professionally accountable and nonpartisan respect for civilian political direction. Unlike civilian editors and politicians, army officers junior and senior wrote virtually nothing about the costs or benefits of annexation and war for the United States as a whole. Many officers from Taylor on down were Whigs or inclined in that direction socially, but remarkably few expressed their opposition to expansionism in writing, and only one seems to have done so in a public forum. This quietude had two sides, of course, for it signified that officers would not refuse to serve in the execution of an expansionist policy many personally opposed. Similarly, the officer corps' conception of itself as a nonpartisan group dedicated to national goals seems to have discouraged officers from commenting on the sensitive issue of slavery or the potential of annexation and expansion for sectional gain or conflict.[45]

Recent historians have re-envisioned the impetus for Manifest Destiny in fears for the survival of the Jeffersonian social order amidst growing urbanization and industrialization, but army officers rarely expressed republican or other ideological sentiments in any detail or in any form save that of antipartisanship, which suited their sense of nationalism and complemented their desire for career security regardless of electoral change. Indeed, much of this inarticulateness should be attributed to the officer corps' nascent professional ethic, which stressed national service in the politically and ideologically neutral form of "duty" rather than "mission." In other words, American officers aspired to a sort of putatively "objective" responsibility to the nation-state which employed them rather than a subjective one to the ideals of agrarian republicanism, "free institutions," or the ethnocultural community of romantic nationalists. The officer corps' political behavior and its concept of accountability to civilian control is therefore best encapsulated in the phrase "careerist neutrality," which implies not political isolation or alienation, nor—and this is significant—simple self-interestedness, but antipartisan nationalism and a focus on the internal bureaucratic politics of promotions, postings, and the allocation of resources and power among different branches of the army. Officers certainly did not lack ties to political elites, but their demands on civilian society were usually limited to increases in military spending and compensation, professional command over the militia and volunteers in time of war, and attempts to control entry into and the values of the officer corps by requiring specialized training and socialization at West Point. Regular officers left analyses of the war's costs and benefits to different sectors of society to the growing political and editorial professions.[46]

Individual officers reacted to service in Texas in ambiguous ways shaped largely by personal considerations. Most officers took it for granted that Mexico was no match for the United States. Indeed, they expected the army's advance to the Rio Grande to go uncontested, and most believed that this would compel Mexico to peacefully submit to U.S. dictates, but prior to 1846 few of them advocated or expected that the United States take advantage of Mexico's weakness to seek further expansion. Indeed, while many officers sought duty in Texas, significant numbers tried to avoid it, and most found it difficult to sustain their initial enthusiasm as the months dragged by without a resolution to the crisis. The close quarters and tedium of camp life dampened the corps' ardor, and restlessness bred dissension, demoralization, and talk of resignation. "A camp where there is no active service is a dull and stupid place," wrote Lieutenant George Meade in the fall of 1845: "[I]t seems we are not even to have the consolation of a little glory, but are to remain here rusting in idleness, or rather in drilling and parading." As early as that September Lieutenant John Porter Hatch asserted that "promotions from resignations are quite rapid"; he suggested that he would not mind a transfer to Florida since Texas was so isolated, while a substantial number of officers suggested that resignation was preferable to a long wait without prospect of combat.[47] Both Meade and Ulysses Grant wrote constantly about securing leaves of absence with which to visit their loved ones, and the two lieutenants commented extensively on other officers' efforts to do so. Indeed, as late as the beginning of March, Grant assured his fiancée that "I do not think that I will stand another year of idleness in camp."

Among more senior officers, President Polk's ruling that Colonel David Twiggs's seniority in permanent rank overrode that of William Worth in brevet led the latter, one of the army's most experienced, distinguished, and (until then) responsible commanders, to submit his resignation and head for Washington to argue his case. Worth returned as soon as he heard of the Mexican advance across the Rio Grande, but he was too late to command his troops at Palo Alto and Resaca de la Palma.[48]

By the beginning of 1846 the Army of Occupation seemed to be gripped by a malaise, and Lieutenant James Wall Schureman relayed the news that "the excitement of the contemplated campaign, the ardor for distinction, and all the soldier's incentives have one by one vanished and left them sad and gloomy. . . . The state of the Army of Occupation is the prostration of a patient after the fever has subsided; our Regiment has cause to be thankful that it is not there." Zachary Taylor confirmed that "one of the principal diseases now among the officers . . . is homesickness," and he typified the officer corps in this as well as his lack of enthusiasm for expansion: "All the pomp & parade of [the Army of Occupation is] lost on me; I now sigh for peace & quiet with my family around me." On the other hand, personal considerations did spur officers to hope for battle as soon as possible, because they blamed Mexico for the interminable negotiations that kept them far from their families while waiting for some resolution. "There will not be a hostile gun fired, but we shall have to drag through a hot and tedious summer here without our families, infinitely worse than all the horrors of war. It is nonsense for our government to temporize any longer with the Mexico," Captain Philip Barbour wrote impatiently in April, and these tensions impelled some officers to hope for a quick battle in order to convince Mexico of American invincibility. As was so often the case, George Meade's attitudes probably typified the officer corps' feelings after several months of inactivity had passed. Meade was consumed with longing for his wife but hoped to draw some prestige out of his sacrifice; he wrote to her in February that "I hope for a war and a speedy battle, and I think that one good fight will settle the business; [for] really, after coming so far and staying so long, it would hardly be the thing to come back without some laurels."[49]

As this language suggests, the interplay between personal frustration and organizational accountability was ultimately both dialectical and symbiotic. The growth of the Whig party combined with constant Democratic criticism of the army and its officers during the early 1840s may have made the officer corps more hesitant to draw congressional fire by taking overt positions on the desirability of expansion, while the irritation which officers stored up waiting for the war to begin seems to have reinforced the desire to prove themselves that was spurred by congressional attacks. Whatever officers' frustrations, resignations were actually rare, and the corps remained properly quiescent until events provided them with the opportunity to unleash their energies against Mexico. The final reactions of officers awaiting combat were a sense of duty that showed neither elation nor alienation from the task at hand: "I go to meet the enemy with my feelings all schooled to do my duty regardless of personal consequences," wrote Philip Barbour. This mind-set of dutiful service ultimately typified army officers' attitudes toward the coming of war with Mexico, helping to account for the surprising rarity of ardently warlike or expansionist sentiments in the officer corps. Whatever the initial elation displayed by some, the army's overwhelming reaction to service in Texas was simple boredom, and few regulars found satisfactory relief in attention to their professional duties or analyses of the political and diplomatic context they were performed in. When the war came the officer corps fought skillfully, courageously, and successfully, but conflict seemed so unlikely that few officers could sustain much enthusiasm for the prospect until hostilities had actually begun. Until then, the attitude that characterized the corps best was George Meade's hope "that the whole affair will be settled before spring, [to] enable me and many other victims to rejoin our disconsolate wives."[50]

Army officers' unenthusiastic responses to the opportunities presented by expansion demonstrate the close links between institutional maturity, occupational monopoly, elite class and nation-state formation, and professional accountability in the development of the commissioned officer corps during the period between 1815 and 1846. The officers who came to dominate the army's lower commissioned ranks once West Point began to provide the majority of the army's new lieutenants could not pursue their dreams of foreign conquest as independently as their predecessors on the southern frontiers, for they lacked the social, political, and regional prominence that officers like Andrew Jackson or James Wilkinson (the commanding general from 1796 to 1812, and a notorious intriguer) had used to bypass the legal and constitutional channels of national civilian authority in quest of personal, sectional, and national aggrandizement. Though appointed through political influence, the junior officers of the 1830s and '40s were not gentry leaders or party politicians themselves, and by the 1830s unrestrained individualism no longer seemed a successful mode of action and personal advancement to men from middling social origins who aspired to genteel status and prestige in a less deferential society. The professional rhetoric of neutral duty, service, and responsibility proved materially and psychologically attractive to such men, and they increasingly made the army a long-term career rather than a temporary avocation. As American society became more fluid and democratic, officers felt a growing threat to their livelihoods and their ability to command respect, but rather than resigning their commissions to pursue the growing economic opportunities in the competitive civilian marketplace, officers responded with a strong distaste for disorder and a pursuit of structured advancement through a bureaucratic hierarchy —in short, through careerism in its institutional form. For the army officer corps, the answer to uncertainty and the means of social ascent lay in the availability of a fledgling bureaucracy that could fuse officers' material needs (for security at a socially "respectable" level) with their pretensions to disinterested social service, authority, and legitimacy. Duty, honor, and country came to mean that officers won honor, glory, and reputation by dutifully serving their country, whether as peacekeepers and law enforcers or directors—but not initiators—of conquest.

These changing occupational circumstances influenced officers' nuanced responses to the complex foreign policy problems they confronted. The army was the first public-sector employer on a national scale in the United States, and its officers espoused centralist values that served, but were also shaped by, their duties and interests. Their occupational roles as the principal defenders of national and federal sovereignty fostered a strong personal and institutional interest in increasing the federal government's power and legitimacy, and their ongoing search for personal and organizational security bred a yearning for order and stability that regulars expressed in the stern idiom of legalism and national sovereignty. Their vocation challenged by Americans' fondness for the locally controlled militia and its extralegal counterpart, the filibustering expedition, regular officers increasingly responded by stressing the importance of centralized national control over the organized use of military force. These biases were clearly present in their disdain for the Canadian and Texan rebels, who elevated doctrines of natural right and democracy over the rule of domestic and international law while usurping the regulars' jobs as managers of organized violence. Filibustering was a threat to domestic law and social order and a demonstration of the limits of the government's sovereignty over its own people, whereas the officer corps sought national security through orderly processes of centralized diplomatic negotiation and military preparation, which provided employment for the army and posed little danger of serious conflict with the army's civilian employers.

This lack of enthusiasm for expansion does not mean that army officers were isolated or alienated from their society, though some of its values irritated and even disgusted them, for their sense of accountability to civilian direction was enhanced not by an ideological faith in the glories of democracy and republicanism but by their occupational position as members of an organization dependent on republican political processes (congressional appropriations and confirmation of executive appointments) for its authority and survival. Historian Thomas Hietala has recently demonstrated that in the 1840s "many Democratic expansionists viewed the acquisition of land and markets as essential to their program for sustaining the unique character of American social and political life." While neither insensible to these desiderata nor incapable of profiting from their pursuit, army officers no longer lived within the Jeffersonian world that the civilian expansionists were attempting to preserve and restore. Their service within increasingly formalized bureaucratic institutions led them to a broadly Whiggish (yet institutionally nonpartisan) perspective which valued order, restraint, and stability in all aspects of personal and national life, and as the putatively neutral servants of the nation-state, army officers essentially sat out what Hietala calls the central cultural conflict of the decade.[51]

Surprising as it may seem, careerist self-interest actually made the regular officers of the 1830s and '40s less likely to seek expansion and war or to willfully violate American neutrality and foreign borders than their predecessors. Professional military men often find war unattractive because of the likelihood that it will disrupt the organizational (and thus personal) stability built up in times of peace, a consideration that naturally grows in strength as an army becomes more institutionally mature. Commanders before and after 1820 both spoke in the cautious language of realism, preparation, and national interest and sought to defend U.S. sovereignty along the frontiers, but officers committed to lifelong army careers and increasingly sensitive to the fragility of the social order and their place within it came to fear that American national honor and security were endangered by unauthorized military action. The personal and occupational security provided by a national bureaucracy encouraged accountability as well as laxity, and men with careers as secure as those of army officers did not need Manifest Destiny to advance themselves: they had a definite stake in orderly national expansion, but they did not need to take the political and military risks of urging or precipitating it. The army's accountability to civilian political control flowed both directly and ironically from its employment by the nation-state, and the officer corps' role and interests as the principal defenders of American national sovereignty came to mesh quite smoothly with their individual and organizational searches for prestige, authority, and legitimacy, but not in the simple monolithic form of support for Manifest Destiny and empire.

NOTES

1. "Agents of Empire" is Francis Paul Prucha's title for his chapter on the officer corps in *The Sword of the Republic: The United States Army on the Frontier, 1783–1846* (London: Macmillan, 1969).

2. See William Earl Weeks, "New Directions in the Study of Early American Foreign Relations," *Diplomatic History* 17 (Winter, 1993): 73–95. Many elements of my argument will be familiar to readers of William B. Skelton, *An American Profession of Arms: The Army Officer Corps, 1784–1861* (Lawrence: University Press of Kansas, 1992), although he sees a good deal more enthusiasm for expansionism than I do. Most previous studies have located the officer corps' professionalization in the post—Civil War era; see e.g. Edward M. Coffman, *The Old Army: A Portrait of the American Army in Peacetime, 1784–1898* (New York: Oxford University Press, 1986); Russell F. Weigley, *History of the United States Army* (New York: Macmillan, 1967); and Allan R. Millett, *Military Professionalism and Officership in America* (Columbus: Mershon Center of Ohio State University, 1977). The form and content of the officer corps' professionalism varied widely depending on the circumstances and issues in question; I would maintain that its greatest success lay in the development of accountability to civilian political control (however centralized in the nation-state). In turn, employment by the nation-state was indispensable to the regular officer corps and its professionalization project, for this sponsorship enabled the army to carve out a legal monopoly unavailable to the other occupations aspiring to professional status during this era. I have not explored the nuances of accountability to executive direction versus that to congressional oversight, matters dealt with at some length for the post—Civil War era in Samuel P. Huntington, *The Soldier and the State: The Theory and Practice of Civil-Military Relations* (Cambridge, Mass.: Harvard University Press, 1957). There are no monographic treatments devoted primarily to this subject for the years between 1800 and 1865.

3. See Reginald C. Stuart, "Special Interests and National Authority in Foreign Policy: American-British Provincial Links during the Embargo and the War of 1812" *Diplomatic History* 8 (Fall, 1984): 311–28, on similar problems from an earlier period; see Stephen Peter Rosen, "Alexander Hamilton and the Domestic Uses of International Law," *Diplomatic History* 5 (Summer, 1981): 183–98, and Daniel G. Lang, *Foreign Policy in the Early Republic: The Law of Nations and the Balance of Power* (Baton Rouge: Louisiana State University Press, 1985), regarding the identification of domestic and international law and order in the mind and actions of an earlier conservative.

4. Skelton, "High Army Leadership in the Era of the War of 1812: The Making and Remaking of the Officer Corps," *William and Mary Quarterly* 51 (April, 1994): 258 (table 2), surveys the geographic origins of the army's field and general officers appointed between 1808 and 1815, and *An American Profession of Arms*, table 9.1 (p. 155), provides an assessment of the geographical origins of the officers on the 1830 and 1860 army lists.

5. See Robert E. May, "Young American Males and Filibustering in the Age of Manifest Destiny: The United States Army as a Cultural Mirror," *Journal of American History* 78 (December, 1991): 857–86. Officers often found the Jacksonian sense of boundlessness somewhat daunting, and they were generally reluctant to accept the implications of the "self-made manhood" increasingly applauded in civilian society. Many felt themselves unsuited to the more demanding tempo of business life and found the army's ordered pace attractive. See Skelton, "The Army Officer as Organization Man," in *Soldiers and Civilians: The U.S. Army and the American People*, ed. Garry D. Ryan and Timothy K. Nenninger (Washington, D.C.: National Archives, 1987), pp. 61–70, especially 62–64.

6. Army officers generally espoused values that harked backward to the ideal of the eighteenth-century gentleman. Though primarily from middle-class rather than elite economic backgrounds, army officers learned and espoused genteel values of social distance (i.e., hierarchy), personal decorum, and honor, to aspire to public fame and reputation rather than material wealth. Army officers fit more comfortably into the republican society of the early national period than the liberal or democratic one of the Jacksonian era; see Richard L. Bushman, *The Refinement of America, 1750–1850: Persons, Houses, Cities* (New York: Alfred A. Knopf, 1993) for an analysis of what might be called "the gentrification of the middle class" during this era and a recognition of the survival of aristocratic values in the early republic.

7. See Anna Kasten Nelson, "Destiny and Diplomacy, 1840–1865," in Gerald K. Haines and J. Samuel Walker, eds., *American Foreign Relations: A Historiographical Review* (Westport, Conn.: Greenwood Press, 1981), p. 53, echoing the argument first set out by Norman A. Graebner, *Empire on the Pacific: A Study in American Continental Expansion* (New York: Ronald Press, 1955).

8. Lt. George Meade to his wife Margaretta, September 18, 1845, in *The Life and Letters of George Gordon Meade, Major-General United States Army, Volume I*, text by George Meade (New York: Charles Scribner's Sons, 1913), p. 26: "General Taylor . . . is a staunch Whig, and opposed *in toto* to the Texas annexation, and therefore does not enter heart and soul into his present duties." "He is said to be very tired of this country, and the duty assigned to him, and is supposed will return on the arrival of General Worth." Meade warned his wife not to repeat the rumor. Holman Hamilton, *Zachary Taylor: Soldier of the Republic* (Indianapolis: Bobbs-Merrill, 1941), p. 167, suggests that Taylor's thoughts of retirement were common gossip in the Army of Occupation.

9. See Isaac J. Cox, *The West Florida Controversy, 1790–1813: A Study in American Diplomacy* (Baltimore: Johns Hopkins Press, 1918); Rembert W. Patrick, *Florida Fiasco: Rampant Rebels on the Georgia-Florida Border, 1810–1815* (Athens: University

of Georgia Press, 1954), and Wanjohi Waciuma, *Intervention in Spanish Florida, 1801–1813: A Study in Jeffersonian Foreign Policy* (Boston: Branden Press, 1976), on U.S. aggression against Florida prior to the War of 1812; David S. Heidler and Jeanne T. Heidler, *Old Hickory's War: Andrew Jackson and the Quest for Empire* (Mechanicsburg, Pa.: Stackpole Books, 1996), provides the most thorough narrative of Jackson's invasions. See Harris Gaylord Warren, *The Sword Was Their Passport: A History of American Filibustering in the Mexican Revolution* (Baton Rouge: Louisiana State University Press, 1943), pp. 244–51, and Capt. William C. Beard's letters to Jackson and Ripley, as enclosures to Jackson's report dated July 24, 1819, in file J-55, Office of the Secretary of War: Letters Received, Registered Series (hereafter SW: LR-Reg.), Record Group 107, National Archives, concerning the Long expeditions. Though unsuccessful as a leader of filibusters, Eleazar Ripley maintained his connections in the world of southwestern affairs and eventually served as a congressman from Louisiana between 1835 and 1837. Jesup's plans are discussed in Chester L. Kieffer, *Maligned General: The Biography of Thomas Sidney Jesup* (San Rafael, Calif.: Presidio Press, 1979), pp. 55–58.

Jackson was certainly not foreclosing future options, for in December, 1820, he remarked to Calhoun that "if we do not possess the Floridas, I have supposed we would take possession of Texas . . . to the Rio Grande." Nevertheless, Jackson cautioned Secretary of State Adams against demanding Texas in the Transcontinental Treaty lest he jeopardize the primary strategic objective of securing Florida and the southern flank. See Jackson to Calhoun, December 21, 1820, Jackson Papers, Library of Congress (hereafter LC), and Charles F. Adams, ed., *Memoirs of John Quincy Adams, Comprising Portions of His Diary from 1795 to 1848*, 12 vols. (Philadelphia: J. B. Lippincott, 1874–1877), vol. 4, p. 239. See William Earl Weeks, *John Quincy Adams and American Global Empire* (Lexington: University Press of Kentucky, 1992), concerning the Transcontinental Treaty.

Like Ripley, Winfield Scott mixed republican zeal and practical caution in his views on the provision of aid to revolutionaries in Spanish Latin America; see Scott to Secretary of State Monroe, November 18, 1815, and March 19, 1816, from Paris and Liverpool, in the Winfield Scott Papers, United States Military Academy Library at West Point (hereafter abbreviated USMA) (originals in the State Department Archives in Washington, D.C.). Scott reported the secret discussions he had held with liberal Spanish general Espoz y Mina, but noted his caveat that aid would be supplied solely by purchase, and only if the United States were at war with Spain. (Whether Scott's caution was primarily directed toward protecting himself or the U.S. government is unclear.) Scott gave Mina letters of introduction to U.S. officials and met with him again in New York later that year. See Warren, *The Sword Was Their Passport*, pp. 149–51.

10. Scott to Secretary of War Calhoun, August 20, 1820, file S-37, SW: LR-Reg.
11. Taylor to Jesup, January 20, 1824, Taylor Papers, series 2, reel 1, LC. Reginald C. Stuart, *War and American Thought, from the Revolution to the Monroe Doctrine* (Kent, Ohio: Kent State University Press, 1982), provides an analysis of American attitudes toward war generally applicable to the army officer corps. Stuart sees increasing expansionism as a threat to the European-derived "limited-war

mentality" he attributes to the early national period, which was ultimately true for army officers who feared the loss of national and occupational control embodied in the actions of filibusters and the use of volunteers. Military officers absorbed European standards and sensibilities to a greater degree than most Americans and therefore constitute an excellent example of the declining sense of American exceptionalism (via the growing acceptance of European principles of international law) that Stuart observes in the realm of foreign relations in *United States Expansionism and British North America, 1775–1871* (Chapel Hill: University of North Carolina Press, 1988), p. 84. See Bradford Perkins, *Castlereagh and Adams: England and the United States, 1812–1823* (Berkeley: University of California Press, 1964) on Anglo-American relations; John M. Belohlavek, *"Let the Eagle Soar!": The Foreign Policy of Andrew Jackson* (Lincoln: University of Nebraska Press, 1985), ch. 1, and Douglas M. Astolfi, *Foundations of Destiny: A Foreign Policy of the Jacksonians, 1824–1837* (New York: Garland, 1989), ch. 1, for the decline of republican internationalism among Jacksonians in the 1820s; and John J. Johnson, *A Hemisphere Apart: The Foundations of United States Policy toward Latin America* (Baltimore: Johns Hopkins University Press, 1990) on U.S. reactions to the revolutions. Richard C. Rohrs, "American Critics of the French Revolution of 1848," *Journal of the Early Republic* 14 (Fall, 1994): 359–77, suggests the increasing conservatism of U.S. responses to liberal revolutions in Europe.

12. Major William Jenkins Worth to Secretary of War Joel R. Poinsett, February 12, 1838, in Worth's official letterbook, LC (Worth hereafter cited as simply "Worth to x," unless another source has been used). See Albert B. Corey, *The Crisis of 1830–1842 in Canadian-American Relations* (New Haven: Yale University Press, 1941), p. 49 (note 17) for Poinsett's instructions to Scott, which the State Department relayed to the British. The Neutrality Act of March 10, 1838, permitted the seizure of arms upon probable cause and authorized the use of military force to aid the civil authorities, but the latter were still necessary to provide warrants for searches, seizures, and arrests.

13. Like most scholars, I use the contemporary term "Patriots" to refer to the initial rebels, their U.S. supporters in the winter of 1837–38, the Canadian Refugee Relief Association, the "Sons of Liberty," the "Hunters' Lodges," and any other organizations devoted to filibustering against Canada during this period, for neither army officers nor other commentators seem to have differentiated closely between them. Corey, *The Crisis of 1830–1842 in Canadian-American Relations*, p. 78, notes that of 140 filibusters taken prisoner by the British in November, 1838, near Windmill Point, "practically every man was a laborer, dependent for the most part upon seasonal employment." The wages offered by the Patriots were eight dollars a month, the same as those of a private in the U.S. Army at the time. John J. Duffy and H. Nicholas Muller stress the social and psychological dimensions of the Patriot fever in *An Anxious Democracy: Aspects of the 1830s* (Westport, Conn.: Greenwood Press, 1982), observing that Vermont professionals almost uniformly opposed the movement because of a mindset that stressed order and stability, while many businessmen supported it, even against their own interests (p. 50).

14. See Stuart, *United States Expansionism and British North America*; Howard Jones,

To the Webster-Ashburton Treaty: A Study in Anglo-American Relations, 1783–1843
(Chapel Hill: University of North Carolina Press, 1977); and Kenneth R. Stevens,
*Border Diplomacy: The Caroline and McLeod Affairs in Anglo-American-Canadian
Relations, 1837–1842* (Tuscaloosa: University of Alabama Press, 1989). See Corey,
The Crisis of 1830–1842 in Canadian- American Relations, ch. 6; Gordon Stewart,
The American Response to Canada since 1776 (East Lansing: Michigan State
University Press, 1992), pp. 42–44; and Stuart, p. 143, for examples of conservative
opinion. See Frederick Merk (with the collaboration of Lois Bannister Merk), *The
Monroe Doctrine and American Expansionism, 1843–1849* (New York: Alfred A.
Knopf, 1966) and Thomas R. Hietala, *Manifest Design: Anxious Aggrandizement in
Late Jacksonian America* (Ithaca: Cornell University Press, 1985), regarding U.S.
fears of encirclement.

15. Lt. (and assistant adjutant general, or AAG) Robert Anderson to Representative
    Gouverneur Kemble of New York, January 12, 1839, Robert Anderson Papers, LC;
    Worth to Poinsett, February 12, 1838. I have found very few comments about the
    possibility of expansion into Canada in officers' correspondence from this period.
    Worth's later interest in filibustering to the south is discussed in May, "Young
    American Males and Filibustering in the Age of Manifest Destiny," pp. 879–80, and
    Skelton, *An American Profession of Arms*, pp. 330–31, uses Worth as a prime
    example of expansionism and Anglo-Saxon racialism in the officer corps; the
    contrast to his attitudes toward the Patriots is therefore all the more instructive.

16. Major Benjamin F. Larned to Robert Anderson, April 23, 1839, Anderson Papers,
    LC; Scott to Poinsett, January 12, 1839, in Stacey, p. 412; Worth to Capt. William R.
    Montgomery, December 19, 1838; Brady to Adjutant General Jones (December 6,
    1838), Scott (February 26, 1838), and Jones (June 29, 1838), in Francis Paul Prucha,
    ed., "Reports of General Brady on the Patriot War," *Canadian Historical Review* 31
    (March, 1950): 56–68 (hereafter cited only as "Brady to *x*," unless a different source
    from Brady has been used).

17. "Disorganizers": Brady to Jones, February 26, 1838, and Anderson to Kemble, op.
    cit.; "agitators": Worth to Scott, February 13, 1838, and March 21, 1839;
    "adventurers": Worth to Jones, February 23, 1838, and Worth to Poinsett, March 3,
    1838 (in Stacey, p. 408) ("miserable"), and deputy quartermaster general Henry
    Whiting to Robert Anderson, March 14, 1840, Anderson Papers, LC
    ("unprincipled").

18. Brady to Jones, June 8, 1838; Brady to Scott, January 14, 1838; Worth to Lt. Col.
    Newman Clarke, November 1, 1838.

19. Worth to Scott, February 9, 1839, and to Poinsett, February 12, 1838; Brady to Jones,
    June 27 and June 8, 1838, and to Scott, February 2 and 15, January 14, and March 14,
    1838; Worth to Poinsett, November 15, 1838, and to the British Officer
    Commanding at Kingston, November 23, 1838. All of these attitudes were common
    in "respectable" civilian society, the press, and official circles outside the border
    region; see Corey, *The Crisis of 1830–1842 in Canadian-American Relations*, ch. 6.

20. Anderson to Kemble, January 12, 1839, and Whiting to Anderson, March 14, 1840,
    Anderson Papers, LC; Worth to Col. Abraham Eustis, November 20, 1838.

21. Worth to Poinsett (March 3, 1838) (in Stacey, p. 408), Scott (February 26, 1838, and

March 10, 1839), "A. Bacon and other Gentlemen of Ogdensburg" (November 17, 1838). Brady reported "a meeting of the most respectable citizens of Detroit" to Scott (March 14, 1838), and he often referred to "respectable" citizens in general.

22. Worth to Major Benjamin K. Pierce (February 14, 1839), and Col. Clarke (November 1, 1838); Scott to Poinsett, January 12, 1839 (in Stacey, p. 411).

23. Scott to Poinsett, January 12, 1839, and Worth to Poinsett (private), December 25, 1838, in Stacey, pp. 411 and 409; Worth to U.S. District Attorney Nathaniel Benton (February 17, 1838), Scott (February 17, 1838), and Capt. Giles Porter (February 17, 1839).

24. Worth to Scott, February 17, 1838, and to the Adjutant General of New York, January 7, 1839; Brady to Scott, February 15, 1838; Scott to Poinsett, December 15, 1838, in Stacey, pp. 409–410; Worth to Brigadier General King (the Adjutant General of New York), January 30, 1839; Brady to Scott, January 6 and February 15, 1838, and to Poinsett, November 23, 1838; Worth to Governor William L. Marcy, March 5, 1838, to Scott, February 15, 1838 and March 21, 1839, and to Governor William Seward, March 28, 1839. See Harwood P. Hinton, "The Military Career of John Ellis Wool, 1812–1863" (Ph.D. dissertation, University of Wisconsin, 1960), pp. 143–47, 150–56, and 159, on Wool's problems preventing the Vermont militia from aiding the filibusters. Worth eventually became concerned that the frontier arsenals had been so largely stripped of arms by the Patriots that there would be insufficient weapons available to arm the militia should the British attack across the border in force (Worth to Scott, February 9, 1839).

25. See e.g. Worth to Scott, February 13, 1838, and to A. W. Rogers (recently acting U.S. district attorney), February 14, 1838; Lt. Morris S. Miller (one of John Wool's aides-de-camp) to his mother, Maria, October 30, 1838, in the Morris S. Miller Papers, USMA; and Brady to Adjutant General Jones, November 22, 1838.

26. Brady to Jones, December 6, 1838; Worth to Scott, February 9, 1839, and February 13, 1838. See Kenneth Bourne, *Britain and the Balance of Power in North America, 1815–1908* (Berkeley: University of California Press, 1967), ch. 4, for an account of British military preparations.

27. Worth to Scott (December 12, 1838), Capt. Giles Porter (February 17, 1839), and a Capt. Williams Sandom of the Royal Navy (November 1, 1838).

28. Worth to Capt. William Montgomery (November 4, 1838), Nathaniel Benton (November 14, 1838) (regarding a Deputy Marshal Malcolm), George McWhorter (January 7, 1839), Bishop Perkins (February 21, 1839), and Major Pierce (April 10 and March 20, 1839). Worth cautioned Montgomery that any arrest would be "a painful and delicate duty to be performed with great discretion and judgement and under the clearest evidence of criminal design," and that he must "deliver the person arrested to the civil authority" "with all possible diligence" (January 24, 1839, from Worth's AAAG to Capt. Porter, Worth letterbooks, LC.

29. Worth to Poinsett (March 8, 1839), Capt. Montgomery (November 4, 1838), Scott (February 14, 1839), Messrs. Bacon, Hill, and Sherman (the Trustees of Ogdensburg) (March 9, 1839), and Major Pierce (March 20 and 21, 1839).

30. Worth to Jones, February 23, 1838 (see also Worth to Scott, February 20, and to

Governor Marcy, March 5, 1838), Major Pierce (March 21, 1839), Scott (March 21 and April 10, 1839), and John Hine (December 27, 1838).

31. Worth to Eustis (November 16, 1838), and Scott (April 10, 1839); Corey, *The Crisis of 1830–1842 in Canadian-American Relations,* p. 115. Scott initiated this unofficial policy of cooperation and confirmed it in a confidential circular on April 15, 1839: "should you, at any time, doubt your means of prevention, under the neutrality laws, you will (as heretofore instructed) not for a moment hesitate to give immediate information . . . to the nearest British commander, in part acquittance of our obligations of good faith towards friendly neighbors" (copy in the Robert Anderson Papers, LC).

    Officers were also active as facilitators of better relations between influential New Yorkers and the British. Worth provided a citizen's committee investigating arsons on U.S. soil with a letter of introduction to a British Lt. Col. Taylor (March 19, 1839), and British Major Richard P. Webb wrote to Major Nathaniel Young thanking him for Young's earlier letter, which was delivered by U.S. army surgeon Henry Heiskell and transmitted the names of the members of an apparently friendly grand jury (Webb to Young, June 14, 1838, in the Nathaniel Young Papers, LC). Worth also acted to reduce tensions by easing barriers to civilian movement and by limiting the chance that his officers might become involved in incidents with angry Canadians; see Lt. H. Taylor to a Capt. Tuthill of the New York volunteers, March 4, 1838 (Worth letterbooks, LC), Worth to a British colonel Cameron, March 5, 1838, and to Capt. Joseph Bonnell, December 30, 1838.

32. Scott to Worth, December 12, 1837, as cited in Charles Winslow Elliott, *Winfield Scott: The Soldier and the Man* (New York: Macmillan, 1937), p. 336, note 14; Worth to Scott, January 11, 1838, Winfield Scott Papers, LC. On the whole, Scott can be considered a transitional figure in the history of early national civil-military relations: exposed to the intrigues of the pre-1812 army, socialized in the gentry style of personal independence and political activism rather than the West Point ideal of neutral duty, and still considering it his right and duty to advise his civilian superiors on political matters, but accountable enough to wait for civilian sanction before carrying any of his bellicose thoughts into practice.

33. See Skelton, *An American Profession of Arms,* pp. 329 and 339, for expressions of Anglophobia during the 1840s; for different views on the Oregon crisis, see Lt. William F. Barry and Lt. Henry J. Hunt to Capt. James Duncan, April 3, 1846, and March 17, 1844, Duncan Papers, USMA; Captain W. W. S. Bliss to Lt. Col. Ethan Allen Hitchcock, May 18, 1845, Ethan Allen Hitchcock Papers, LC; and Lt. Col. Sylvanus Thayer to J. R. Chadbourne, June 28, 1846, Thayer Papers, USMA. See Merk, *The Monroe Doctrine and American Expansionism,* ch. 4; idem., *Albert Gallatin and the Oregon Problem: A Study in Anglo-American Diplomacy* (Cambridge, Mass.: Harvard University Press, 1950); and idem., *The Oregon Question: Essays in Anglo-American Diplomacy and Politics* (Cambridge, Mass.: Harvard University Press, 1967), concerning Oregon, in which officers left few traces of interest prior to the mid-1840s. Merk, *The Monroe Doctrine and American Expansionism,* examines the possibility of European intervention in North America during the 1840s; Bourne, *Britain and the Balance of Power in North America,* ch. 5,

treats British military preparations against the United States after 1842; see also Kinley J. Brauer, "The United States and British Imperial Expansion, 1815–1860," *Diplomatic History* 12 (Winter, 1988): 19–37. England's influence led topographer George Meade and his fellow captain Ephraim Kirby Smith to conclude that the solutions to the Oregon and Texas disputes were dependent on one another; see Meade to his wife Margaretta, January 10 and February 24, 1846, in *The Life and Letters of George Gordon Meade,* pp. 44 and 49, and Smith to his wife, April 19, 1846, in *To Mexico With Scott: Letters of Capt. E. Kirby Smith to His Wife,* ed. Emma Jerome Blackwood, with an introduction by R. M. Johnson (Cambridge, Mass.: Harvard University Press, 1917), p. 37. See David M. Pletcher, *The Diplomacy of Annexation: Texas, Oregon, and the Mexican War* (Columbia: University of Missouri Press, 1973), for a thorough survey of Polk administration policy.

34. Gaines, March 11, 1823, file G-136, SW: LR-Reg.

35. Gaines to Taylor, March 1, 1827, quoted in K. Jack Bauer, *Zachary Taylor: Soldier, Planter, Statesman of the Old Southwest* (Baton Rouge: Louisiana State University Press, 1985), p. 46; Calvin Reese, "The United States Army and the Indian: Low Plains Area, 1815–1854" (Ph.D. dissertation, University of Southern California, 1963), p. 317; Colquohoun to Major James Hook, February 24, 1829, in Records of the Headquarters of the Army, Letters Received, Record Group 108, National Archives.

36. Gaines to Jackson, March 20, 1830, Adjutant General's Office, Letters Received, Record Group 94, National Archives; Reese, "The United States Army and the Indian," pp. 319–24.

37. Jubal Anderson Early to his father, November 8, 1835, Jubal Anderson Early Papers, LC. Early was commissioned in 1837 and promoted to first lieutenant the following year, but he resigned within a month of his promotion to pursue the less circumscribed opportunities open to civilians. As his impatient rhetoric and rapid resignation indicate, Early did not take to the slow-paced routines of peacetime army life, and his ideologically outspoken views were uncharacteristic of the majority of officers, particularly those with more experience and those from the North. For further context see Michael A. Morrison, "Martin Van Buren, the Democracy, and the Partisan Politics of Texas Annexation," *Journal of Southern History* 61 (November, 1995): 695–724; idem., "The Westward Curse of Empire: Texas Annexation and the American Whig Party," *Journal of the Early Republic* 10 (Summer, 1990): 221–49; and John H. Schroeder, "Annexation or Independence: The Texas Issue in American Politics, 1836–1845," *Southwestern Historical Quarterly* 84 (October, 1985): 137–64.

38. Ethan Allen Hitchcock to his mother, Mrs. Lucy Hitchcock, April 9, 1836, Hitchcock Papers, Vermont Historical Society Collections, reprinted in "Ethan Allen Hitchcock and the Texas Rebellion: A Letter Home," ed. Marshall M. True, *Vermont History* 45 (Spring, 1977): 104–105.

39. See James W. Silver, *Edmund Pendleton Gaines, Frontier General* (Baton Rouge: Louisiana State University Press, 1949), ch. 9, for a narrative of Gaines's actions in 1836.

40. Reese, "The United States Army and the Indian," pp. 335–37; Hitchcock to

Secretary of War John C. Spencer, March 20, 1842, Hitchcock Papers, LC; Spencer to Taylor, March 26, 1842, SW: LS; Taylor to Adjutant General Jones, December 23, 1842, and March 28, 1843, cited in Brainerd Dyer, *Zachary Taylor* (Baton Rouge: Louisiana State University Press, 1946), pp. 138–40. See Joseph M. Nance, *After San Jacinto: The Texas-Mexican Frontier, 1836–1841* (Austin: University of Texas Press, 1963), and idem., *Attack and Counterattack: The Texas-Mexican Frontier, 1842* (Austin: University of Texas Press, 1964), for a narrative of the ongoing border strife. Robert Wooster provides the most directly comparable assessment with the post—Civil War officer corps in "The Army and the Politics of Expansion: Texas and the Southwestern Borderlands, 1870–1886," *Southwestern Historical Quarterly* 93 (October, 1989): 151–67, with conclusions generally similar to my own.

41. Gaines to Taylor, July 27, 1843, reprinted from the St. Louis *Evening Gazette* in the *Army and Navy Chronicle & Scientific Repository* 2 (August 17, 1843): 206–207; Burgwin to Lt. Abraham Johnston, July 27, 1843, Abraham Robinson Johnston Papers, USMA; Prucha, *The Sword of the Republic*, pp. 377–78.

42. Gaines to Taylor, July 27, 1843, reprinted from the St. Louis *Evening Gazette* in the *Army and Navy Chronicle & Scientific Repository* 2 (August 17, 1843): 206; Silver, *Edmund Pendleton Gaines,* ch. 12.

43. Bauer, *Zachary Taylor,* p. 129. Winfield Scott remained on the sidelines throughout this period, and in the summer of 1843 he cautioned the adjutant general against overreacting to rumors of a Mexican invasion (August 25, 1843, Headquarters of the Army, Letters Sent, Record Group 108, National Archives). As commanding general, Scott was essentially an administrative figure, headquartered at the center of government in Washington, which distanced him mentally as well as geographically from the urgent expansionism of the frontier. Scott was also the army's best-known Whig and had been considered as a presidential candidate ever since his diplomatic successes on the Canadian border in the late 1830s. Taylor had the Whig's sense of restraint without Scott's political connections and ambition, and besides Gaines the other senior officers with southwestern commands were too old for active command.

44. Lt. Napoleon Jackson Tecumseh Dana to his wife, Sue, November 1, 1845, in *Monterrey is Ours!: The Mexican War Letters of Lieutenant Dana, 1845–1847,* ed. Robert H. Ferrell (Lexington: University Press of Kentucky, 1990), p. 29; Cadet William T. Dutton to his fiancée and cousin, Lucy Matthews, March 6, 1845, William Dutton Papers, USMA. *The Life and Letters of George Gordon Meade* provides the most extensive examples of this pattern of response. It may be true that "the officer corps greeted the outbreak of fighting in 1846 with an enthusiasm bordering on mania" (Skelton, *An American Profession of Arms,* p. 294), but this enthusiasm was quite limited until the war began. My "Manifest Destiny and Military Professionalism: A New Perspective on Junior U.S. Army Officers' Attitudes Toward War With Mexico, 1844–1846," *The Southwestern Historical Quarterly* 99 (April, 1996): 467–98 elaborates on the analysis herein, emphasizing the influence of careerism and the inner life of the officer corps (especially considerations of family and health) in officers' responses to being stationed in Texas. The classic analyses of Manifest Destiny and expansionism are Alfred K.

Weinberg, *Manifest Destiny: A Study of Nationalist Expansionism in American History* (Baltimore: Johns Hopkins Press, 1935); and Merk, *Manifest Destiny and Mission in American History: A Reinterpretation* (New York: Alfred A. Knopf, 1963).

45. For examples of the scholarly consensus on officers' enthusiasm, see Skelton, *An American Profession of Arms*, ch. 17 (especially p. 330), and William H. Goetzmann, *Army Exploration in the American West, 1803–1863* (New Haven: Yale University Press, 1959), p. 68: "Almost to a man, for example, the officers of the Corps [of Topographical Engineers] were in accord with the policy of Manifest Destiny." Fremont's expedition was certainly an exception to the pattern I am presenting, but both Fremont and the Corps of Topographical Engineers to which he belonged were unusual in the degree of their political involvement and support for expansionism because of their duties as explorers and the romantic *mentalité* they produced. Examining George Meade, a topographical engineer in the Army of Occupation, provides a much more nuanced example of officers' motives and concerns than Fremont, who was not a West Pointer and had not undergone the professional socialization most regulars shared.

Gaines often included pejorative references to abolitionism in his letters and memorials to Congress, as other officers did in private correspondence, but they did so from fear of political and cultural "fanaticism"—social disorder and sectionalism—not (with the exception of Gaines) as Southerners per se. A fair proportion of the officer corps (including Zachary Taylor) were slaveholders, and junior Southern officers expressed sentiments characteristic of that region, but few officers commented on slavery as an issue during the annexation crisis, and I have found none who overtly sought an empire for slavery or expressed the hopes proclaimed by civilian expansionists that Texas would serve as a racial safety valve and an alternative to emancipation. Lt. Napoleon Dana and Capt. Philip Barbour noted that several officers' slaves had fled across the Rio Grande to freedom, and Barbour felt that officers would have to resort to white servants as a result, but the two officers viewed these incidents as personal rather than political affairs. See Napoleon Dana to Sue Dana, April 11 and 17, 1846, in *Monterrey is Ours!*, pp. 42 and 45; Barbour, April 4, 1846, in the *Journals of the Late Brevet Major Philip Norbourne Barbour and His Wife Martha Isabella Hopkins Barbour Written during the War With Mexico–1846,* ed. with a foreword by Rhoda van Bibber Tanner Doubleday (New York: G. P. Putnam's Sons, 1936), p. 42.

Similarly, few officers spoke of the war as a means of national unification or as a moral good in itself, nor did they debate the impact of imperialism and colonialism on American society and its institutions. Skelton, *An American Profession of Arms*, offers only one citation (on p. 340) of an officer from the Mexican War era directly advocating war as a means of national unification, from Lieutenant John J. Peck, October 31, 1845, in *The Sign of the Eagle: A View of Mexico–1830 to 1855*, ed. Richard F. Pourade (San Diego: Union-Tribune Publishing, 1970), pp. 7–9, and I have been unable to find any others from that period.

46. See Huntington, *The Soldier and the State*, ch. 4, concerning objective and subjective civil-military relations, and William B. Skelton, "Officers and Politicians: The Origins of Army Politics in the United States Before the Civil War," *Armed*

Forces and Society 6 (Fall, 1979): 22–48, and *An American Profession of Arms*, ch. 15, for more historically specific analyses.

47. George Meade to Margaretta Meade, November 3 and October 21, 1845, in *The Life and Letters of George Gordon Meade*, pp. 35 and 33; John Porter Hatch to Eliza Hatch, September 10, 1845, Hatch Papers, LC. Army officers did not articulately express the sort of attitudes described in such detail in Reginald Horsman, *Race and Manifest Destiny: The Origins of American Racial Anglo-Saxonism* (Cambridge, Mass.: Harvard University Press, 1981). Skelton, *An American Profession of Arms*, pp. 330–31, asserts that the officer corps "had come to accept the idea of a distinct Anglo-Saxon race" as described by Horsman, but gives only one citation that directly supports this, and I have only found one such statement (from Lt. Richard Stoddard Ewell to his sister Rebecca Ewell, July 30, 1844, Richard Stoddard Ewell Papers, LC). As on the Canadian border, officers' conscious attitudes toward their likely adversaries were (at least initially) conditioned primarily by class sensibilities. While ethnocentric and often casually racist, they did comment favorably on Mexican officers and their treatment of U.S. prisoners of war, and a number considered the elite Mexicans of Corpus Christi "much the most respectable portion of the inhabitants" (Lt. John Porter Hatch to his sister Eliza, October 28, 1845, John Porter Hatch Papers, LC), in contrast to their rare but almost uniformly negative comments on the Anglo Texan frontiersmen. From the officer corps' perspective the most important fact about the Mexicans before the war was that they were not Indians—victories against them would be respected and acknowledged by the American people, unlike those in the recent Seminole War. Although the bitterness of war spurred a growing racialization of officers' attitudes, they initially saw Mexican officers, their professional counterparts and opponents, as gentlemen of European blood, however tainted by the characteristics (especially cruelty) Anglo-Saxons associated with Spanish descent. See James M. McCaffrey, *Army of Manifest Destiny: The American Soldier in the Mexican War, 1846–1848* (New York: New York University Press, 1992), ch. 5, for the overwhelmingly negative reactions to Mexicans and their culture among U.S. troops during the war. My argument here is simply that they demonstrated little interest in Mexico and its inhabitants before the war began, just as they showed little interest in foreign policy and affairs, the issues involved in war, or their own professional preparation, and that what interest they did show was conditioned more by class than by race or ethnicity.

48. Grant to Julia Dent, March 3, 1846, in *The Papers of Ulysses S. Grant*, p. 75. Philip Barbour noted that Worth's "resigning at this time is considered by nearly the whole army a false step from which he can never recover and, should we have an engagement, [it] will dim forever the luster he has thrown around his name" (April 9, 1846, in *Journals of the Late Brevet Major Philip Norbourne Barbour*, pp. 31–32). See also Edward S. Wallace, "General William Jennings Worth and Texas," *Southwestern Historical Quarterly* 54 (October, 1950): 159–68; and Darwin Payne, "Camp Life in the Army of Occupation: Corpus Christi, July 1845 to March 1846," *Southwestern Historical Quarterly* 73 (January, 1970): 326–42.

49. Schureman to his mother, January 26, 1846, Schureman Papers, USMA; Taylor to

his daughter Mary Elizabeth Taylor, December 15, 1845, quoted in Hamilton, *Zachary Taylor*, p. 168; Barbour, April 15, 1846, in *Journals of the Late Brevet Major Philip Norbourne Barbour*, p. 37; George Meade to Margaretta Meade, February 18, 1846, in *The Life and Letters of George Gordon Meade*, p. 48.

50. Barbour, May 1, 1846, in *Journals of the Late Brevet Major Philip Norbourne Barbour*, pp. 50–51; George Meade to Margaretta Meade, November 12, 1845, in *The Life and Letters of George Gordon Meade*, p. 36.

51. Hietala, *Manifest Design*, pp. 7–8.

Anglophobia and the Annexation of Texas

THE QUEST FOR

NATIONAL SECURITY

Sam W. Haynes

The annexation of Texas has often been viewed as the starting point from which the nation began its slow descent into the vortex of Civil War. No issue before it had so inflamed the passions of North and South, or proved so ill-suited to amicable compromise. While earlier political battles had prompted some national leaders to worry for the future of the young republic, not until the Texas crisis would prominent statesmen of both sections advocate disunion if the matter were not resolved to their satisfaction. So controversial was the annexation issue that its reverberations continued to be felt long after Texas became a state in 1845. As many opponents of the measure had predicted, the acquisition of territory formerly owned by Mexico sparked a diplomatic impasse with that country that soon led to war, additional territorial conquests, and a new round of debates over the expansion of slavery. By the 1850s Texas had become, as James Buchanan noted ruefully, the Trojan horse "that entered our camp."[1]

And yet for all the sectional rancor generated by the Texas crisis, annexation was never simply a political contest between two sharply divided regions of the country. Extremists on both sides played key roles in shaping the annexation debate, but for a majority of Americans the expansion of slavery represented only one dimension of a complex matrix of issues that comprised the seemingly insoluble Texas question. It is this very complexity which has sometimes been lost by historians who, writing from a postbellum perspective, have studied annexation primarily in terms of its significance as an ingredient of North-South discord. There were many factors, acting either in concert or as separate agents, that served to make annexation the most divisive and hotly debated political question of its day.

No issue illustrates the tangled dynamics of the annexation controversy better than the expansionists' charge that Her Majesty's government was seeking to bring Texas within the orbit of the British Empire. From the outset of the long and bitter debate over the Tyler administration's efforts to annex Texas, proponents of the measure argued that the British government aimed to gain control of the Lone Star Republic in order to promote abolitionism there. Such a plan, the pro-annexation lobby maintained, would if successful undermine not only the social order of the Deep South but the economic and political institutions of the United States as well. To Northern opponents, however, the charge that Great Britain planned to turn Texas into a British satellite was merely a ruse by Southerners to acquire a vast new domain for the slave empire. Whigs and many Northern Democrats accused the administration of raising the specter of Anglophobia in order to instill an irrational fear of the British among Northern voters and thereby obtain biregional support for a policy of exclusive benefit to the South.

Several historians of Texas annexation have been inclined to view the anti-British alarm raised by annexationists with some skepticism. David Pletcher states that the fear of British intrigue "lent itself admirably to exaggeration and propaganda," while Paul Varg argues: "The expression of interest by Great Britain in maintaining Texas independence played, at most, a minor part in annexation." Frederick Merk goes even further, regarding Anglophobia as a false phantom, a shibboleth conjured up for political purposes by Southern leaders. In no less than four books that deal with U.S. expansionism in general and which examine, to varying degrees, annexation in particular, Merk insists that expansionists sought to frighten a gullible electorate with allegations of a British conspiracy in Texas, which would divert attention from their proslavery objectives. While Merk exhibits little patience for any of the politicians and pundits who championed the Manifest Destiny agenda, he reserves his greatest scorn for the Tyler administration, which engaged in a propaganda campaign characterized by "misconception, misrepresentation, and outright falsehood" as part of its campaign to bring about the annexation of Texas.[2]

In recent years, historians have not been so ready to dismiss the political rhetoric of pro-annexation leaders. William Freehling, while agreeing with Merk that the Texas annexation movement was engineered by Southern statesmen with a slaveholding agenda, argues that the president and his advisers "were not paranoids," but "coherent ideologues" whose efforts in defense of the peculiar institution must be viewed in the broader context of "established patterns of slavery politics." Thomas Hietala, on the other hand, in his study of the dynamics of U.S. expansionism, views annexation as a measure with legitimate national appeal. Although he argues that the Lone Star Republic was coveted by expansionists primarily "as a potential outlet for their country's unwanted black population," Hietala examines many anxieties that shaped the thinking of U.S. policy makers, including the desire to check England's position as the preeminent commercial rival of the United States.[3]

This essay will seek to build upon the work of these two scholars in an effort to present a more broad-based and direct critique of the Merk thesis, and in so doing attempt to shed some light on the impact of Anglophobia on the annexation controversy. Although their fears were largely unfounded, pro-annexation Democrats viewed alleged British meddling in Texas with genuine alarm, a response that is by no means surprising given the fact that their political culture had been shaped, to a considerable degree, by a deep-seated hostility toward Great Britain and the antirepublican, oligarchic tendencies which that nation appeared to represent. If Southern leaders, who were often found at the vanguard of the annexation crusade, tended to react to the perceived British threat with a higher degree of hysteria than their Northern counterparts, it was only because that threat carried with it the specter of abolitionism, and as slaveholders they had more to lose.

Anglophobia, moreover, was not a fear that gripped U.S. expansionists alone. While many Whigs and Northern Democrats cried that the charges of a British conspiracy had been introduced into the annexation debate as a foil to conceal an insidious plot to expand the slave empire, their own rhetoric betrayed similar fears of British aggrandizement that actually served to legitimize their opponents' apprehensions. Unmoved by expansionist claims that British meddling in Texas represented a threat to national security, they nonetheless denounced British activities along the Canadian border and vowed to challenge Britain's commercial supremacy in the Western Hemisphere. In short, while it constituted a shared experience for millions of Americans in the 1840s, Anglophobia manifested itself in ways that reflected regional concerns, and thus could only go so far in uniting the nation against a common enemy. Ironically, when coupled with the slavery issue in the debate over annexation, it would contribute to the sectional tensions that would ultimately tear the nation apart.

Thirty years after the war of 1812, Americans remained keenly suspicious of Great Britain; indeed, this fear had grown as the United States increasingly defined its economic and strategic interests in terms that extended beyond its own borders. Despite close commercial ties with Great Britain, Americans regarded British economic power with a combination of envy and distrust. In the global marketplace, Britain's far-flung empire reigned supreme, greatly inhibiting U.S. opportunities for overseas commercial development.[4] Nearer to home, Great Britain enjoyed close relations with Texas and Mexico and seemed well poised to block U.S. expansionist ambitions in the West. Allowing their imaginations free rein, many Americans saw a sinister purpose behind Great Britain's interest in Texas (as well as Mexican-held California), convinced that Her Majesty's government aimed to encircle the United States and thereby render the republic virtually defenseless in the event of war between the two countries.

When the Tyler administration embarked upon a policy to acquire Texas in 1843, the annexation question had been dormant for six years. Despite continued support in Texas for the measure, leaders of both parties had little interest in pursuing an issue so dangerously freighted with sectional discord, and which carried with it the added risk of war with Mexico. The possibility of annexing Texas seems to have been on President Tyler's mind for some time; he is first known to have broached the subject to Daniel Webster, then secretary of state, in the fall of 1841. Tyler's narrow political base made such an event unlikely, however, causing him to reject two overtures from Texas in 1842; early the following year he complained to Texas minister Isaac Van Zandt that the outlook for annexation looked bleak.[5]

But in 1843 the administration was galvanized into action by reports that the United States was not the only power interested in the fate of the Lone Star Republic. Great Britain had abolished slavery in its colonial possessions in the West Indies ten years earlier, a decision which, as even Her Majesty's government conceded, had been an economic disaster. This had given rise to the fear among Southern slaveholders that Her Majesty's government was now seeking to undermine the institution throughout the Western Hemisphere in an attempt to restore the colonies' economic competitiveness. According to this theory, Great Britain aimed to turn the Texas Republic, where slavery was not yet firmly entrenched, into a colonial dependency to destabilize the institution in the American South. The Tyler administration had received intelligence from Duff Green, a confidential U.S. agent in London, that British Foreign Minister Lord Aberdeen had offered the financially strapped republic a loan in exchange for emancipation. Charles Elliot, the British chargé d'affaires in Texas, helped to lend credence to these rumors when the New Orleans press broke the story that he had proposed to his superiors in Whitehall a scheme by which the Republic would be induced through lucrative commercial treaties to abolish slavery. Operating under the wholly mistaken impression that Texas leaders might support such an idea, Elliot envisioned a pro-British satellite which would serve as a haven for free black labor. This prospect was particularly disturbing to Southern slaveholders, who feared that an independent Texas under British control would offer asylum to the slaves of the Deep South, or worse, incite slave rebellions in neighboring states. Soon thereafter, in the spring of 1843, British diplomats sought to turn their government's influence with Mexico to good account by offering to mediate a peace between that country and Texas. Once again, a guarantee that Texas abolish slavery was rumored in the United States to be the price of British mediation.[6]

Alarmed by these reports, the Tyler administration embarked upon a bold new policy that would ultimately lead to the incorporation of Texas into the Union as the twenty-eighth state. To promote public support for such an initiative, the administration orchestrated a propaganda campaign that raised the specter of Great Britain while systematically presenting the manifold advantages of annexation to Americans of all sections. The opening salvo of this campaign took the form of a series of articles entitled "The British Conspiracy," believed to have been written by Tyler's secretary of state, Virginia-born Abel P. Upshur, in the *Daily Madisonian,* the administration news organ. Early the following year, secret negotiations were underway between Upshur and Texas diplomats in Washington.[7]

There can be little doubt that while reports of British designs contained a germ of truth, on the whole they represented a far less sinister danger than Southerners imagined.[8] While Her Majesty's government made no secret of its commitment to worldwide abolition, it showed little willingness to go beyond modest diplomatic pressure to achieve that objective. Elliot's plan for a free black state in the American Southwest fell on deaf ears in Whitehall, while Lord Aberdeen, anxious to allay Southern concerns, moved quickly to deny reports that he had offered Texas leaders a loan contingent upon emancipation. British efforts to mediate a permanent peace between Texas and Mexico never seem to have stood much chance of success, given the reluctance of those countries' respective governments to give ground on any issue, and by early 1844 negotiations had collapsed, never to resume.

But if Tyler and Upshur acted on the basis of false information, it was information they nonetheless believed to be credible, and which posed, in their view, a very real threat to U.S. national interests. Frederick Merk, among others, has argued that the administration viewed slavery with a monomania that blinded it to all other concerns, and which prompted it to press forward on annexation with a reckless disregard for either the facts or national unity. This thesis hinges largely upon the administration's misplaced faith in Duff Green, who is often credited with having first sounded the alarm regarding British intrigues in Texas. Green's fear of British designs was not limited to slavery, however—he was equally concerned that Her Majesty's government aimed to stifle the growth of U.S. commerce—nor can it be characterized as the alarmism of the moment. A lifelong Anglophobe, Green in 1866 was still blaming the sectional tensions that had caused the Civil War on a British conspiracy.[10] Moreover, though Green's report of a British loan to Texas played a key role in rousing the Tyler administration to action in 1843, it was by no means the only basis for the annexation initiative that followed. Green's allegations were later corroborated by a much less excitable non-administration source, Ashbel Smith, the Texas minister in London, who was equally alarmed by the influence of British antislavery forces on Her Majesty's government and its Texas diplomacy. Many years later, Smith endeavored to exculpate himself of any blame in contributing to the Tyler junto's misapprehensions by offering a version of events discrediting Green, a self-serving account which has not met with the critical scrutiny from historians that it deserves.[11]

Fears of British meddling in Texas affairs were also confirmed by reports which Tyler and Upshur were receiving from Texas, and which added to the body of evidence on which the administration based its decision to embark upon a new annexation initiative. The mere presence of British citizens on the streets of Galveston was enough to convince U.S. chargé d'affaires William S. Murphy when he arrived in June that a British plot was afoot to infiltrate Texas with British agents.[12] Wild as these allegations may seem today, they too were corroborated by a source outside the administration. Washington D. Miller, the private secretary of Texas President Sam Houston, had written a letter to Tyler in January, 1843, presumably at Houston's direction, in which he painted a dark scenario of British intrigue and urged him to act before it was too late.[13] Six months later Miller penned another, even more anxious missive to the U.S. president, imploring him to take immediate steps on behalf of annexation. "Every day that the action of the US is delayed the prospects of GB are brightening. Will Mr. Upshur permit another year to elapse without doing something effective? Will you not do it?"[14] Similar letters describing British activities in the Lone Star Republic poured into Washington from private citizens in Texas.[15] In short, in the months before it launched its annexation initiative, Washington had been inundated with reports from London and Texas, from sober-minded correspondents and hysterical ones, all of whom came to pretty much the same conclusion: that Great Britain was intent on establishing a satellite on the southwestern border of the United States. Little wonder, then, that Tyler and Upshur paid no attention in the fall of 1843 to a more circumspect assessment of British intentions from Edward Everett, the U.S. minister to England, a Boston-born Whig whose antislavery views were well known.[16]

The argument that the Tyler administration acted precipitately in its defense of slavery against British interference also ignores the broader context of Anglo-American relations in 1843–44. No doubt the administration would have been inclined to place credence in reports of British intrigue in Texas whatever their source, if only because they confirmed what Americans already believed about the long-range intentions of Her Majesty's government. Relations between the United States and Great Britain, never good, had grown increasingly turbulent in recent years. Southern leaders raged in vain against Whitehall's policy of freeing slaves found aboard U.S. vessels forced into ports in the British West Indies as a result of inclement weather or other mishap. In the Northeast, talk of a third war with Great Britain had been rife for several years, owing to a series of incidents along the U.S.-Canadian border, culminating in the celebrated McLeod affair in 1841.[17] The Webster-Ashburton treaty aimed to settle these and other outstanding grievances between the two countries, but despite Senate ratification by a wide margin in August, 1842, dissatisfaction with the agreement had been mounting steadily ever since. Southerners complained that the treaty was silent on the subject of the extradition of fugitive slaves, while confusion over the specific terms of the treaty regarding Britain's right to search U.S. ships suspected of carrying on the slave trade added to the controversy. Expansionist-minded Americans fumed that the agreement surrendered five thousand square miles of land they believed rightfully belonged to the United States. The subsequent revelation that the British Foreign Office had in its possession during the negotiations a map buttressing the U.S. territorial claim only reinforced American suspicions that Her Majesty's government would not hesitate to resort to devious and duplicitous means to serve its own interests.[18] Finally, the unauthorized seizure of Hawaii by a British naval commander in the spring of 1843, though later disavowed by Her Majesty's government, was interpreted by U.S. policy makers as yet another signal that Great Britain stood ready to thwart American commercial interests at every turn.[19]

The net effect of these rising tensions was to create an atmosphere of suspicion and distrust that led Washington policy makers to view even the most innocuous actions on the part of Her Majesty's government with a jaundiced eye. In 1842 Texas leaders had proposed that the three major powers—Great Britain, France, and the United States—might use their combined influence to prevail upon Mexico to cease its policy of border harassment against the republic. Though warmly endorsed in Washington and Paris, the suggestion met with a cool reception in London, which was anxious not to upset its close relations with Mexico. In some quarters in the United States, however, Britain's refusal to participate in the tripartite agreement was viewed as evidence of a darker purpose. "Her object doubtless was to be free from the observation and the responsibility of her associate pacificators," declared one suspicious Tennessee Democrat, "in order to hold such confidential counsels with Mexico as would promote her ulterior schemes."[20] The public declarations of high-ranking members of Parliament and Her Majesty's government seemed to offer further evidence to Southerners in the Tyler administration that Great Britain was actively engaged in an effort to promote emancipation in Texas. In a debate in the House of Lords in mid-August, 1843, renowned antislavery leader Lord Brougham offered the opinion that the abolition of slavery in Texas would ultimately lead to the collapse of the institution throughout the Southern states. When pressed by Brougham to comment on the government's policy toward the Lone Star Republic, Foreign Secretary Lord Aberdeen admitted frankly, if ambiguously, that the Peel ministry desired to see the abolition of slavery in Texas and throughout the world, a statement that lent itself to ominous misinterpretation in Washington.[21]

Even without the initiative from Washington, a pro-annexation groundswell was already well underway in the Southern states by the early 1840s. The revolt of Anglo-Texans against Mexico in 1835–36 had met with the universal approbation of the Deep South. But with the collapse of the annexation movement in 1837, Southerners quickly became reconciled to the emergence of a rival cotton-growing republic on their western border. As long as Texas remained politically viable, its existence occasioned little concern; this mood changed, however, when a series of military setbacks at the hands of Mexico in 1841 and 1842 brought Texas to the verge of collapse. Rumors that Great Britain had financed Mexican incursions along the Texas frontier in an attempt to check the spread of slavery were circulated widely in the Southern press.[22] Though some Texas leaders may have doubted their veracity, these reports helped give rise to a climate of suspicion that intensified with the arrival in Galveston in the fall of 1842 of Charles Elliot, Britain's visible and energetic chargé d'affaires. Making no secret of his abolitionist sympathies, Elliot soon aroused the apprehensions of Southern slaveholders, and by the summer of 1843 these fears seemed amply confirmed by reports of the British diplomat's scheme to promote emancipation in Texas. Elliot's activities coupled with the continued decline of the Republic's economic fortunes punctured Texans' inflated claims of nationhood. Georgia-born Mirabeau B. Lamar, the Texas leader most prominently associated with the fledgling republic's imperial ambitions, quickly abandoned his dreams of empire when confronted with evidence of a British abolitionist conspiracy in Texas. "I paused in my opinions, and turned to seek for my country a shelter from the grasp of British cupidity beneath the only flag under which her institutions could be saved from the storms that threatened her."[23]

The specter of British abolitionism that so worried slaveholders like Lamar was not a figment of excitable imaginations. Southerners had watched with unconcealed horror as British antislavery forces, fresh from their triumph in obtaining passage of the Emancipation Act in 1833, turned their attention to the United States. With organizational assistance, guest lecturers, and financial aid from England, the militant abolitionist efforts of William Lloyd Garrison, Theodore Weld, and Lewis Tappan began to show immediate results. Southerners charged that Northern antislavery leaders were merely the deluded minions of their British counterparts, attributing even the abolitionist petitions which had led Congress to impose the famous gag rule in 1834 to antislavery extremists in Parliament.[24] While these charges were untrue, American antislavery societies in Boston and Philadelphia took their lead from the British and Foreign Anti-Slavery Society, owing much of their success to the assistance they received from London. But by the mid-1840s, for all their crusading zeal, American antislavery groups had yet to develop broad-based support in the Northern states, and could be dismissed as a crankish if vocal minority. The British and Foreign Anti-Slavery Society, on the other hand, was a very different matter. The organization enjoyed close access to the highest circles of power in Whitehall and had already demonstrated a formidable ability to influence the foreign policy of Her Majesty's government.[25]

While Southerners regarded the activities of British abolitionists with frenzied alarm, like many Americans they believed that Great Britain's opposition to slavery represented a much broader assault on the United States. Leaders of both sections and parties were convinced that their republican system was locked in a historic, ideological contest with the monarchies of Europe, and many Northern pro-annexation Democrats viewed the abolitionist movement as an instrument Britain intended to use in that struggle. According to this line of reasoning, Her Majesty's government had seized upon emancipation in a deliberate effort to agitate the American slavery question, the Achilles heel of the young republic. Alert to the tensions between North and South, Great Britain sought to exploit the slavery issue to "dissolve the Union" and thereby check the inexorable spread of U.S. political institutions. "This is the discord which England will touch most successfully," said Pennsylvanian Charles Jared Ingersoll, House chairman of the Foreign Affairs committee.[26] The real goal behind British abolitionism, insisted Moses Norris, a New Hampshire Democrat, was "to array the North against the South, and thus to weaken the ties that bind us together, and finally consummate her long cherished desire(s) by a dissolution of our Union . . ."[27]

Few expansionists believed, however, that British efforts to undermine the stability of the United States were confined to slavery alone. Rather, Great Britain's campaign to sow the seeds of North-South discord was viewed as only the first step in a broader, insidious plot to cripple its principal economic rival in the Western Hemisphere. The suggestion that Great Britain would resort to commercial warfare against the United States was hardly a novel one when the Tyler administration raised the issue during the annexation debate, being generally accepted as an article of faith for Americans of both parties. The Texas annexation crisis only served to heighten these long-standing anxieties, prompting expansionists regardless of section to join in a rising chorus of outrage against British imperialism. The *New Hampshire Patriot,* a Democratic organ sponsored by the supporters of Levi Woodbury, viewed "British rapacity and ambitious schemes of commercial aggrandizement," as the principal issue in the annexation debate. "In comparison with it, the consideration of slavery and the consideration of relative benefit to the North and South, sink into insignificance." Britain's chief aim, the *Patriot* declared, was "to cripple our prosperity, and destroy her most formidable rival in manufactures and commerce. And the blow is to be aimed as much at the North as the South."[28]

Southern hard-liners, though all too often characterized strictly in terms of their zealous defense of slavery, also viewed British abolitionist activities as but one phase of a protracted and wide-ranging campaign on the part of

Great Britain to disrupt the economy of its former North American colonies. Not long after the War of 1812, John C. Calhoun had warned his colleagues in the House of Representatives that the conflict with Great Britain was far from over. A new struggle for commercial supremacy was about to begin, in which the United States "will have to encounter British jealousy and hostility in every shape, not immediately manifested by force or violence, perhaps, but by indirect attempts to check your growth and prosperity."[29] Thirty years later Calhoun saw no reason to modify these views. "Her object is power and monopoly, and abolition but the pretex[t]," he wrote in 1844. "She unites in herself the ambition of Rome and the avarice of Carthrage [sic]."[30]

Whether Great Britain would succeed in its plot to destroy the United States as a commercial rival depended on the future of Texas, annexationists argued. Great Britain had for several years been engaged in a search for new sources of cotton to reduce its dependence on the plantations of the Deep South. Crop yields in India were at long last beginning to show promising results, while Texas offered yet another attractive area for development. Southerners feared that Her Majesty's government would seek to block the Lone Star Republic's entrance into the Union and, with British capital investment, boost agricultural productivity in the region, making it a serious competitor to the United States as a source of supply within a few years. This prospect heightened Southern fears dating back to the "Tariff of Abominations" that Great Britain might retaliate against U.S. protectionist policies by imposing high duties on U.S. cotton and other raw materials. It required little imagination on the part of Southerners long uneasy about their dependence on British markets and profoundly suspicious of British abolitionism to suspect that Her Majesty's government's interest in Texas stemmed from a well-conceived plot to strangle the mainstay of the Southern economy.

The annexation of Texas would not only eliminate these concerns, supporters of the measure contended, it would actually reverse the roles that presently existed between the two rival nations, making Great Britain economically dependent upon the United States. With one stroke, the United States could acquire a monopoly over the cotton-producing regions of North America, giving it the commercial leverage to neutralize Great Britain as a military or economic threat. Mindful of the calamitous effects which a cotton embargo would have on its textile industry, Great Britain would think seriously before it opposed American interests again. A monopoly of cotton, the Tennessee Democrat Andrew Johnson argued, would compel Great Britain "to keep the peace for all time to come."[31]

Anxious to offset antislavery sentiment, as always the chief obstacle to the annexation of Texas, the Tyler administration and its expansionist allies made a concerted effort to win the support of powerful Northern interest groups. If Great Britain managed to establish strong commercial ties with the Republic, they charged, the consequences would be disastrous to Northern manufacturers. British-made goods would be allowed to enter the port of Galveston duty-free, effectively eliminating U.S. manufacturers from the growing Texas market. Furthermore, with Texas under its control, Great Britain might then attempt to circumvent high tariffs in the United States, flooding the country with its surplus manufactured products. Many expansionists also insisted that annexation would pay long-term maritime dividends, allowing the United States to gain a competitive edge over Great Britain in important global markets. Without a navy of its own, Texas would rely on the merchant fleet of New England, giving U.S. ships command of the Gulf of Mexico. Should the United States reject Texas, one Texan argued, "the trident of this important sea passes into the hands of England."[32] Other expansionist claims regarding the benefits of Texas annexation were rather more far-fetched. Andrew Jackson, among others, blithely accepting the Republic's dubious claim to the Rio Grande as its western boundary, viewed Texas as an essential stepping stone to the Pacific, the ports of which "would give protection to all our Eastern Whalers."[33] "No heavier blow could be given to British power and commerce," a pro-Calhoun broadside declared optimistically in 1843. Annexation would "open to us the trade of the Western coast of the two Americas," and thus "the trade of the East Indies, Russia in Asia, and the rich commerce of the Chinese Empire . . . and a market for the products of the South and the manufactories of the North."[34]

It was, of course, politically expedient for the Tyler administration to emphasize the economic benefits that would accrue to the North in the event of annexation. But such efforts should not be dismissed as a cynical attempt to divert attention from the issue of slavery, as Merk and other historians have argued. Privately as well as publicly, administration leaders maintained a consistent if not always equal regard for the interests of both sections. Fearful that British efforts to thwart annexation might lead to a devastating race war that would engulf the South, Upshur and other Southerners in the administration quite naturally viewed the protection of slavery as their paramount concern. But they were by no means ignorant of the larger dangers which Great Britain seemed to pose to the nation at large. Far from being oblivious to sectional antagonisms, Southern leaders, like so many Americans, were troubled by the growing rift over slavery. And yet they remained hopeful that the threat from Great Britain might serve to neutralize these tensions and give rise to a renewed sense of national purpose.

In a letter to John C. Calhoun in August, 1843, Upshur outlined in considerable detail the administration's reasons for reviving the annexation question. Even as he expressed his mounting irritation with the North's reluctance to stand by the South on the issue of slavery, the secretary feared that the British would exploit these tensions to bring about "a separation of the Union." Though admitting that annexation would be received initially with "a brush of repugnance" in the North, Upshur believed that the failure to bring Texas into the Union would be detrimental to the economic well-being of both sections. "To the South it is a question of *safety;* to the North, it is one of interest," the secretary of state wrote of annexation, adding, "I have never known the North to refuse to do what her interests required."[35] Thus Upshur viewed annexation not simply as a means of protecting the institutions of the South, but as a policy initiative that would awaken both sections to their mutual advantage, strengthening the Union as it prepared to meet this most recent challenge from Great Britain, at a time when a North/South accord was needed more than ever before.

Even more compelling than the economic arguments in favor of annexation was the direct threat of military aggression from Great Britain. Here again, expansionist propaganda did not so much shape public opinion as capitalize on anti-British sentiment that was already fully formed. Western Americans needed no prodding from the Tyler administration to imagine British forces using Texas as a base of military operations. No American accepted this scenario more unreservedly than Andrew Jackson, who in February, 1843, warned Tennessee congressman Aaron V. Brown that with Texas under its aegis, Great Britain could at its convenience march an army to the Sabine River, where it would be poised to strike Louisiana and Arkansas and threaten the entire Mississippi valley. Nor were the dangers of British abolitionism lost on the slaveholding ex-president, who feared that Great Britain would incite U.S. slaves to revolt against their masters, fomenting a destructive race war.[36]

The annexation crisis invited comparison with the War of 1812, an event that resonated in the collective memory of western Americans. Former Tennessee senator Alexander O. Anderson viewed annexation "as the greatest question which has arisen since our last bloody conflict with Great Britain."[37] The opposition of New England on both occasions seemed to make the analogy particularly appropriate. Anderson viewed antislavery spokesmen as agitators who, much like the Hartford Convention Federalists, harbored pro-British sympathies and were working actively to subvert U.S. institutions. Indiana congressman William J. Brown expressed similar sentiments when he declared: "There is a British party in the United States, and that party has existed since the days of the Revolution. It existed during the last war; it showed itself in the halls of Congress, by the act of those who refused to vote supplies to our famishing army; it was seen in the blue lights that burned along the shores of New England; and is now exhibiting itself in those who, with anti American spirit, oppose the extension of our territory, and the spread of civil and religious liberty."[38] Invoking the memories of earlier conflicts with Great Britain proved a popular theme at Democratic association meetings in communities throughout the West. The Kentucky *Yeoman* recalled with pride the heroics of an earlier generation when it declared that the "brave and chivalrous Kentuckians who met and vanquished the British Lion when he assailed our homes in 1812 . . . will again pour out rivers of blood before he shall set his polluting foot upon the soil of the young republic [of Texas]."[39]

Robert J. Walker emphasized the threat of British aggression forcefully in what was surely the most compelling and influential treatise on behalf of annexation, his *Letter on the Re-Annexation of Texas*, published in February, 1844. Historians have focused most of their attention on the Democratic leader's novel argument that Texas would serve as a safety valve for slavery by drawing off a growing black population in the Upper South, where the need for slave labor was declining. But Walker's attempt to exploit Northern racist fears of a mass exodus of blacks into the Northern states constituted only a part of his famous *Letter,* much of which was a scathing polemic against British imperialism. "Though saturated with blood, and gorged with power," Walker raged, "she yet marches on her course to universal dominion; and here, upon our own borders, Texas is next to be her prey."[40] The Democratic leaders of Carroll County, Kentucky, who had asked Walker to author his famous open letter and to whom it was addressed, used the document to drum up anti-British feeling among the party faithful at a meeting in April, 1844. The editor of the *Kentucky Yeoman,* citing the recent Maine boundary negotiations, British claims to the Pacific Northwest, and rumors of designs on Texas, declared that Great Britain would soon "bestride our country like a vast Colossus, and crush our interests beneath the weight of her military empire."[41]

While the vulnerability of the western frontier was a particular concern in the trans-Appalachian states, it represented part of a still larger geopolitical problem for many expansionists: the threat of British encirclement. Fears that Great Britain aimed to restrict U.S. territorial growth did not originate with the Texas annexation question and had rarely been articulated by Southerners prior to 1843; prominent Northern Democrats like Sidney Breese, Lewis Cass, and James Buchanan, however, had long been suspicious of British designs in the West and had been especially vocal in calling for the United States to assert its claim to all of Oregon. In his message referring the annexation treaty to the Senate in April, 1844, President Tyler borrowed freely from the political rhetoric of Democratic expansionists when he pointed to the fact that the United States was "already almost surrounded" by European powers—by which he meant, of course, Great Britain—and that commercial arrangements with Texas "would complete the circle."[42] Andrew Jackson would harp upon this theme with increasing vehemence until his death in 1845. "She is the Key to our safety in the South and the west," Jackson said of Texas in a letter to the *Nashville Union* on the eve of the 1844 Baltimore convention. "Let us take it and lock the door against future danger."[43] In near-apocalyptic terms the aging general warned that if Great Britain managed to establish a permanent foothold in the Southwest it would form an "iron Hoop around the United States" that would cost the nation "oceans of blood, and millions of money to Burst asunder."[44] Committed Anglophobes like Jackson harbored no illusions that annexation would mean the end of British aggrandizement in the Western Hemisphere; the Texas crisis represented merely one of several battlegrounds in the competition for empire between the United States and Great Britain. "England wants Texas, next Cuba, and then Oregon," Jackson predicted in 1844, and in the years that followed, expansionists would add Mexico, the Yucatan, and Central America to the list of territories targeted for conquest by Her Majesty's government.[45]

Beyond the issues of economic advantage and national security, many Americans bristled at the idea that Great Britain would attempt to involve itself in a matter that was strictly the concern of the United States and Texas. Democrats reminded voters that while Her Majesty's government had officially declared that it would not seek to influence Texas, it had only promised to do so "provided other states act with equal forbearance."[46] For Alexander Everett, a Harvard-educated former Whig and erstwhile editor of the *North American Review,* such an admission "amounts, in short, to an indelicate interference in the internal concerns of the Union, with which Great Britain has nothing to do."[47] Similarly, Sidney Breese of Illinois was one of many Democratic statesmen who took umbrage when Great Britain, "with that arrogance so peculiarly her own, presumes to question the propriety of our conduct in attempting the acquisition of Texas."[48] Anglophobia also offered Democrats uncomfortable with the extension of slavery an opportunity to focus attention instead on British social problems. European criticism of their institutions, peculiar or otherwise, had long rankled Jacksonian Americans, who pointed with smug satisfaction to the squalid living conditions of the English working class as evidence of the hypocrisy of the British government's putative humanitarianism. The landed aristocracy was a favorite target of U.S. editorialists, which one Northern Democratic newspaper denounced as "the oppressors of a population more enslaved, harder worked, poorer fed, more beastly and more degraded than the world ever saw."[49]

Despite the administration's efforts to promote the issue as a national measure, Tyler's Texas treaty stood at best only a slim chance of success given the fierce opposition in the North to the expansion of slavery. The outlook for ratification grew bleaker still with Upshur's untimely death in late February, 1844, a victim of the USS *Princeton* explosion. Upshur's successor, John C. Calhoun, proved to be a signally disastrous choice, and in April he proceeded to scuttle Northern support for Tyler's treaty by penning the famous "Pakenham letter," one of the most controversial episodes of the South Carolinian's long and turbulent career. The letter was written in response to an earlier statement by Lord Aberdeen, in which the British Foreign Secretary sought to allay Southern fears that his government would "do nothing secretly or under-handed" to abolish slavery in Texas.[50] Far from satisfied, Calhoun testily observed that while Great Britain's commitment to emancipation in its own colonies was no concern of the United States, his government would take strong exception to British efforts regarding abolition in Texas, since any effort to undermine slavery in the Republic would impinge directly upon the stability of the institution in the American South. Had Calhoun stopped there, the letter might not have become a lightning rod for sectional controversy. Instead the secretary of state went on to lecture the British minister on the advantages of slavery to both races. Citing spurious census data, Calhoun attempted to demonstrate that free blacks in the Northern states experienced abnormally high rates of mental and physical disease, leading him to conclude that slavery was the natural condition of African Americans.[51]

Contemporaries no less anxious than Calhoun to see Texas annexed were appalled by the letter, which they regarded quite correctly as a colossal tactical blunder that would only alienate Northern support for the treaty, upon which its success depended. Andrew Jackson groaned upon reading the secretary's letter: "How many men of talents want good common sense."[52]

Writing some years later, Tyler himself laid much of the blame for the Senate's failure to ratify the treaty on Calhoun's ill-advised and unnecessary appeal to sectional interests. Some of Calhoun's fiercest critics, such as Thomas Hart Benton, even charged him with purposely attempting to sabotage his own treaty in order to stir up secessionist sentiment in the South, although no evidence exists for such an accusation.[53]

Several historians, equally perplexed by the Pakenham letter, have offered various theories to explain Calhoun's conduct.[54] Most tend to agree that the unabashed proslavery tone of the correspondence was a deliberate and calculated effort by the South Carolinian to rally the South behind the cause of annexation. Calhoun's correspondence in the months before he became secretary of state supports this assertion, but it is worth noting that many of his friends did not initially view the Pakenham letter as a Southern call to arms. From New York and Philadelphia, Calhoun received letters from supporters who, like so many of their countrymen, had long resented British criticism of American customs and institutions, and praised the secretary of state on that basis alone.[55] In a similar vein, Charleston resident John R. Mathewes saw merit in the letter because "it is the only means by which we can obtain a patient hearing from Europe whose eyes have been blinded & ears deafened by England against us."[56]

In their effort to tease meaning from the Pakenham letter, scholars have looked closely for portents of disunion but have generally paid less attention to Calhoun's unabiding hostility toward Great Britain than this facet of his political makeup deserves. As already noted, Calhoun had been a relentless opponent of all forms of British aggrandizement in North America since his election to the War Hawk Congress more than thirty years earlier. Recent events, moreover, seemed to offer fresh evidence of British designs. Less than a month before the secretary wrote his first letter to Pakenham, he had received information that British agents had plotted to foment a slave revolt in Cuba.[57] Like Upshur before him, Calhoun did not feel the need to wait for corroboration of these reports; Britain's policy to subvert U.S. institutions was too well established to require further investigation. While Northern abolitionists railed against annexation as part of a plot to expand the slave power, Calhoun saw a conspiracy of his own, one with international dimensions. Like Mirabeau Lamar and other Southerners, Calhoun was a relative latecomer to the annexation crusade, embracing the cause in the end because he believed British machinations left him no other choice. Certainly there is no reason to suspect that Calhoun was being disingenuous when he stated, as he did on more than one occasion, that the offer to annex Texas "was forced on the government of the United States, in self-defence," as a result of British abolitionist intrigues.[58]

Calhoun's lifelong Anglophobia stirred another, more recent concern, one even more troubling because of the danger it posed to the Union: the growing strength of antislavery opinion in the North. Since all patriotic Americans had a fundamental duty to resist British aggression in whatever form, the zeal with which Northern political leaders championed the cause of British abolitionism could only be viewed as treasonous behavior by the Southern ideologue. From Calhoun's point of view—one which admittedly demonstrated a remarkable facility for trimming the facts to fit a Southern perspective—his section had been quick to come to the defense of the North in two wars against Great Britain, and more recently in the region's quarrel over the Maine boundary. But now, "when our very safety is at stake," he complained, "the great body of the enlightened portion of the North either holds back, or oppose."[59] Though frequently characterized as a Southern extremist, Calhoun in 1844 remained faithful to the union as he understood it, a compact based on reciprocal obligations, with each section willing to set aside its own parochial interests and rise to the defense of the other. Though anxious for the future, the Southern leader was reluctant to accept the unwelcome possibility that the North might fail to fulfill its duty to the South and defend its institutions against foreign aggression.

The furor that followed the publication of Calhoun's Pakenham letter, however, seems to have confirmed the South Carolinian's worst fears of Northern disloyalty. "There is something wrong in all this, and not a litle ominous to the duration of our system," Calhoun wrote to a friend, although he was not yet ready to adopt extreme measures to defend the institutions of the South.[60] He took comfort from the fact that despite fierce opposition to annexation in the Northern states, the measure enjoyed strong support in the rest of the country, and to those who harbored more radical, secessionist views he counseled against disunion, which he felt was inadvisable "at this time."[61]

During the ensuing debate in Congress and the national press over Tyler's Texas treaty, opponents of the measure dismissed the grim scenarios which expansionists claimed would befall the United States should it fail to annex the Lone Star Republic. With regard to the fear that a British ally on the southwestern border of the United States was a threat to national security, Whig spokesmen pointed to the fact that the Northern states shared a two-thousand-mile border with Canada, a country which, unlike Texas, was indisputably a part of the British Empire. Antiexpansionists argued, not implausibly, that if Great Britain intended to launch an offensive against the United States, it was already well poised to do so from military bases that had long been established on the Great Lakes and St. Lawrence River. Whigs also held up to ridicule the suggestion that Great Britain would strike at New Orleans from the pine forests of East Texas, observing that an attack upon the Crescent City from the sea would seem to be a far more practical military strategy. The argument that Great Britain intended to circumvent U.S. tariff schedules by using the Republic as an entrepôt for its manufactured goods was shown to be similarly unfounded. If Her Majesty's government seriously intended to establish smuggling operations into the United States, antiexpansionists explained, it would already have done so from Canada.[62]

Despite these counter-arguments, Whigs and Northern Democrats were unable to entirely dispel the concerns raised by the apostles of annexation, for the simple reason that an intense distrust of Great Britain was not unique to U.S. expansionists. While their Anglophobia tended to be much more subdued than their Democratic counterparts, many prominent Whigs were no less convinced that Her Majesty's government felt threatened by the emergence of the United States as a rival power in the Western Hemisphere. Rarely during the annexation debates did opponents attempt to minimize the danger of British aggression, for many had used equally strident invective to condemn British actions in the Maine boundary dispute and the McLeod affair.[63] Few shared the sanguine opinion of South Carolina Whig Waddy Thompson, who insisted that the United States had nothing to fear from Great Britain, in view of the strong commercial ties which worked to the mutual benefit of the two countries.[64]

Notwithstanding the tensions over slavery which the Texas question unleashed, politicians on both sides of the expansion issue viewed Great Britain as the principal obstacle to U.S. economic progress. The anti-British harangues of Democratic expansionists in this regard during the annexation debates in 1844 had an uncomfortably familiar ring for many Whigs, who had been unsparingly critical of British free trade policies in their successful campaign for a higher tariff two years earlier. In 1842 Whigs asserted that Great Britain, motivated by "the deepest jealousy" at U.S. commercial growth, was engaged in a relentless program of economic warfare against the United States. "Shall we madly cut asunder the great link of national independence forged by our protective policy, and place ourselves in a condition to be humbled, and grieved, and ruined . . . [by] the mandate of British power . . . ?" asked one Whig congressman.[65] The Peel ministry's apparent willingness to relax its trade restrictions on U.S. foodstuffs was only a ruse to induce the United States to lower its duties on British-made goods, Whigs maintained. "I have no faith in such heartless professions," declared R. W. Thompson, a Whig congressman from Indiana, "especially when they are opposed by the constant and persevering practice of those who utter them."[66] Instead of trade reciprocity, Whigs charged, Great Britain intended to flood the U.S. market with British manufactures, incurring short-term losses to destroy its principal industrial competitor.

Similarly, while many antiexpansionists scornfully dismissed the idea that Texas was essential to the national defense, they pointed with alarm to the dangers of British military aggression in other parts of the hemisphere. Although Whigs and antislavery Democrats refused to believe that an attack was imminent, or that the British would choose to launch an invasion of the United States along its southwestern border, many nonetheless accepted the idea that a day of reckoning between the two countries would occur at some point in the not too distant future. Even as he derided expansionist claims that the British intended to strike at the United States through Texas, Congressman Samuel Rathbun pointed to the danger which Great Britain posed to the Northeast in Canada. "Here they will find the lion in his lair," the New York Democrat declared.[67] Many Whigs, such as Kentucky abolitionist Cassius M. Clay, believed that the two countries would eventually come to blows in the West over Oregon.[68] And while they scoffed at the annexationists' charge that Great Britain's interest in Texas was part of a long-range plot to encircle the United States, few Whig leaders questioned the encirclement theory itself. Indeed, one year after the annexation of Texas, the Whig magazine *American Review* would employ the same line of reasoning to urge Washington to establish U.S. sovereignty over California. Firmly entrenched in the West Indies, Canada, and Halifax, and with a loyal ally in Mexico, Her Majesty's government aimed to acquire California in order to ensnare "us as completely in her net, as the bloodiest intentions of extermination could possibly desire."[69]

Even the most zealous antislavery advocates in the United States rejected the argument that philanthropic motives guided British diplomacy. In a well-known treatise against annexation, Van Buren Democrat Theodore Sedgwick acknowledged that Americans had every reason to be suspicious of England, which seemed "urged on by an insatiable lust of dominion."[70] John Quincy Adams, who had gone so far as to publicly urge the British to promote abolitionism in Texas, nonetheless viewed the altruistic rhetoric of Her Majesty's government with a hefty dose of skepticism. British efforts to maintain Texas' independence, Adams believed, had more to do with balance-of-power geopolitics—specifically the need to protect Mexico from the territorial ambitions of the United States—than the lofty goal of emancipating Texas slaves.[71]

Unable to successfully lay to rest U.S. fears that Great Britain represented a threat to national security, some opponents of annexation chose to characterize the Texas Republic as a bulwark against British aggression, emphasizing the affinity which Texans felt for U.S. institutions. "All that is said of the probability of Texas becoming a colony of Great Britain is but a disguise of the real question," declared the New York *Evening Post*, an antislavery Democratic newspaper. "Texas can exist as an independent nation as well as Sweden or Denmark."[72] As former citizens of the United States, Missouri senator Thomas Hart Benton argued, Texans could be counted upon to resist British influence. Alarming reports that Texas would "throw herself forthwith into the arms of Great Britain" should annexation be rejected was "a libel upon the people of Texas. They are not monarchists or British adherents, but republicans and Americans."[73]

Benton was only partly right. To be sure, Texans were no less Anglophobic than citizens of the United States, but it was precisely this fear which had undermined their willingness to maintain their national sovereignty. Indeed, as Mirabeau Lamar's comments cited earlier make clear, the widespread allegations of British intrigues alarmed many Texans and destroyed their pretensions of independence. Even as opponents of annexation in the United States maintained that the Republic would stand guard against British encroachment in the Southwest, Texans were seeking refuge from that very threat in the protective embrace of the United States.

Finally, opponents of annexation could point to what they must have regarded as their trump card—the complete absence of substantive evidence that might prove allegations of a British conspiracy. Antiexpansionists complained that Her Majesty's government had repeatedly stated that it had no desire to interfere in the affairs of Texas. Theodore Sedgwick wondered why Great Britain, if indeed it harbored designs on the Lone Star Republic, had not acted on them already. "She might have offered bounties upon Texas cotton; she might have colonized her with emigrants; she might have made her peace with Mexico; she might have lent her money; she might have endeavored to undermine her slavery; she has done nothing of all these things that she might have done."[74]

But as is invariably the case with conspiracy theories, no burden of proof was required; indeed the very absence of direct evidence to support charges of foreign subterfuge only served to legitimize the contention that Britain's efforts to cloak its activities in a veil of secrecy had been successful. "Much is concealed as regards the ultimate designs of England," Mississippi senator Robert J. Walker noted darkly, in a classic example of conspiracy reasoning, "for to acknowledge them now would be to defeat them."[75] For expansionists like Walker, Britain's repeated denials that it sought to gain control of Texas bolstered their claim that a sinister plot was afoot to achieve that very object. Long wary of British intrigues, few Americans, it seems, were swayed by Thomas Hart Benton's argument that Her Majesty's government was "too proud to lie," many no doubt preferring to believe, with Pennsylvania senator James Buchanan, that in spite of its repeated disavowals, "England has long had her ever-watchful eyes intently fixed upon Texas; and she has strained every nerve to acquire an influence over that republic."[76]

But if widespread fears of British activities in the Western Hemisphere transcended partisan lines, these concerns by themselves were not enough to salvage Tyler's Texas annexation treaty. What Tyler, Upshur, and Calhoun failed to realize was that the Texas question—by fusing two vitally important issues, national security and slavery—represented a momentous turning point in the long and painful history of the sectional controversy. Calhoun continued to hope that the nation's hostility toward Great Britain would muffle if not completely silence antislavery agitation in the United States. But there could be no escaping the fact that the acquisition of Texas would almost double the size of the slave empire, a prospect anathema to abolitionists and troubling even to Northern moderates. Consequently, no other issue with which slavery had been associated—the tariff, western public lands, or congressional representation—was so designed to arouse the passions of the North. At the same time, supporters of annexation felt no less determined to push the measure forward, regarding the British threat as one of the gravest crises the country had faced in recent years. The question was therefore non-negotiable; unlike so many nagging problems that plagued antebellum national leaders, it did not lend itself to compromise or deferral. Once unleashed, it could not be governed by the normal institutional processes that had kept contentious issues at bay, demanding resolution from a two-party system ill-suited to swift and decisive action. Thus the fear of Great Britain, which expansionists believed would foster a national purpose and unite the country's principal sections, served as a wedge to drive them further apart.

The explosive nature of the Texas question became woefully apparent when leaders of both parties proved powerless to deny annexation a place at the forefront of the political agenda. In 1844 party leaders Henry Clay and Martin Van Buren assumed the question would fade quietly away, as it had once before in 1837. In April, to keep the annexation controversy from roiling the political waters on the eve of the presidential campaign, both men issued carefully worded policy statements opposing Tyler's Texas treaty. With the upcoming nominating conventions in May regarded largely as a formality for both candidates, Clay and Van Buren intended their statements to serve as position papers for their respective parties in the fall campaign. The fact that the two letters were published on the same day fueled plausible if unproven speculation that Clay and Van Buren had agreed upon a strategy to neutralize the Texas issue during a meeting several months earlier.[77]

Far from disappearing as a political issue, however, the annexation question continued to shape the course of events in ways that neither Clay nor Van Buren could have imagined. No one factor, of course, can account for the remarkable resiliency of the annexation issue. The holders of Texas land scrip represented a powerful lobby that Democratic politicians could ill afford to ignore, while many party leaders had long resented the dominance of the Van Burenite faction and saw an opportunity to rejuvenate their increasingly fractious party under the banner of militant expansionism. But the specter of Great Britain in 1844 provided a dimension of urgency to the annexation crisis that did not exist when the issue was first broached in 1837. No longer merely a question of advantage to the South, annexation had been transformed into an issue essential to the security of the nation.

To some extent, both Clay and Van Buren anticipated the electorate's concern and sought to reassure anxious voters that they would act resolutely to combat British aggression if elected. In his famous "Raleigh letter," Clay went on record opposing annexation and dismissed the likelihood that any European nation harbored designs upon Texas; nonetheless he felt obliged to add that any attempt by a foreign government to undermine the republic's sovereignty would meet with determined resistance from the United States. Van Buren declined to support annexation "at this time," but left open the possibility that Texas might be brought into the Union at a later date, provided Mexico's consent could be secured, a position which he no doubt hoped would satisfy all but the most rabid Southern expansionists. Like Clay, Van Buren attached an important proviso by which the United States would exercise its right to "self-defence" should Texas become "a dependency or colony" of Great Britain.[78]

These caveats notwithstanding, the Texas position papers of Van Buren and Clay left both candidates vulnerable to the charge that they had dangerously underestimated the threat from Great Britain. Although Henry Clay won the Whig presidential nomination by acclamation, he had clearly misjudged the depth of public support for annexation among Southern Whigs, and he would spend much of the fall campaign trying to clarify his Texas position. Van Buren's equivocal position enraged Democratic expansionists, who had been disappointed with the New Yorker's performance in the last election and now seized this opportunity to discredit him. Mexico, they argued, took its orders from Her Majesty's government, and therefore would not consent to annexation at any time or under any circumstances. Should the New Yorker receive the nomination, one Virginia editorialist raged, the "lone star" would soon be found "twinkling luridly, under the flaming Red Cross of St. George," and would henceforth be known as "BRITISH TEXAS!"[79] At the Baltimore convention in May, Democrats jettisoned the New Yorker as their candidate for president, nominating an avowed expansionist, James K. Polk.

By the early summer of 1844, the Texas annexation treaty had become such a lightning rod for sectional grievances that its defeat in the Senate had become a foregone conclusion. Most members of the Whig party—which enjoyed a majority in the Senate—already regarded Tyler as a political pariah for his strong states' rights views, while Calhoun's Pakenham correspondence had done much to sabotage the administration's efforts to promote the issue as a national measure. On the Democratic side, angry Van Burenites, who blamed the party's expansionist wing for the defeat of their candidate, needed little prodding to cast their votes against the treaty. As a result, the Senate defeated the measure by a comfortable 35–16 margin when it came up for a vote in June.

Far from quieting the clamor for annexation, the Senate vote served only to add more fuel to the controversy. Determined to redeem his much-maligned administration, Tyler announced that he would try to annex Texas again by means of a joint resolution when the next session of Congress convened in December. With the Democratic candidate also running on a platform that promised the annexation of Texas, expansion became the central issue of the 1844 presidential contest. Inevitably, fears of British ambitions remained a prominent feature of the political debate, albeit one that was increasingly obscured by concerns over the future of slavery. In July Henry Clay issued a second policy statement on the annexation issue which, not unlike the position taken by Van Buren, suggested that the acquisition of Texas might be accomplished at some point in the future if Mexican cooperation could be obtained.[80] Democrats excoriated Clay for his new stand, using the argument that Mexico's political leadership served as the mouthpiece for Her Majesty's government, which they had employed to such good effect against the former Democratic front-runner. The news that Queen Victoria had conferred a medal upon Antonio López de Santa Anna prompted Robert J. Walker to declare that the Mexican president was now a "British nobleman."[81] Democrats pointed gleefully to anti-British remarks which Clay had made earlier in his career as evidence that the Whig nominee had not always been an eager lackey of British interests. In answer to the question "Who forbids the union?" of Texas and the United States, Democrats like Chesselden Ellis of New York had a ready answer: "it is England and the Whig party!"[82]

It is impossible to gauge the extent to which expansionist efforts to tar the Whigs with a British brush affected the U.S. electorate in 1844; the presidential contest was an exceedingly close one—Polk failed to gain a popular majority—and in many states local issues competed with annexation for voters' attention. Nonetheless, when the second session of the Twenty-eighth Congress convened in December, many Whigs felt compelled to establish their credentials as Anglophobes more forthrightly than Henry Clay had done in the recent election. The second session annexation debates differed little in substance from those of the first, beyond the constitutional question of acquiring territory by joint resolution instead of a treaty. But while the party line remained unchanged, a number of Whigs took pains to point out that their opposition to annexation should not be construed as truckling to the British. Luther Severance, a Whig representative from Maine, warned his colleagues not to engage in a "grab game" with Great Britain. "She has been rather apt to take a hand in all such operations, and generally takes the lion's share."[83] Americans fearful of British military power could not have found much comfort in the assurances of John J. Hardin, a Whig congressman from Illinois, who dismissed "this dreaded British influence" on the grounds that Great Britain was too preoccupied with its policies of aggression in Asia to trifle with nascent republics in the American Southwest.[84] James Pollock, a Pennsylvania Whig opposed to annexation, mocked Great Britain's professed desire to see slavery abolished worldwide. "I have long distrusted the policy of England," Pollock stated. "It is crafty, far-seeing, widely grasping, and deeply laid. It begins and ends in her own intense selfishness."[85]

In the final analysis, party discipline outweighed concerns for the extension of slavery, the interference of Great Britain, or any other factor in resolving the annexation crisis. With few exceptions, members of both houses cast their ballots in late February, 1845, along party lines, approving the measure by a comfortable margin in the House and a slender 27–25 vote in the Senate. But the appearance of party unity was deceptive on both sides. The Texas issue had placed an intolerable strain on the two-party system, leaving the political landscape dominated by an ever widening sectional fault line that would threaten the structural integrity of both party organizations in the years ahead.

The debate over annexation was a complex one, involving a broad range of concerns and anxieties for Northerners and Southerners alike. While the expansion of slavery was the most combustible element of this debate, the fear of Great Britain greatly intensified its explosive properties. Antislavery opponents of annexation had successfully blocked the measure when it was first raised after Texas won its independence, but in 1844 they faced a far more determined pro-annexation lobby. At the core of this newfound resolve among the agents of expansion lay a profound distrust of Great Britain and a sense that the future prosperity if not the very survival of the Union might be in danger if this threat was not addressed promptly.

But if Anglophobia was a nationwide phenomenon, why did it not serve at least to mute the sectional antagonisms that were rapidly gaining ground in the United States? Why were so many in the North, who felt little affinity for the cause of abolitionism, so thoroughly unmoved by Southern pleas for aid to combat British aggression? The answer lies in the fact that Anglophobia lent itself to many permutations. While all Americans could agree that Great Britain posed a threat to the United States, each section or interest group viewed the precise nature of the British danger differently. Alarmed by alleged British ambitions insofar as their own region or interests were concerned, Anglophobes reacted frequently with ambivalence and even disdain when the cry of British aggression was raised in other quarters. The specter of Great Britain proved to be an amorphous, chimerical one, capable of taking many sinister forms, but never assuming monolithic definition for the nation as a whole.

Thus Thomas Hart Benton could scoff at Southern claims of a British abolitionist conspiracy in Texas, characterizing it as a "cry of wolf where there was no wolf." But his newfound skepticism surprised even British diplomats, who had not forgotten his furious denunciations of the Webster-Ashburton treaty as a treasonous betrayal of Western interests.[86] John C. Calhoun could work himself into an apoplectic frenzy over British meddling in Texas, but he fretted that Western calls to disregard the British title to the Oregon territory might lead to war and the disruption of the cotton trade.

Even the most vocal leaders of the radical Whig faction were not averse to expansion on their own terms and harbored their own apprehensions of British interference. New York Whig William Seward believed that the real battlefield upon which the United States and Great Britain would ultimately clash would be the markets in the Far East, while John Quincy Adams, who argued eloquently and consistently for a rapprochement between the United States and Great Britain during the first half of the decade, demanded in 1846 the occupation of "All Oregon" with an enthusiasm that rivaled even the most bellicose midwestern Democrats.[87]

There were, then, many vectors of Anglophobia, all crossing the political axis at separate points, but never intersecting to generate a cohesive response. The United States was still a nation of disparate parts; a threat to one was not automatically perceived to be a threat to all. The ideal of an organic union lay far in the future; partisan, sectional, and parochial differences remained formidable obstacles to the development of a strong, national identity. The divisiveness that accompanied the U.S. reaction to the dangers which Great Britain seemed to pose during this period therefore stands in sharp contrast to the broad consensus that characterized U.S. public opinion one hundred years later, when the nation perceived itself to be locked in another epochal contest for global economic and political hegemony with the Soviet Union. During the 1840s, expansionists expected the citizens of the republic—North and South, Democrat and Whig—to stand together in the face of an external enemy, not an unreasonable expectation in view of the widespread Anglophobia that existed at that time. Rather than demonstrate how much Americans had in common, however, the annexation issue—and its corollary anxiety over British ambitions—exacerbated the tensions that continued to divide them.

NOTES

1. James C. N. Paul, *Rift in the Democracy* (Philadelphia: University of Pennsylvania Press, 1951), p. 183.
2. David Pletcher, *Diplomacy and the Annexation of Texas* (Columbia: University of Missouri Press, 1973), p. 122; Paul Varg, *United States Foreign Relations, 1820–1860* (East Lansing: Michigan State University Press, 1979), p. 140; Frederick Merk, *Slavery and the Annexation of Texas* (New York: Alfred Knopf, 1972), p. xii.
3. William W. Freehling, *The Road to Disunion: Secessionists at Bay, 1776–1854* (New York: Oxford University Press, 1990), p. 356; Thomas R. Hietala, *Manifest Design: Anxious Aggrandizement in Late Jacksonian America* (Ithaca: Cornell University Press, 1985), p. 11.

4. For more on U.S. opposition to British commercial imperialism, see Kinley J. Brauer, "The United States and British Imperial Expansion, 1815–60," *Diplomatic History,* vol. 12 (Winter, 1988) no. 1: 19–37.

5. Van Zandt to Jones, April 19, 1843, in George P. Garrison, ed., *Diplomatic Correspondence of the Republic of Texas* (Washington, D.C.: GPO, 1908–11), Part 2, p. 165.

6. For more on the Peel ministry's diplomatic policy toward Texas, see Ephraim D. Adams, *British Interests and Activities in Texas* (Gloucester: Peter Smith, 1963), chs. 5–6.

7. *Daily Madisonian,* September 23, 25, 27, 28, 1843. The thesis that the Tyler administration planned to promote Texas annexation by spreading the alarm against the British is presented in Merk, *Slavery and the Annexation of Texas,* ch. 1.

8. Most historians accept the findings of Ephraim D. Adams, who in his examination of Her Majesty's government's diplomatic initiatives in Texas found little evidence to support allegations of undue British influence in Texas affairs.

9. Green has generally received rough treatment at the hands of recent historians. David Pletcher characterizes the Southern politician as "an irresponsible rumor-monger," while Frederick Merk describes him as a "restless manipulator and propagandist." *The Diplomacy of Annexation,* p. 123; *Fruits of Propaganda in the Tyler Administration* (Cambridge: Harvard University Press, 1971), p. 17.

10. Green develops this thesis fully in *Facts and Suggestions, Biographical, Historical, Financial and Political* (New York: Richardson, 1866).

11. Ashbel Smith, *Reminiscences of the Texas Republic* (Galveston, 1876), pp. 50–51; 54–58.

12. William S. Murphy to John Tyler, March 16, 1844, *The Papers of John C. Calhoun,* ed. Robert L. Meriwether et al. (Columbia: University of South Carolina Press, 1959–96), vol. 13 (1844), p. 85. See also William Murphy to Hugh S. Legaré, June 5, 1844, no. 1, Despatches from United States Ministers to Texas, vol. 20, National Archives.

13. Washington D. Miller to President Tyler, January 30, 1843, Washington Daniel Miller Papers, Texas State Archives.

14. Ibid., September 16, 1843, Miller Papers.

15. Anonymous Texas to John C. Calhoun, April 20, 1844, *Calhoun Papers,* 18: 296; W. W. T. Smith to John C. Calhoun, May 20, 1844; *Calhoun Papers,* 18: 547.

16. Edward Everett to Upshur, November 16, 1843, cited in Merk, *Slavery and the Annexation of Texas,* pp. 31–32; Edward Everett to John C. Calhoun, April 17, 1844, *Calhoun Papers,* 18: 263.

17. For more on the McLeod affair and other sources of conflict between the United States and Great Britain in the Northeast, see Kenneth R. Stevens, *Border Diplomacy: The Carolina and McLeod Affairs in Anglo-American-Canadian Relations, 1837–1842* (Tuscaloosa: University of Alabama Press, 1989).

18. Howard Jones, *To The Webster-Ashburton Treaty, A Study in Anglo-American Relations, 1783–1843* (Chapel Hill: University of North Carolina Press, 1977), ch. 9.

19. Pletcher, *Diplomacy of Annexation,* 208.

20. Alexander O. Anderson, *The Letter of Alexander Anderson, of Tennessee . . .*, August 21, 1844.

21. Justin Smith, *The Annexation of Texas* (New York: AMS Press, 1971 reprint), p. 73.

22. Joseph Milton Nance, *Attack and Counter-Attack* (Austin: University of Texas Press, 1964), p. 138; Smith, *Annexation of Texas,* p. 123.

23. Mirabeau Lamar to T. P. Anderson and Others, in Charles Gulick, ed., *The Papers of Mirabeau Lamar* (Austin: A. C. Baldwin, 1921–27), 4: 113.

24. Robert Barnwell Rhett, January 21, 1845, *Congressional Globe,* 28th Cong., 2nd Sess., p. 143.

25. Betty Fladeland, *Men and Brothers, Anglo-American Antislavery Cooperation* (Urbana: University of Illinois Press, 1972), chs. 10–11.

26. Charles Jared Ingersoll, *Charles Jared Ingersoll's Views of the Texas Question,* May 1, 1844, p. 12.

27. Moses Norris, Jr., *Appendix to the Congressional Globe,* 28th Cong., 2nd Sess., p. 192.

28. *New Hampshire Patriot,* February 24, 1845.

29. Speech on the Revenue Bill, *Calhoun Papers,* January 1816, 1: 321.

30. Calhoun to Upshur, August 27, 1843, *Calhoun Papers,* 17: 381.

31. Andrew Johnson, January 21, 1845, *Appendix to the Congressional Globe,* 28th Cong., 2nd Sess., pp. 222–23. For more on the Tyler administration's cotton diplomacy, see Hietala, *Manifest Design,* 64–70, 178–80.

32. Guy Bryan to Rutherford B. Hayes, December 21, 1843, in "The Bryan-Hayes Correspondence," *Southwestern Historical Quarterly* 25 (October, 1921): 111.

33. Andrew Jackson to Aaron V. Brown, February 9, 1843, in John Spencer Bassett, ed., *The Correspondence of Andrew Jackson* (Washington D.C.: Carnegie Institute of Washington, 1926–35), 6: 202.

34. *Ximenes, Mr. Calhoun—Mr. Van Buren—Texas* [July 1, 1843].

35. Upshur to Calhoun, August 14, 1843, *Calhoun Papers,* 17: 356.

36. Andrew Jackson to Aaron V. Brown, February 9, 1843, *Correspondence of Andrew Jackson,* 6: 202.

37. Alexander O. Anderson, *The Letter of Alexander Anderson, of Tennessee . . .*, August 21, 1844, p. 3.

38. William Brown, *To the People of the Fifth Congressional District of the State of Indiana,* 1844, p. 7.

39. *Kentucky Yeoman,* April 12, 1844.

40. Robert J. Walker, *Letter on the Re-Annexation of Texas,* p. 19.

41. *Kentucky Yeoman,* April 12, 1844.

42. *A Compilation of the Messages and Papers of the Presidents,* ed. James D. Richardson (Washington D.C., U.S. Congress, 1898), 5: 2163.

43. Andrew Jackson to Nashville Union, May 13, 1845, *Correspondence of Andrew Jackson,* 6: 291.

44. Andrew Jackson to Sam Houston, March 15, 1844, in Eugene Barker and Amelia Williams, eds., *The Writings of Sam Houston* (Austin: Jenkins Publishing Co., 1938–41), 4: 266.

45. Andrew Jackson to Andrew Jackson Donelson, December 2, 1844, *Correspondence of Andrew Jackson,* 6: 335.

46. Lord Aberdeen to Richard Pakenham, December 26, 1843, *Calhoun Papers,* 18: 54.

47. Alexander Everett, "The Texas Question," *United States Magazine and Democratic Review,* 15 (September, 1844): 264.

48. *Congressional Globe,* 28th Cong., 1st Sess., p. 543.

49. *New Hampshire Patriot,* February 24, 1845.

50. Aberdeen to Pakenham, December 26, 1843, *Senate Documents,* 28th Cong., 1st Sess., no. 341.

51. Calhoun to Pakenham, April 18, 1844, *Calhoun Papers,* 18: 276–78.

52. Andrew Jackson to Francis Blair, May 11, 1844, *Correspondence of Andrew Jackson,* 6: 287.

53. Thomas Hart Benton, *Thirty Years' View* (New York: Appleton & Co., 1854–56), 2: 581–90.

54. For a summary of various viewpoints, see William Cooper, *The South and the Politics of Slavery, 1828–1856* (Baton Rouge: Louisiana State University Press, 1978), 375–76.

55. William Hale to John C. Calhoun, May 18, 1844, *Calhoun Papers,* 18: 547; Charles Augustus Davis to John C. Calhoun, May 22, 1844; *Calhoun Papers,* 18: 583–84.

56. [John R. Mathewes] to John C. Calhoun, May 12, 1844, *Calhoun Papers,* 18: 495.

57. T[homas] M. Rodney to Secretary of State, March 26, 1844, *Calhoun Papers,* 18: 114–15.

58. John C. Calhoun to Benjamin Green, April 19, 1844, *Calhoun Papers,* 18: 283.

59. Calhoun to Francis Wharton, May 28, 1844, *Calhoun Papers,* 18: 649.

60. Ibid.

61. Calhoun to Henry Conner, July 3, 1844, *Calhoun Papers,* 19: 254.

62. Junius [Calvin Colton] *Annexation of Texas,* New York, 1844; C. Hudson, January 20, 1845, *Appendix to the Congressional Globe,* 28th Cong., 2nd Sess., p. 335.

63. Benton, *Thirty Years' View,* 2: 300.

64. "Letter of Waddy Thompson, upon the Annexation of Texas," *National Intelligencer,* July 3, 1844.

65. David Wallace, July 9, 1842, *Appendix to the Congressional Globe,* 27th Cong., 2nd Sess., p. 918.

66. R. W. Thompson, June 20, 1842, ibid., 959.

67. Samuel Rathbun, January 22, 1845, *Appendix to the Congressional Globe,* 28th Cong., 2nd Sess., p. 131.

68. Cassius Clay, *Speech of Cassius M. Clay on the Annexation of Texas,* December 30, 1844.

69. "California," *American Review,* vol. 3, no. 1 (January, 1846): 94.

70. [Theodore Sedgwick], *Thoughts on the Proposed Annexation of Texas to the United States,* 1844, p. 25.

71. John Quincy Adams, *Memoirs of John Quincy Adams* (Philadelphia: J. B. Lippincott, 1874–77), 11: 406–407.

72. New York *Evening Post,* quoted in *The Anti-Texass* [sic] *Legion,* Albany: 1844.

73. Thomas Hart Benton, May 16, 1844, *Congressional Globe*, 28th Cong., 1st Sess., p. 484.

74. [Theodore Sedgwick], *Thoughts on the Proposed Annexation of Texas to the United States*, 26–27, 1844.

75. Walker, *Letter on the Re-Annexation of Texas*, p. 17.

76. Benton, *Thirty Years' View*, 2: 612; Buchanan, June 8, 1844, *Congressional Globe*, 28th Cong., 1st Sess., 727.

77. Paul, *Rift in the Democracy*, 37–38.

78. Henry Clay to the Editors of the Washington *Daily National Intelligencer*, April 27, 1844, in *The Papers of Henry Clay*, ed. James F. Hopkins, et al. (Lexington: University of Kentucky Press, 1959–1992), 10: 41–46; Washington *Globe*, April 27, 1844.

79. [Seth Barton], *The Randolph Epistles; To the Delegates of the National Democratic Convention* [1844].

80. Henry Clay to Thomas M. Peters and John M. Jackson, July 27, 1844, *Clay Papers*, 89–91.

81. [Robert J. Walker], *The South in Danger, Address of the Democratic Association*, Washington D.C., September, 1844.

82. Thomas Morgan, *A Glance at Texas . . .*, 1844; *Appendix to the Congressional Globe*, 28th Cong., 2nd Sess., p. 43.

83. Luther Severance, January 15, 1845, *Appendix to the Congressional Globe*, 28th Congress., 2nd Sess., p. 369.

84. John J. Hardin, January 15, 1845, *Appendix to the Congressional Globe*, 28th Cong., 2nd Sess., p. 274.

85. James Pollock, January 22, 1845, *Appendix to the Congressional Globe*, 28th Cong., 2nd Sess., p. 356.

86. *Appendix to the Congressional Globe*, 28th Cong., 1st Sess., p. 485; Smith, *The Annexation of Texas*, p. 266.

87. Glyndon Van Deusen, *William Henry Seward* (New York: Oxford University Press, 1967), p. 105; John Quincy Adams, *Memoirs*, 11: 406–407.

Manifest Destiny's Filibusters

Robert E. May

Had the American filibusters finally appeared? Ever since the fall of 1851, when reports reached the Hawaiian kingdom that 160 filibuster "young bloods" from San Francisco were heading their way, Sandwich Islanders[1] had dreaded their arrival. The king and his ministers created a defensive military force, arranged to have the troops trained by a U.S. naval officer, and persuaded U.S. commissioner in Honolulu Luther Severance that a U.S. warship ought to be deployed so as to intercept any incoming filibusters. Sensing "how few here . . . would favor a Fillibusters operation," Severance promised the Hawaiians that "the gov't of the US will treat them in perfect faith, giving no countenance, direct or indirect, to Fillibusters." Good to his word, Severance asked the U.S. customs collector in San Francisco to prevent filibusters from leaving port. But even though the collector stopped and searched vessels for filibusters, and even though the reports of 160 filibusters proved to be a false alarm, apprehensions continued to fester in Honolulu. "We still continue to hear ominous outgivings of further Fillibuster movements from San Francisco," Severance reported in a March, 1852, dispatch to U.S. Secretary of State Daniel Webster. News of American William Walker's filibuster to Mexican Baja California late the following year increased the tension. Officials held military drills or reviews every day but Sunday in preparation for a showdown.[2]

Now, on the night of March 3, 1854, the Hawaiians' nightmare appeared to be coming true. Severance's replacement as U.S. commissioner, David L. Gregg, explained in his next day's dispatch: "Towards ten o'clock a rumor was put afloat that a vessel lying off & on, outside the harbor, contained a detachment of 'filibusters' from California, who were to land on a signal from their associates on shore, which was to be the simultaneous firing of the houses of the natives. The alarm was at once given in every direction. All the troops within reach were called out, and stationed in the best positions for defense in the town and along the shore. An intense excitement pervaded the entire population." Gregg reported that the suspected filibuster ship had proved to be merely a "harmless" merchant vessel, but added that the danger was far from over. Months later, he informed Washington that Hawaiian troops had spent a night under arms because of "the supposed presence of 'filibusters.'" [3]

Unlike Severance, who had cautioned Washington that filibustering might cause Hawaiian authorities to ask Britain and France, perhaps even Russia, for a protectorate over the islands, Gregg dared hope that the islanders would seek annexation to the United States as better security. The Hawaiian chiefs, he believed, were almost unanimous in favoring incorporation into the Union "in preference to continual domestic disturbances, and the apprehension of 'filibustering' expeditions from the American Coast." What should he do, Gregg inquired of Secretary of State William L. Marcy, if Hawaiian authorities approached him about annexation? Marcy, believing that the United States had a "duty" to "accept the sovereignty of these Islands" given evidence that power could no longer be "retained in the feeble hands of the native rulers," encouraged Gregg to negotiate annexation if the opportunity presented itself. [4]

Would Manifest Destiny leap some two thousand miles from the Pacific Coast to the Sandwich Islands? When first articulated in the summer of 1845 by New York editor John L. O'Sullivan, the expansionist ideology implied North American continental limitations. O'Sullivan, in a *Democratic Review* column, had complained that European intrigues in the Republic of Texas threatened to restrict American "greatness" by "checking the fulfilment of our Manifest Destiny to overspread the continent allotted by Providence for the free development of our yearly multiplying millions." Just months afterwards, in a column for the New York *Morning News* about his country's dispute with Britain over Oregon, he had invoked his country's "manifest destiny to overspread and to possess the whole of the continent which Providence has given us." [5]

Washington, in fact, had refrained from seeking Hawaii's annexation, despite the growing role of Americans in the islands' government, economy, and society. Although President John Tyler and his secretary of state, Daniel

Webster, in 1842 provided a kind of Monroe Doctrine umbrella over Hawaii by threatening "a decided remonstrance" should any other power try to take the islands, Tyler had informed Congress that the United States sought "no exclusive control over them." Years later, Secretary of State John M. Clayton had confirmed that the United States "do not want the islands" in a communication to Gerrit P. Judd, an American serving as Hawaii's finance minister.[6]

By the time of the Hawaiian filibuster panic, however, the U.S. national mood seemed to be shifting. As early as October, 1852, students of Western Reserve College's Philozetian debating society argued: "Ought the Sandwich Islands to be annexed to the U.S.[?]" A San Francisco sheet thought so. It reported that young American eaglets had been "trimming their wings for a trip to the Sandwich Islands." Perhaps the time had come to extend O'Sullivan's now familiar maxim across the Pacific. "Their manifest destiny," proclaimed the Cincinnati *Daily Enquirer*, "is to become a portion of the American domain."

That filibustering and Manifest Destiny reached Hawaii at approximately the same time should hardly surprise us. After all, none other than John L. O'Sullivan had been a filibuster. O'Sullivan had joined Cuban exile Narciso López's filibustering movement in 1849, describing himself as "deeply interested" in it that August. He remained a Cuba filibustering conspirator for several years. It is common for U.S. history textbooks to credit O'Sullivan for his notions of Manifest Destiny. None that I have read add that O'Sullivan was twice arrested by U.S. authorities for his filibustering activities.[8]

Americans do not know very much about filibustering and its relationship to Manifest Destiny, even though the two were inextricably linked long before either term was coined. Too bad. We need to understand, as D. W. Meinig reminds us in his geopolitical study, *The Shaping of America,* that this country's growth was often achieved by violence and that filibustering provided one of three means, along with military invasions and revolts, by which force was applied to U.S. expansion.[9]

What was the nineteenth-century meaning of the term "filibustering"? Who were the filibusters? Exactly how did filibustering play its part in the expansion of the United States? Did filibusters always facilitate the fulfillment of Manifest Destiny, or did they sometimes inhibit the nation's territorial growth? The rest of this essay explores these questions.

When it entered the U.S. lexicon, apparently in 1850, the term *filibuster* carried far different connotations than it conveys today.[10] Filibusters were persons who, lacking either the explicit or implicit consent of their own governments, planned, abetted, or participated in private military invasions or intended invasions of foreign nations or dependencies with which their own countries were at peace.[11]

This definition is more cumbersome than Charles H. Brown's contention that filibusters were "adventurers taking part in forays against friendly nations to foment revolution or capture the government."[12] It diverges from how pre–Civil War critics regarded filibusters. Playing off the term's descent from the Dutch word for freebooter *vrijbuiter*, contemporary antagonists condemned filibustering as nothing more than piracy by land.[13] And it excludes certain famed Americans such as Andrew Jackson and John C. Frémont, who conducted quasi-official invasions of foreign domains. Jackson, commanding some three thousand men, invaded Spanish Florida in 1818. Frémont led an intrusion into Mexico's Alta California in 1845 and participated the following year in the "Bear Flag" revolt there against Mexican rule. We may never know whether Jackson was lying when he claimed prior authorization for his invasion by means of a message from the Monroe administration transmitted through a third party. Most likely we will also never know, for sure, whether U.S. Marine Lieutenant Archibald Gillespie, who tracked Frémont down in May, 1846, conveyed a signal from the Polk administration that Frémont revolutionize California.[14] But neither Jackson nor Frémont qualify as filibusters because they both were commissioned officers of the U.S. Army in command of federal troops at the moment they crossed into foreign territory,[15] and because both men apparently had the implicit approval of their government for their aggressions.[16]

However, my definition holds true to the meaning of filibustering after the term was coined. It takes into account filibustering's illegal character in the United States—the country primarily associated with the phenomenon by persons living throughout the Western World.[17] It finds room for persons who organized and underwrote expeditions but did not themselves enroll in invading forces. It also avoids the mistake of reducing the adventurers' varied intentions to merely one or two categories.

Most importantly, this definition distinguishes U.S. filibustering from most private military expeditions occurring in other countries over the course of world history. The Spanish conquistador Coronado led a privately financed sixteenth-century invasion of North America in search of the legendary Seven Cities of Cíbola. The British East India Company, a private enterprise, conquered much of the Indian subcontinent in the eighteenth century. But were either Coronado or the company filibustering? Consider that Spanish conquistadores ventured forth with royal license, expecting that their efforts would be rewarded with land, titles of nobility, and governmental authority. Antonio de Mendoza, first viceroy of New Spain, loomed behind Coronado's fruitless meanderings in what is today the American Southwest. Consider, too, that the British government encouraged, rather than obstructed, the East India Company's aggressions.[18]

Whatever one's definition of filibustering, the term was long overdue when it was coined. Americans since the birth of the republic had been in the habit of conducting private military invasions into foreign lands, and they had been doing it despite a sequence of federal laws and prosecutions in federal courts designed to discourage that very behavior.

By the American Revolution, it was an axiom of international law that governments must prevent their own territory from being used for private military attacks against the domains of other countries. The nation's early leaders, committed to founding a government based on law, authorized Congress in Article 1, Section 8 of the United States Constitution to "define and punish" "Offenses against the Law of Nations."[19] Acting in the spirit of this charge, Congress passed enactments in 1794, 1797, 1800, 1807, 1818, and 1838 to prevent what would later be termed filibustering. The most important of these laws, the "Neutrality Act" of 1818, provided fines of up to three thousand dollars (a considerable sum in those times) and imprisonment for up to three years for any person within U.S. jurisdiction committing the misdemeanor of beginning, setting on foot, or providing the means for "any military expedition . . . against the territory or dominions of any foreign prince or state, or of any colony, district, or people, with whom the United States are [at] peace."[20]

Virtually all of this nation's first filibusters set their sights on Spanish dominions—usually those in North America, but occasionally on Spanish holdings further south. In 1793 Citizen Edmond Charles Gênet, minister from the revolutionary French Republic to the United States, commissioned George Rogers Clark, of Revolutionary War fame, to raise Kentuckians for the conquest of New Orleans. In 1796–97 William Blount, one of Tennessee's first U.S. senators, and other westerners hatched abortive plots to attack New Orleans and New Madrid as part of a three-pronged invasion of Spanish Louisiana. Ten years later, in New York City, some two hundred men participated in Francisco de Miranda's unsuccessful attempt to overthrow Spanish rule in his native Venezuela.[21]

France's sale of Louisiana to the United States in 1803 and French emperor Napoleon Bonaparte's invasion of the Iberian peninsula in 1807 created conditions so conducive to American filibustering that a spate of private expeditions departed U.S. territory immediately prior to and during the War of 1812. With Spain absorbed in its "Peninsular War," Latin American discontent with rule from overseas erupted in revolutions that by the mid-1820s eradicated the Spanish and Portuguese empires in the Western Hemisphere except for the Spanish islands of Cuba and Puerto Rico.

Capitalizing on Spain's difficulties, Americans formed military parties bound for adjacent Spanish territory. Some of these groups intended to support Latin revolutionary elements in their struggles for independence. Others intended piratical schemes or to facilitate the absorption of Spain's North American colonies into the United States.

American Reuben Kemper and some sixty to seventy followers filibustered on Mobile Bay's eastern shore in Spanish West Florida in 1810. Resigned U.S. army officer William Magee and hundreds of other Americans participated in Mexican revolutionary Don José Bernardo Gutiérrez de Lara's attempt to overthrow Spanish rule in New Spain's province of Texas in 1812. Virginia native and St. Louis physician John Hamilton Robinson invaded Texas in 1814.[22]

Former U.S. representative and Georgia governor and militia general George Mathews's botched "liberation" of Spanish East Florida in 1812 split the difference between filibustering and covert federal operation. In January, 1811, the seventy-two-year-old Mathews met with President James Madison and secured an appointment as secret U.S. agent for the purpose of acquiring East Florida in pursuit of a recent congressional resolution authorizing U.S. occupation of the province should Spanish officials there agree to U.S. possession or if a "foreign government" (meaning Great Britain) tried to occupy it. Mathews's instructions allowed him to apply to U.S. army and naval officers in the vicinity should he require assistance in what was obviously intended as an effort to revolutionize East Florida according to a model established two years earlier in West Florida. In the prior incident, former Americans residing in West Florida had captured the Spanish fort at Baton Rouge, raised the flag of an independent republic, and requested and received speedy annexation into the United States.

Mathews raised an army primarily of southern Georgians but also some Americans residing in Florida and even some Spaniards living there, created a bogus government for East Florida, and, on March 18, captured the smuggler's nest of Fernandina on Amelia Island just off Florida's Atlantic coast below Florida's border with Georgia. After sending off suggested terms of annexation to U.S. Secretary of State James Monroe, Mathews led his band toward St. Augustine and put the provincial capital under siege. U.S. naval commodore Hugh Campbell helped in the attack on Fernandina by threatening Spanish positions with U.S. gunboat fire. Subsequently, U.S. army troops and marines participated in the occupation of the town. Although Monroe, in a letter dated April 4, revoked Mathews's powers on the grounds that he had exceeded instructions, and although the Madison administration never officially recognized the rebels' government, U.S. forces remained at Fernandina as well as encamped near St. Augustine, fought a bloodless engagement with Spanish troops at St. Augustine, and did not fully evacuate East Florida until the spring of 1813. Some of the Patriots hung on in Florida well after the U.S. withdrawal, winning a skirmish against Spanish loyalists as late as August, 1813.[23]

Americans renewed their private expeditions into Spanish and ultimately Mexican domains immediately after the War of 1812. They participated in the revolutionary government of Luis de Aury at Galveston, Texas, in 1816. They helped finance and joined the Don Francisco Xavier Mina expeditions of 1816 and 1817 to Galveston and Mexico, respectively. In June, 1817, recruits from Baltimore, Savannah, Charleston, and other U.S. communities participated in Scottish soldier-of-fortune Gregor McGregor's seizure of Amelia Island. And from 1819 to 1821, Natchez merchant James Long revolutionized Texas. In 1819, with some three hundred men, Long took Nacogdoches and established a revolutionary regime. After Spanish forces expelled his men while he was absent in Galveston seeking assistance, Long organized yet another filibuster—this incident occurring in 1821 after Mexico achieved its independence from Spain.[24]

U.S. filibustering surged again during the Texas Revolution of 1835–36. Although the revolt began as an uprising of legal and illegal Anglo colonists already resident in the Mexican state of Texas-Coahuila assisted by some Tejanos, it quickly evolved into a filibustering episode as Americans rushed to lend their assistance. They generally came in volunteer units, such as the two companies of "New Orleans Greys" who participated in the rebels' capture of San Antonio in December, 1835. Over three quarters of the soldiers in the revolutionary cause between January and March of 1836 arrived in Texas after October of the preceding year. The following spring, after news spread to the States that Mexicans had massacred Texans at the Alamo and Goliad, the filibuster trickle became a flood. Some reached Sam Houston's Texan army in time to participate in the battle of San Jacinto—the turning point of the uprising. Other filibusters, such as onetime Mississippi governor John A. Quitman and his small band of Natchez volunteers, arrived too late for the San Jacinto engagement, but in time to ensure that Mexican forces would evacuate rather than reconquer Texas. That October, fittingly, Mississippi filibuster Felix Huston succeeded Sam Houston in command of Texas's army, after Houston gained election as the republic's first president.[25]

Not long after Texans established their republic, U.S. filibustering took a rare swing northward. In 1837 rebellion erupted in the British North American provinces of Upper and Lower Canada (today's Ontario and Quebec, respectively). Borderland Americans rallied to the "Patriot" side after British authorities repressed the insurrection, causing rebels to flee across the U.S. boundary. Regrouping in the States, rebel leaders found plenty of Americans willing to filibuster into Canada for Canadian freedom, and bonuses of land and silver.

Just two days after Upper Canada revolutionary leader William Lyon Mackenzie arrived in Buffalo, for instance, twenty-four men under New Yorker Rensselaer Van Rensselaer occupied Navy Island—above Niagara Falls and near the Canadian side of the Niagara river—preparatory to an intended invasion to liberate Canada. Soon afterward, over five hundred additional recruits, primarily Americans, reinforced the Navy Island assemblage. The adventurers unfurled their republican flag and issued a proclamation promising the Canadian people more democratic political and legal institutions, greater religious freedom, and economic development. When loyalist Canadians under a British militia commander destroyed the *Caroline,* a vessel carrying recruits and supplies to Navy Island, they not only created an issue that would aggravate U.S.-British relations for years, but also made filibustering more likely by alienating additional Americans living near the border. Mackenzie's Navy Island occupiers, beset by bitterly cold weather and the opposition of U.S. general Winfield Scott (who had been sent to pacify the border by the Van Buren administration), withdrew on January 13, 1838. However, Americans, usually as affiliates of secret societies such as the Canadian Refugee Relief Association, the Sons of Liberty, and the Patriot Hunters (or Hunters' Lodges) filibustered regularly into the Canadas for the next twelve months. Scores of these filibusters died in skirmishes such as the November, 1838, "Battle of the Windmill" below Prescott on the St. Lawrence river, or were taken prisoner by Canadian authorities. Some of the latter endured years of captivity at the British penal colony in Van Dieman's Land, Tasmania, before being pardoned for their transgressions.[26]

Southward filibustering climaxed, however, between the Mexican War and the Civil War—the years immediately following John L. O'Sullivan's coining of the term Manifest Destiny. During this interval, private expeditions to foreign domains became a national epidemic. Not a day passed when Americans, somewhere, were not organizing or participating in filibusters; often several filibusters to different countries were in simultaneous progress.

Filibusters, sometimes for weeks or months at a time, caught the nation's attention: congressmen praised and damned them; presidents, their cabinet members, judges, army and navy officers, customs collectors, and U.S. commissioners, marshals, and district attorneys grappled with how to stifle them; newspapers devoted headlines and columns to filibuster personalities, plans, campaigns, issues, and legal proceedings; advertisers seized on familiar filibuster names to draw attention to their products; books, magazines, pamphlets, poems, songs, and plays chronicled filibuster expeditions; and public lectures, parades, dances, serenades, and bond sales raised support for filibusters. Not only did college students formally argue about filibustering in their debating societies, but some even dropped out of school to venture into the filibuster wars. Meanwhile, foreign observers watched America's filibustering addiction in stunned amazement, often in disgust or anger. As one British minister to the United States put it in a private letter, this was the land of "Filibustero-ism."[27]

The Narciso López invasions of Cuba and the William Walker expeditions to Mexico and Nicaragua attracted more headlines than any other filibusters of the day. López, a native Venezuelan and Cuban exile, would have invaded Cuba in 1849 had U.S. naval vessels not blockaded the five hundred American volunteers assembled for his expedition at a Round Island rendezvous off eastern Mississippi's Gulf coast. He *did* invade Cuba with an army of 521 men, only 5 of them Cuban exiles, in May of 1850, when his troops captured a Spanish garrison at Cárdenas on Cuba's northern coast before they encountered Spanish reinforcements and were forced to flee to the United States. López would have invaded Cuba a second time in April, 1851, with a force of apparently several thousand men, had not federal authorities seized vessels connected with the operation at New York City and at South Amboy, New Jersey. He *did* invade Cuba a second time the following August with some four hundred men, leaving hundreds, perhaps a couple of thousand, recruits behind for lack of transportation. López and many of his followers perished in this expedition, some from battle wounds, others by execution after their capture.

Walker, a native Tennessean, invaded Mexican Baja California and Sonora from November, 1853, to May, 1854, first proclaiming an independent "Republic of Lower California," later superseding his own creation by announcing a sovereign "Republic of Sonora" with Lower California and Sonora as its two states. Though lucky to escape from Mexico with his life, Walker, commanding fifty-six men, filibustered to Nicaragua in the spring of 1855—a mere year after the conclusion of his half-year stint in Mexico. By November, he controlled the Nicaraguan military establishment and held virtual power in a government headed by a Nicaraguan figurehead. Inspired by his success, hundreds, eventually over two thousand, adventurous American males poured into Nicaragua to serve in his army for the rank, pay, and land bonuses that he was promising. Many more tried to go, only to be frustrated by federal efforts to interdict their "emigration." In July, 1856, following a long-sought recognition of his regime by the U.S. government and a rigged election, Walker staged his own inauguration as Nicaraguan president. Though expelled from Central America in May, 1857, Walker mounted a series of subsequent Nicaraguan expeditions lasting until the very eve of the Civil War. His final adventure never reached its destination. Walker died at the hands of a Honduran firing squad on September 12, 1860—less than two months before Abraham Lincoln's election as president.[28]

The above summary, however, by no means exhausts Manifest Destiny's filibustering story. Americans enlisted and died under commanders other than López and Walker between the mid-1840s and the Civil War. Generally, these other filibusters put in their service in Mexico.

U.S. adventurers, for instance, joined the 1848–49 filibuster to the breakaway Mexican state of Yucatán.[29] Starting in mid-1848, they associated as "Owls" in a "Buffalo Hunt" to carve an independent Republic of the Sierra Madre out of northern Mexico. In this capacity, they reinforced borderland revolutionary José María Jesús Carbajal (sometimes "Carvajal" or "Carabajal") after he captured Camargo in September, 1851, and participated in the insurgents' capture of Reynosa and unsuccessful siege of Matamoros the following month. When Carbajal crossed the Rio Grande in 1852 and 1853, he took U.S. filibusters, such as Captain A. H. Norton, whose men sacked Reynosa during the 1853 invasion, with him. Meanwhile, in 1851, other U.S. filibusters invaded Mexico by sea from California.[30] That year, California quartermaster general and former Mexican War officer Joseph Morehead boarded forty-five men on the bark *Josephine* out of San Diego and set sail for Mazatlán, apparently intending a subsequent invasion of Sonora.[31]

Mid-decade brought more Mexico-bound expeditions, though scholars argue about whether Americans in the Zerman expedition of October–November, 1855, from San Francisco to Baja California, intended a filibuster.[32] Far to the east, that same October, Texas Ranger captain James Hughes

Callahan and some 115 followers eluded U.S. army troops at Fort Duncan near Eagle Pass, Texas, swam their horses across the swollen Rio Grande river, and burned the village of Piedras Negras before returning to the United States after encountering heavy resistance from Mexican troops and their allied Indian bands.[33]

Not much more than a year after Callahan's retreat, former California state senator, editor, and U.S. Senate candidate Henry A. Crabb led eighty-four filibuster followers of his "Arizona Colonization Company" to their bloody deaths at Caborca, Sonora. Some died in battle. The rest, with a single exception, were executed by Mexican troops following their surrender as supposed prisoners of war. When the sole survivor returned a few days after the battle, he discovered that the exuberant Mexicans had severed Crabb's head from his body after the executions and preserved it in an earthen jug filled with vinegar. Reinforcements from Tucson under Granville ("Grant") Oury, later the Arizona Territory's delegate to the Confederate Congress, were lucky to escape with only four men killed after encountering resistance at Caborca's outskirts.[34]

Gringo filibustering plagued Mexico to the very eve of the U.S. Civil War. Texas Rangers crossed into Mexico on several occasions in 1860. Twice in 1860, George Bickley instructed the "castles" of his secret "Knights of the Golden Circle" to mobilize at the Rio Grande for invasions of Mexico. That same year, Texas Governor Sam Houston considered unleashing fellow Texans to filibuster into Mexico. Had Houston assumed command of a filibuster army, as he threatened on several occasions, he likely would have drawn thousands of recruits to his cause.[35]

Any accounting of the era's filibustering should note the forty or so Californians who participated in former Ecuadorian president Juan José Flores's attempt in 1852 to regain power in that country, an escapade that cost the lives of about half of the U.S. intruders when their ship exploded.[36] But it should especially reserve space for John A. Quitman's Cuba plot and the Henry L. Kinney filibuster to Nicaragua's Mosquito Coast.

Quitman, who had recently served a second term as Mississippi's governor, contracted in 1853 with Cuban exiles in the United States to serve as "civil and military chief" of their movement to overthrow Spanish rule in their native land. Conspiring with conspicuous public figures of the day including congressmen, state legislators, governors, judges and editors, Quitman and his agents enlisted men, raised funds, stockpiled war matériel, and engaged vessels to transport a projected 3,000-man army to Cuba, before encountering serious federal interference as well as evidence that Spanish authorities in Cuba had the military resources to crush his army. Quitman resigned his command on April 29, 1855, just five weeks before Kinney and eighteen followers left New York harbor on the schooner *Emma* bound for Central America. Kinney's "Central American Colonization Company" claimed the right to settle the Mosquito Coast, then a British protectorate, by virtue of its acquisition of an approximately 22,500,000-acre land grant conferred in 1839 by the "king" of Mosquitia upon another party—a grant that had since been revoked. Kinney would have taken several hundred men on his filibuster had not U.S. authorities commenced legal proceedings against him and put the steamship that he had chartered under surveillance. Even in his seriously reduced condition, he managed to reach San Juan del Norte (or Greytown), the southernmost port on Mosquitia's Caribbean Coast, where he had himself proclaimed "Civil and Military Governor" by a supposed convention of the town's denizens. Kinney hung on at San Juan del Norte until July, 1857, despite hostility from filibuster competitor William Walker. In April, 1858, Kinney staged a ridiculous comeback: he returned to San Juan del Norte with six followers, informed the mayor that the people of the community had asked him to take over, and seized an ex-mayor as his prisoner. Luckily for Kinney, a humane U.S. naval officer intervened to arrange his exit, sparing him from a vengeful mob.[37]

Perhaps, too, there were filibusters, or aborted filibusters, in this period that historians have yet to identify or fully to describe. The day's press and diplomatic correspondence carried a stream of rumors about expeditions other than those described above. Most likely, at least a few of these reports picked up on expeditions that were ultimately cancelled while still in preliminary planning stages.

It is easy enough to dismiss as fanciful a State Department special agent's dispatch that ten thousand men might be readying a filibuster against distant Japan.[38] Similarly, there is little cause to take seriously "General" N. S. Reneau's claim in an 1859 letter to President James Buchanan that he had five thousand Americans mobilized for a descent upon Cuba, and that he only needed Buchanan to give him five U.S. warships to bring the island into the Union! Reneau, according to contemporary accounts, was psychologically disturbed. His request was bizarre.[39] But rumors regarding filibusters to Venezuela and Peru may have had some basis,[40] as may have a series of reports between 1850 and 1852 that a "Dominican Encampment of the Brotherhood of the Union" intended an invasion of the Dominican Republic, Haiti, or the Spanish colony of Puerto Rico. John T. Pickett, who commanded the Kentucky battalion in Narciso López's first invasion of Cuba, approached Hungarian revolutionary Louis Kossuth during the latter's visit to New Orleans in early 1852 and suggested that they cooperate in the conquest of Haiti. President Franklin Pierce took such reports seriously. His December, 1853, annual message to Congress expressed satisfaction that no "unauthorized expeditions" had set out for Puerto Rico since Congress's last adjournment.[41] Perhaps, too, some U.S. filibusters intended an Atlantic crossing. In 1856, federal authorities arrested thirteen naturalized Irish immigrants belonging to the "Irish Emigrant Aid Society of Ohio" for plotting an invasion of the Emerald Isle.[42]

What was it about the pre–Civil War years, in particular, that spawned U.S. filibustering? Each filibuster, of course, had his own agenda. Certainly it is difficult to read broad patterns into some of the explanations that American males gave regarding their personal decisions to join expeditions, such as Californian E. J. C. Kewen's intimation to a newspaper correspondent that his "sole object" in joining William Walker's Nicaraguan army was to avenge the earlier death of his brother in Walker's service.[43]

When trying to comprehend filibustering as an American phenomenon, we also need to acknowledge that filibustering in no small measure derived from particular local needs that can hardly be projected upon the whole country. Some New Orleans merchants supported Cuban filibustering, for instance, in the hope that the conquest of Cuba would end tariffs that discriminated against U.S. goods, and provide new markets for trade out of their port. Some New York shipping magnates supported William Walker's Nicaraguan filibusters as a means of controlling international trade and transit across the Central American isthmus.[44]

Texans had racial feelings about and grievances against Mexicans unique to their historical experience and geographical position that made them more prone to filibuster southward than other Americans. Thus Texans filibustered to retaliate against Indians who raided isolated settlements and then found refuge in Mexican sanctuaries. "Some have styled this a fillibustering movement. I do not so regard it . . . I do not want anything that belongs to Mexican or Indian on Mexican soil," explained one Texan in a letter to his governor. Rather, he invaded Mexico to avert Texas's frontier being "drenched with the blood of helpless women and innocent children." Many of the Texans who joined the José Carbajal and James Callahan invasions did so to recover slaves who had escaped bondage by fleeing across the border.[45] Few non-Texans who turned filibuster were motivated by such quests for personal and propertied security.

Still, there were things going on in this country that help explain why Americans as a people resorted so frequently to filibustering in the antebellum years. Socioeconomic changes transforming the United States during the antebellum period, including rapid urbanization, high rates of immigration, improvements in communications and transportation, economic dislocations, and deteriorating parental authority all facilitated the outbreak of filibustering. Young urban American males, living on their own during turbulent economic times in cities spawning a violent lower-class subculture, read telegraph reports about pending expeditions in the penny press, and rushed to a filibuster rendezvous, sometimes in company with unemployed immigrants, and naturally without confiding to their parents that they planned to violate the law.[46]

Not all filibusters, by any means, fit this model. Many hailed from rural areas. Many informed their loved ones about their intentions to join expeditions, or sent them letters proudly recounting their subsequent experiences. "I intend having my Dugaretype [sic] taken and sent home and have you folks to exhibit me as a live Fillabuster," one promised. Plenty of young Americans of the day simply thought of filibuster soldiering as romance, high adventure, their chance for fame and glory, an opportunity to travel virtually for free to exotic foreign lands. "I am determined to visit the lands of Cuby and this is the very way that I prefer going," one volunteer admitted to John Quitman. It would be impossible to overstate the macho camaraderie of filibuster camp life as an inducement to enlistments. Many defeated filibusters, returning to the United States, found it difficult to erase from their thoughts the "glorious fellows," sometimes exotically clad, that they had fought besides. One filibuster, recalling a captain attired in "dancing black plume" as well as some of his other recent comrades, dreamed of again "tipping a glass of *aguadente* [sic] with every mother's son of them." Filibuster ranks filled with repeaters. Many filibusters searched out comradeship in new expeditions immediately upon their return from former invasions. In the case of the Cuban filibusters in particular, this comradeship, especially among officers and expedition organizers, drew reinforcement from Masonic brotherhood. López, Quitman, and many of the others, whether U.S. citizens or Cuban exiles, belonged to Masonic lodges.[47]

Yet surviving documents do highlight how socioeconomic dislocations prompted filibustering as one route to monetary gain or to what today we might call career enhancement. Filibuster recruiters promised land bonanzas, gold mines, opportunities to plunder, swift promotions, governmental offices, and other incentives to enlistees and officers. Profilibuster newspaper boosterism reinforced their message. Many disoriented Mexican War veterans, unsuccessful California forty-niners, U.S. army officers stuck in low ranks, apprentices unhappy with their situations, mechanics mired in urban poverty, physicians anxious to hone their skills by treating battle wounds, men rebounding from broken romances, and all sorts of other individuals craving a change in their situation (including some criminals on the run) found such enticements seductive.

Consider the free Southern black who ventured to William Walker's Nicaragua because so many "grand opportunities were presented according to the papers." Ponder the case of the Mexican War veteran "at a loss for something to earn a living" after being mustered out of the army, who learned about Narciso López's first Cuba plot upon meeting a wartime comrade and immediately signed up. Review the story of Mexican War U.S. army lieutenant Albert Tracy. A onetime art student of telegraph inventor Samuel F. B. Morse, Tracy had rendered some battlefield paintings during the war, but struggled to make a living as a civilian artist after the fighting ceased. He considered signing on with López. Then, too, there was the Quaker who failed in the California mines and almost accepted a lieutenancy in William Walker's Mexican filibuster. When Walker's second-in-command promised him "an ample share in the distribution of the Spoils, and a chance of high position under the new Government," it seemed such an "alluring" "rosy picture" "to a Young Man with no Employment and small means," that he almost forsook his pacifism![48]

Socioeconomic flux, however, only partially explains why antebellum Americans showed a particular affinity for filibustering. The nation's worsening sectional crisis over slavery also lurked behind filibuster episodes. Many late antebellum Southerners believed that one way to strengthen the institution of slavery against Northern antislavery attacks was to spread its influence southward into the tropics, and that filibustering offered the most promising way to attach new slave states either to the Union or to a separate Southern nation.

It is no coincidence that virtually all locales targeted by post–Mexican War filibusters either had slavery, as in the case of Cuba, or were believed by many Southerners capable of supporting a slave labor system. As early as November, 1850, John Henderson, a former U.S. senator from Mississippi and one of the key financial backers of Narciso López, looked upon Cuban filibustering as a "Southern question" of vast magnitude. As the North-South crisis over slavery worsened, more Southerners concluded that filibustering might provide their salvation. Thus John T. Pickett of Kentucky, formerly a lieutenant colonel under López, intimated in 1854 that filibustering should once again be undertaken, this time to bring Mexico as well as Cuba into the Union. Their annexation would provide Southerners with the means to resist "fanatical Northern demagogues" (abolitionists) as well as spare Southerners from being dependent upon "our compromising vacillating brethren" (presumably meaning "doughface" Northern Democrats) for the political strength to offset antislavery initiatives.[49]

John Quitman turned filibuster largely because he and associated Southerners perceived a clear and present danger to southern slavery in the form of an apparent Spanish threat to emancipate Cuba's slaves. "Africanizing" the island, Southerners knew, would eliminate forever any possibility that Cuba might be annexed to the Union as a slave state. Should Cuban emancipation proceed, moreover, Southerners would face a "mongrel empire," as Quitman put it, of freed slaves closer to their coast than Haiti—a model that might inspire their own slaves to revolt for freedom. "[I]f Cuba be africanized," predicted one of John Quitman's plantation overseers, "this glorious land ... will be a howling desert." He would raise "a company of human liberators in less than a week" to help Quitman "pilot the ship to victory."[50]

William Walker legalized slavery in Nicaragua during his tenure as its president, a decision that cost him much of his previous support in the North, but which endeared him to many Southern expansionists. Walker's recruiters afterwards made much of how he represented "the promulgation of the institutions and sentiments of the Southern portion of the United States." During his intervals in the States between expeditions, Walker hobnobbed with public figures notorious for their Southern sectionalism, such as Alabama fire-eater William L. Yancey. In his 1860 autobiographical account *The War in Nicaragua*, Walker reminded readers how liberated slaves in Haiti had used their freedom to "murder and destroy," argued that blacks needed whites to "direct" their labors under the "protection" of slavery, and proclaimed that anyone "born and educated in a slave State of the Union" had a special stake in his cause. Slave state males, in response, dominated Walker's expeditions to recover Nicaragua following his expulsion in 1857. Said a North Carolinian seeking an officer's commission from the filibuster, "I ... would like to engage in some good, some plausible undertaking as a Southern Man, strictly of southern feelings."[51]

George Bickley's Knights of the Golden Circle marked the apogee of sectionalized filibustering. Knights' rituals emphasized the invasion of Mexico and the creation of a vast slave empire. The "Circle" radiated outward from Cuba, included the Southern states, and reached southward through Mexico all the way to South America while extending westward to Kansas. Knights' membership seems to have been exclusively Southern. Although the Knights never did invade Mexico, their initial objective, they played a significant role in agitating secession in Texas, before moving northward and emerging as one of the most notorious "Copperhead" organizations during the Civil War.[52]

But can we afford to overlook the conclusion of a contemporary observer that filibustering was natural in a land "brimful of adventurers and 'manifest destiny men,'"[53] as we try to make sense of antebellum filibustering? That is, did not the ideology of Manifest Destiny itself have something to do with why Americans filibustered during the Age of Manifest Destiny? To put it another way, do ideologies guide human behavior, or do they merely mask more substantive motivations? Just as pursuit of this matter has informed other chapters of U.S. history, such as the American Revolution, so it can illuminate our investigation of filibustering.

Manifest Destiny inspired filibusters with its call upon Americans to share their institutions of representative government with other peoples. In the 1840s, far more than in earlier decades when national leaders had been constrained by fears that growth was inimical to republican institutions, the concepts of expansion and democracy fused together in the American mind. During the national debate over annexing Texas, expansionists regularly invoked a crusade, as Andrew Jackson put it in 1843, to "extend the area of freedom." Americans assumed a mission to bestow their systems of elective offices, extended suffrage, federalism, and religious freedom upon less privileged peoples.[54]

Filibusters of the post–Mexican War period inherited this proclaimed mission to share democracy—most particularly in respect to Cuba, which was ruled from overseas by a monarchical power that denied the island political representation, yet censored Cuba's press, imposed high taxes, fees, and tariffs on the island's population, maintained a large standing military establishment in Cuba, and excluded Creoles from the bloated bureaucracy that it established on the island. López and his subordinate officers regularly inspired their followers with talk of assuming the role of liberators: they could free Cuba from Spain just as foreigners Lafayette, Steuben, Kosciusko, and Pulaski had helped win independence for the American colonies from monarchical England. This liberating vision survived López's death. Thus in 1854 Texas Ranger leader John Ford prepared, in the words of an acquaintance, to join John Quitman's Cuba filibuster because he had heard "from those friendly to the cause of freedom, that an expedition is being fitted out the object of which will be to render 'material' and effective aid to the oppressed and downtrodden patriots" of the island. Using virtually identical phrasing, a Pennsylvanian announced to Quitman that he was prepared to sacrifice his life to "free the people" of "downtrodden" Cuba. This objective inspired other filibusters. P. G. T. Beauregard, the later famous Confederate general, sought an officership under William Walker because he believed in Walker's goal of establishment of a "Central American Republic, based on our own system."[55]

More importantly, Manifest Destiny gave filibusters a racialist and missionary rationale to justify their conquests and attempted subjugation of native peoples. By the end of the Mexican War, Manifest Destiny had sprouted a sequence of derivative teachings, regularly disseminated through the expansionist press, the most salient of which was the notion that American Anglo-Saxons had a mission to regenerate peoples deemed as inferior, and to bring progress, Protestantism, and capitalistic enterprise to backwards, anarchic regions. Not all expansionists internalized these teachings. In fact, during the war, many expansionists backed off from calls to conquer all of Mexico as they came to realize that unless the United States ruled Mexico as a colonial possesssion (thus flaunting the very American tradition of representative government that Manifest Destiny was supposed to extend) it would eventually have to provide citizenship to a lot of dark-skinned, Catholic peoples. Some expansionists escaped this dilemma by espousing primitive versions of "survival-of-the-fittest" thinking: they argued that Mexico's inhabitants, much like U.S. Native Americans, would gradually die out when brought into sustained contact with superior white Americans. But because most Americans recoiled from the prospect of admitting masses of Mexicans to the nation's body politic, the Polk administration and Congress settled in the Treaty of Guadalupe-Hidalgo for merely annexing sparsely populated regions of northern Mexico. Still, the racialist strains of Manifest Destiny survived the peace with Mexico and helped inspire postwar filibustering.[56]

Pre–Civil War American filibuster commanders, their subordinate officers, and their civilian organizers and recruiters, in part as propaganda to cover the brutalities they committed, in part because they had themselves been indoctrinated by others, regularly drew on Manifest Destiny's racialist precepts to raise volunteers and funds and to bid for public support. Filibustering, they explained, would bring "American civilization" and capitalistic development to effete, "imbecile" peoples who had already endured far too many years of misgovernment, economic stagnation, and, in many cases, anarchy and civil war.

William Walker announced to the American people, in an address from Ensenada, Lower California, that he had occupied the peninsula because its "indolent and half civilized people" had failed to utilize the area's "mineral and pastoral wealth" and because the Mexican government neglected providing the Lower Californians with protection from robbers or with means of communication to the outside world. Later, in his inaugural address as president of Nicaragua, Walker promised to bring that country public education and the arts. Henry L. Kinney's newspaper trumpeted that the "industry intelligence and energy of an Anglo American population" would transform the "teeming soil" of the Mosquito Coast. Another filibuster officer inspired his soldiers with oratory about how the filibusters would lead Cubans in the "onward march" of an "age of progress." Governor Sam Houston of Texas even had the effrontery to tell U.S. Secretary of War John Floyd that he might unleash Texans to filibuster into Mexico, because that nation's "regeneration" depended on help from someone who would "deem it his manifest destiny" to begin a rescue mission.[57]

However much we might today dismiss such doctrines as preposterously ethnocentric and self-serving, young American males signed up as filibusters genuinely believing that they would better their fellow man by joining God's design to supplant tropical poverty with U.S. prosperity. We should not automatically dismiss their sincerity, even as we recoil from their fallacies. After all, any filibusters plagued by self-doubts could find the necessary psychological reinforcement, if they just read the right newspapers. While many of the day's sheets expressed dismay about filibustering, plenty of others told filibusters that they were engaged in a holy cause. Thus the New Orleans *Daily Creole* called William Walker's filibusters "bold pioneers" and a New York *Daily Times* reporter envisioned Henry Kinney's "Northmen" supplanting the "tainted, mongrel and decaying race" inhabiting the Mosquito Coast.[58]

Filibusters found such dogma irresistible. "Tell my dear old Aunt Christena not to fit about me," requested one of William Walker's followers in a letter home. "I am right side up with care fighting for the liberty and regeneration of Nicaragua." Another of Walker's filibusters affirmed that it was as "clear as fate" that "the white race are to govern the destinies of this Central American country." John C. Reid signed on as a lieutenant in Granville Oury's Sonoran foray in part because he thought an infusion of Anglo

Americans promised the best "panacea" for the degeneration of Mexico's population.[59]

What particularly needs to be remembered, in explaining why filibustering surged after the Mexican War, is that Manifest Destiny and slavery expansionism tended to be mutually reinforcing rather than contradictory impulses. Slavery expansionists felt no contradiction between extending democracy and spreading slavery, since they never included African Americans within their conception of a legitimate body politic. Rather, as countless recent scholars have observed, antebellum Southerners believed that slavery actually promoted democracy within their own society: since the South's dangerous lower classes were all African American, upper-class Southerners could afford to extend the franchise and officeholding privileges, as well as a modicum of social respectablility, to the region's middling white classes. In fact, they had to share power with less fortunate whites, if they hoped to keep their race united in defense of their right to own slaves. Given this situation, it was only natural for Southern filibusters to organize expeditions to "liberate" Cuba by reinforcing the slaveholding rights of the island's Creoles.[60]

Northerners who filibustered, or who supported filibustering, tended to have greater tolerance for slavery than did filibustering's opponents. Some, in their attitudes, were closet Southerners. John L. O'Sullivan, whose sister married a well-off Cuban planter in 1845, who espoused theories of government similar to those of John C. Calhoun, and who opposed giving the vote to his state's black population, fits this model. When in 1850 O'Sullivan schooled John Quitman to get involved in López's filibuster for Cuban "liberty," he stressed the need to "aid in preserving the social tranquility of the country (I refer to the blacks)." Mike Walsh, New York congressman and behind-the-scenes manipulator for the Quitman Cuba plot, even bragged about how he convinced delegates to a state Democratic convention "to cut loose from ... all pretended democrats who are tainted in any way with abolitionism."[61]

Of course, this very connection between filibustering and slavery expansion stacked the deck against the invaders ever conquering anything. Abolitionists and Free-Soilers charged, in righteous indignation, that the filibusters not only were violating U.S. and international law, but, worse, that they were part of a slave power conspiracy to spread the peculiar institution into the tropics. The validity of such charges did not matter. The important thing is that they put Northerners who might otherwise have supported filibustering on the defensive. For in the decade of the Fugitive

Slave Law and the Kansas-Nebraska Act, Northern politicians had to be wary of incurring the political damage that would attend identification with supposed slave power plots. The presumed connection between slavery and filibustering made it virtually impossible for President Franklin Pierce, who hinted that he might support filibustering, to carry through on such intimations by relaxing enforcement of the Neutrality Law. The outcry against Filbustering [*sic*] has cowed the administration," observed Pennsylvania presidential aspirant George Mifflin Dallas in May, 1854. They also guaranteed that profilibuster initiatives by Southern political collaborators with the filibusters, such as attempts by U.S. senators John Slidell of Louisiana and Albert Gallatin Brown of Mississippi formally to suspend the Neutrality Law, would get nowhere.[62]

The pre–Civil War filibusters never beat the odds, despite a lot of hype about what they would do for this country. The *Democratic Review* believed, for instance, that filibusters would pave the way for new U.S. acquisitions by drawing the attention of Americans to the "vast riches" of the tropics. One of William Walker's biographers does credit that filibuster's Lower California expedition with shocking Mexico into ceding 45,000 square miles to the United States in the "Gadsden Purchase," the only U.S. territorial acquisition from a foreign power during the period between the Mexican and Civil wars.[63] But it is apparent that the filibusters did far more to inhibit than to facilitate U.S. territorial growth.

Certainly James Gadsden, the U.S. minister who negotiated the purchase, does not seem to have felt that filibustering assisted his mission. Official Mexican complaints that the U.S. government had been lax in preventing filibustering put Gadsden on the defensive in his negotiations. About a month and a half before the treaty was signed, Gadsden informed Secretary of State Marcy that he had been encountering difficulty removing Mexican suspicions "that the Government at Washington secretly favored these movements." Concerned about filibustering's influence on his negotiations, he fed information to the U.S. marshal at San Francisco so that additional filibusters would be arrested prior to leaving port. He requested a U.S. naval commander to do a "service to your Govt." by intercepting filibusters at sea. In one dispatch, Gadsden predicted that Walker's *failure* would "have the most favourable influence on the negotiations with which I am charged." Gadsden agreed to an antifilibustering provision in his draft treaty with Mexico, and after negotiating his "Purchase" he continued to declaim against filibusters. Their expeditions gave Mexican reactionaries an excuse to rally public opinion against further inroads of U.S. "institutions" and "progress." Could not the "American system" "propagate itself" without resorting to "auxiliaries" who would "debase and abuse it"?[64] Gadsden's words powerfully indict filibustering as an impediment to Manifest Destiny.

In fact, U.S. filibustering so outraged the peoples and governments of invaded nations, and so threatened other countries, that it helped to eliminate whatever hopes existed, however slim, of annexations in addition to the Gadsden Purchase. Gadsden thought that he might have also acquired Baja California from Mexico had not Walker's "insane expedition" turned Mexican ruler Santa Anna against that cession.[65] Just a few years later, John Forsyth, another U.S. minister to Mexico, observed in an official dispatch that the Crabb expedition undercut his efforts to repair the damage to U.S.-Mexican relations caused by prior filibusters. A "deeply-seated distrust of Americans," Forsyth believed, provided the primary impediment to the peoples of borderland states such as Sonora and Chihuahua from "breaking their feeble ties with the Central Govt., and seeking annexation with us."[66]

In similar fashion, the López filibusters, Quitman plots, and other rumored expeditions against Cuba inflamed U.S. relations with Spain, reducing the likelihood that Spain might voluntarily sell Cuba to the United States. An American consul in Cuba noted how López's first expedition caused a "strong animosity . . . in the minds of the old Spaniards against our Government, and indeed every thing American." U.S. minister to Spain Daniel M. Barringer observed in the wake of the last López invasion that the Spanish government's organ was threatening war against the United States and that even Madrid's more temperate newspapers condemned "our government and people." Memories of these offenses against Spanish sovereignty and pride persisted through the 1850s, undercutting efforts by both the Pierce and Buchanan administrations to effect Cuba's purchase.[67]

Rather than intimidate foreign countries into territorial concessions to the United States, filibustering tended to unify other powers in temporary alliances to forestall such annexations. Spain turned to Great Britain and France for guarantees of her rights to Cuba. Some conservative Mexicans turned to those same powers for protection against U.S. adventurism, at one point even inviting those countries to impose a European prince as ruler of Mexico as a way of warding off the Yankees. Central and South American countries initialed a never-implemented Continental Treaty, containing several antifilibustering clauses, in response to the Walker and Flores movements.[68]

Filibustering also fostered nationalism and patriotism abroad, sentiments counterproductive to U.S. annexationism. To many Central Americans, especially, resistance to the filibusters became a kind of jihad, a way of unifying peoples who previously had not been particularly unified. As the president of New Granada put it, Costa Rica's war against Walker represented "the holiest of causes." Considering such sentiments, E. Bradford Burns concludes in *Patriarch and Folk* that "Nicaraguans forged their nationalism in the fires of war against Walker."[69]

Ultimately, even Commissioner Gregg in Hawaii learned that filibustering would fail Manifest Destiny. Though able to win King Kamehameha III's agreement to a draft treaty of annexation by mid-August, 1854, Gregg found that continued rumors of filibustering undermined the likelihood that the treaty would ever be ratified. Rather than intimidate Hawaii's government into rushing annexation along, the persisting reports caused island officials to seek closer relations with Great Britain and France. By November, Gregg was lamenting to Washington that the British consul general had been successful at engendering "prejudice" against the United States by describing California as a "rendezvous for cut-throats, thieves, filibusters and lawless men" and by harping on the menace of pending invasions. All that Gregg could do, under the circumstances, was to match British and French offers of naval support for the Hawaiians, so that the United States would not be isolated diplomatically in the islands. In a royal proclamation that December, Kamehameha announced that he had accepted U.S., British, and French offers of naval assistance against the danger of being overthrown by "lawless violence." "My independence," the king boasted, "is more firmly established than ever before." Kamehameha died later in December. The next month, Alexander Liholiho, Kamehameha IV, informed Gregg that annexation negotiations should be considered terminated.[70]

Hawaii, of course, eventually became this nation's fiftieth state, and violence by nonresident Americans played a role in its initial annexation story. But the armed sailors who landed from a U.S. cruiser in January, 1893, to help secure the revolution that overthrew the Hawaiian monarchy echoed Andrew Jackson's invasion of Florida and John C. Frémont's adventure in California rather than the filibusters of Narciso López and William Walker. For these sailors were federal employees rather than private performers, and their intervention had been requested by the resident U.S. minister on the grounds that U.S. property and lives required their protection. Americans filibustered long after the Civil War. But filibustering had long since played out its role in American Manifest Destiny.

NOTES

The author would like to express his indebtedness to his mentor and good friend Richard H. Sewell, University of Wisconsin, as well as his Purdue University colleagues Charles R. Cutter, Donald L. Parman, and Raymond E. Dumett, for their thoughtful suggestions regarding an earlier draft of this manuscript.

1. British captain James Cook, "discoverer" of Hawaii in 1778, named the archipelago after John Montagu Sandwich, his nation's first lord of the admiralty. Americans used the designation interchangeably with "Hawaii" during the antebellum period.

2. Luther Severance to Daniel Webster, November 14 (with enclosures), December 8, 1851, March 8, 16, May 3, 31, 1852; Severance to Edward Everett, June 30, 1852; Severance to William L. Marcy, August 15, 1853; Severance to Richard P. Hammond, August 24, 29, 1853; all in Despatches from United States Ministers in Hawaii (hereafter, Despatches, Hawaii), Records of the Department of State, RG 59, National Archives [hereafter, NA] (reel 4, T 30); *The Polynesian* (Honolulu), April 3, 1852, April 30, December 31, 1853; James P. Delgado, *To California by Sea: A Maritime History of the California Gold Rush* (Columbia: University of South Carolina Press, 1990), p. 120; Washington *Daily National Intelligencer,* June 14, 1852. The reported 160 filibusters turned out to be thirty-two or thirty-three passengers who arrived on the *Game Cock* on November 15. Some fifteen of these, including one Samuel Brannan, had reputations for involvement in prior vigilante activity in California. Brannan may have had a vague takeover scheme in mind. Another passenger, former Texan B. F. Hanna, told Severance to expect the imminent arrival of 4,000 filibusters from the Pacific coast. However, the *Game Cock* passengers seem to have come with unrealistic hopes of buying up Hawaiian land cheaply. Brannan and all but three of the others returned to the United States by the following March. Severance to Webster, November 15, December 8, 1851, March 8, 16, May 3, 1852, Despatches, Hawaii (reel 4); *The Polynesian,* March 13, 1852; Andrew F. Rolle, "California Filibustering and the Hawaiian Kingdom," *Pacific Historical Review* 19 (August, 1950): 251–63. Reports of filibuster intentions against Hawaii can be traced to at least 1849. See R. C. Wyllie to Gerrit P. Smith, March 19, 1849 [extract], Despatches, Hawaii (reel 6). Ralph S. Kuykendall in *The Hawaiian Kingdom, 1778–1854* (Honolulu: University of Hawaii Press, 1947), p. 291, notes that Hawaiian authorities abolished a feudalistic land system around this time in part to preempt U.S. filibusters. Allowing inhabitants to acquire fee-simple title for the first time gave landowners a stake in opposing invaders.

3. David L. Gregg to Marcy, March 4, August 7, 1854, Despatches, Hawaii (reel 5).

4. Luther Severance to Daniel Webster, May 3, 1852, Severance to Edward Everett, June 30, 1852, Despatches, Hawaii (reel 4); David L. Gregg to William L. Marcy, January 5, 1854, ibid. (reel 5); Marcy to Gregg, April 4, 1854, Diplomatic Instructions of the Department of State, RG 59, NA (reel 99, M 77); Marcy to James Buchanan, March 11, 1854, in William R. Manning, comp., *Diplomatic Correspondence of the United States: Inter-American Affairs, 1831–1860,* 12 vols. (Washington, D.C.: Carnegie Endowment for International Peace, 1932–39), vol. 7, p. 103.

5. O'Sullivan quoted in Albert K. Weinberg, *Manifest Destiny: A Study of Nationalist Expansionism in American History* (1935; reprint ed., Chicago: Quadrangle Books, 1963), p. 112, and Frederick Merk, *Manifest Destiny and Mission in American History: A Reinterpretation* (New York: Vintage Books, 1963), pp. 31–32. The phrase *Manifest Destiny* appeared in slightly different language even earlier. See Weinberg, *Manifest Destiny*, p. 107. O'Sullivan did not sign either 1845 column using the phrase, but he did sign a January 1846 *Morning News* piece using it. Julius W. Pratt, "The Origins of 'Manifest Destiny,'" *American Historical Review* 32 (July, 1927): 795–98. Pratt notes that it was the December column on Oregon that truly gave the concept a national hearing.

6. Arthur Power Dudden, *The American Pacific: From the Old China Trade to the Present* (New York: Oxford University Press, 1992), pp. 55–57, 59; Sylvester K. Stevens, *American Expansion in Hawaii, 1842–1898* (Harrisburg: Archives Publishing Company of Pennsylvania, 1945), 24–45; Richard W. Van Alstyne, *The Rising American Empire* (1961; reprint ed.: Chicago: Quadrangle Books, 1965), pp. 128, 132–33; John Tyler message, December 30, 1842, in James D. Richardson, ed., *A Compilation of the Messages and Papers of the President, 1789–1908*, 11 vols. (New York: Bureau of National Literature and Art, 1908), vol. 4, pp. 211–12; Daniel Webster to the Commissioners of the Hawaiian Kingdom, December 19, 1842, in Hunter Miller, ed., *Treaties and Other International Acts of the United States of America*, 8 vols. (Washington, D.C.: GPO, 1931–48), vol. 5, pp. 601–602; John M. Clayton to Gerrit P. Judd [no date given], quoted in Dudden, *American Pacific*, 60.

7. Minutes, Philozetian Society, October 6, 1852, Western Reserve College, Case Western Reserve University Archives, Cleveland, Ohio; San Francisco *Herald*, October 27, 1851, quoted in *The Polynesian*, November 22, 1851; Cincinnati *Daily Enquirer*, November 26, 1853.

8. John L. O'Sullivan to John C. Calhoun, August 24, 1849, in *Correspondence of John C. Calhoun*, ed. J. Franklin Jameson, *Annual Report of the American Historical Association for the Year 1899*, 2 vols. (Washington, D.C.: GPO, 1900), vol. 2, pp. 1202–1203; Sheldon Howard Harris, "The Public Career of John Louis O'Sullivan" (Ph.D. diss., Columbia University, 1958), pp. 275–321.

9. D. W. Meinig, *The Shaping of America: A Geopolitical Perspective on 500 Years of History*, vol. 2: *Continental America, 1800–1867* (New Haven: Yale University Press, 1993), p. 209.

10. *The Oxford English Dictionary*, 20 vols. (1933; 2nd. ed., Oxford, Eng.: Clarendon Press, 1989), vol. 5, p. 906, notes that the term "began to be employed" around the years 1850–54. It is my impression that the term was initially coined in 1850, but that it came into common usage in 1851. For an early application of the term, see *The History of the Late Expedition to Cuba, by O.D.D.O., One of the Participants . . .* (New Orleans: Daily Delta, 1850), pp. 26, 39, 43.

11. Whether the countless raids against Native American lands by U.S. settlers comes within this definition is a matter for debate. Given the fact that the U.S. government, starting with the Washington administration, considered Indian tribes as foreign "nations" and signed treaties with them, a case can certainly be constructed that such attacks constituted filibustering. Several scholars explicitly

do so. See, for example, Francis Paul Prucha, *The Sword of the Republic: The United States Army on the Frontier, 1783–1846* (1969; paper ed., Bloomington: Indiana University Press, 1977), pp. 17, 19; Dick T. Steward, "John Smith T. and the Way West: Filibustering and Expansion on the Missouri Frontier," *Missouri Historical Review*, 89 (October, 1994): 69. I am inclined, however, to exclude such raids from the story of filibustering, on the logic that they occurred within the national boundaries of the United States.

12. Charles H. Brown, *Agents of Manifest Destiny: The Lives and Times of the Filibusters* (Chapel Hill: University of North Carolina Press, 1980), p. 3. Other definitions of filibustering abound. See, for example, Janice E. Thomson, *Mercenaries, Pirates, and Sovereigns: State-Building and Extraterritorial Violence in Early Modern Europe* (Princeton: Princeton University Press, 1994), p. 118; Stephen A. Flanders and Carl N. Flanders, eds., *Dictionary of American Foreign Affairs* (New York: Macmillan Publishing Company, 1993), p. 192; Harris Gaylord Warren, *The Sword Was Their Passport: A History of American Filibustering in the Mexican Revolution* (Baton Rouge: Louisiana State University Press, 1943), p. vii; Roy Emerson Curtis, "The Law of Hostile Military Expeditions as Applied by the United States," *American Journal of International Law* 8 (January and April, 1914): 1.

13. Etymologists note that the Dutch *vrijbuiter* passed through several English and Spanish variants, such as the English *flibustier* (pronounced as flib-us-tier) and the Spanish *filibustero*, before it emerged as *filibuster* (often *fillibuster*) in the United States. The term began to assume its modern meaning of obstructing legislative proceedings in the 1880s, though there apparently were occasional earlier applications along these lines. C. T. Onions, ed., *The Oxford English Dictionary of English Etymology* (Oxford, Eng.: Clarendon Press, 1966), p. 355; *Oxford English Dictionary*, vol. 5, p. 906; Mitford M. Mathews, *A Dictionary of Americanisms on Historical Principles*, 2 vols. (Chicago: University of Chicago Press, 1951), vol. 1, pp. 604–605.

14. David S. Heidler, "The Politics of National Aggression: Congress and the First Seminole War," *Journal of the Early Republic*, 13 (Winter, 1993): 505n; Harlan Hague and David J. Langum, *Thomas O. Larkin: A Life of Patriotism and Profit in Old California* (Norman: University of Oklahoma Press, 1990), pp. 112–30; Richard R. Stenberg, "Polk and Frémont, 1845–1846," *Pacific Historical Review*, 7, no. 3 ([no month given], 1938): 216–19, 223.

15. Jackson was a major general in the U.S. Army, commanding its Southern Division, at the time of his invasion of Florida. His force was made up of some 800 U.S. Army regulars, Georgia and Tennessee volunteers, and Indian affiliates. Frémont crossed the Sierras into California in the late fall of 1845 as a lieutenant in the U.S. Army commanding a party of fifteen men in the Army's Corps of Topographical Engineers. Robert V. Remini, *Andrew Jackson and the Course of American Empire, 1767–1821* (New York: Harper and Row, 1977), p. 353; Marquis James, *Andrew Jackson: The Border Captain* (New York: The Literary Guild, 1933), pp. 308–309; William H. Goetzmann, *Army Exploration in the American West, 1803–1863* (1959; paper ed., New Haven: Yale University Press, 1965), pp. 116–23.

16. Remini, *Jackson and the Course of American Empire*, pp. 346–49; William Earl

Weeks, *John Quincy Adams and American Global Empire* (Lexington: University Press of Kentucky, 1992), pp. 109–10, 117–19, 140–45; Harry Ammon, *James Monroe: The Quest for National Identity* (1971; paper ed., Charlottesville: University Press of Virginia, 1990), pp. 423–25; Samuel Flagg Bemis, *John Quincy Adams and the Foundations of American Foreign Policy* (1949; paper ed., New York: W. W. Norton, 1973), pp. 313–15, 314n; George Dangerfield, *The Era of Good Feelings* (1952; paper ed., New York: Harcourt, Brace & World, 1963), pp. 127–36; Thomas R. Hietala, *Manifest Design: Anxious Aggrandizement in Late Jacksonian America* (Ithaca: Cornell University Press, 1985), pp. 83–85. Nothing that Frémont did after the Mexican War began constituted filibustering, since filibusters only attacked nations at peace with their own countries.

17. Janice E. Thomson describes filibustering as "a uniquely American phenomenon" in *Mercenaries, Pirates, and Sovereigns,* p. 118.

18. David J. Weber, *The Spanish Frontier in North America* (New Haven: Yale University Press, 1992), 22–24; James S. Olson, ed., *Historical Dictionary of European Imperialism* (Westport, Conn.: Greenwood Press, 1991), pp. 301–302.

19. Gregg L. Lint, "The Law of Nations and the American Revolution," in Lawrence S. Kaplan, ed., *The American Revolution and "A Candid World"* (Kent: Kent State University Press, 1977), pp. 111–33; Robert W. Tucker and David C. Henrickson, *Empire of Liberty: The Statecraft of Thomas Jefferson* (New York: Oxford University Press, 1990), p. 48.

20. Charles G. Fenwick, *The Neutrality Laws of the United States* (Washington, D.C.: The Endowment, 1913), p. 40, 40n; Dwight F. Henderson, *Congress, Courts, and Criminals: The Development of Federal Criminal Law, 1801–1829* (Westport, Conn.: Greenwood Press, 1985), pp. 10–11, 26, 133; Henry Bartholomew Cox, *War, Foreign Affairs, and Constitutional Power: 1829–1901* (Cambridge, Mass.: Ballinger Publishing Company, 1984), pp. 20–21; "An Act in addition to the 'Act for the punishment of certain crimes against the United States,' and to repeal the acts therein mentioned," April 20, 1818, *Annals of Congress,* 15th Cong., 1st Sess., vol. 2, pp. 2567–70. The 1818 law repealed prior neutrality legislation, including an enactment of the previous year dealing exclusively with the fitting out of vessels for hostilities against "the subjects, citizens, or property, or any prince or state, or of any colony, district or people with whom the United States are at peace." U.S., *Statutes at Large,* vol. 58, pp. 370–71.

21. Stanley Elkins and Eric McKitrick, *The Age of Federalism: The Early American Republic, 1788–1800* (New York: Oxford University Press, 1993), 330–35, 349–50; Robert W. Coakley, *The Role of Federal Military Forces in Domestic Disorders, 1789–1878* (Washington, D.C.: Center of Military History, 1988), pp. 25–26; Arthur Preston Whitaker, *The Spanish-American Frontier: 1783–1795: The Westward Movement and the Spanish Retreat in the Mississippi Valley* (1927; reprint ed., Gloucester, Mass.: Peter Smith, 1962), pp. 187–89; Isaac Joslin Cox, *The West Florida Controversy, 1798–1813: A Study in American Diplomacy* (Baltimore: Johns Hopkins Press, 1918), pp. 24–26; William H. Masterson, *William Blount* (Baton Rouge: Louisiana State University Press, 1954), pp. 301–23; Arthur Preston Whitaker, *The Mississippi Question, 1795–1803: A Study in Trade, Politics, and Diplomacy* (1934;

reprint ed., Gloucester, Mass.: Peter Smith, 1962), pp. 107–15; Harris, "O'Sullivan," pp. 9–10. Since Aaron Burr was arrested on U.S. soil, and since it is still unclear whether or not his famous 1806 expedition intended an attack on foreign territory, it is impossible categorically to either include or exclude him from the record of early American filibustering.

22. Cox, *West Florida Controversy,* pp. 124, 457–86; Warren, *Sword Was Their Passport,* pp. 33–77, 89–95; Donald E. Chipman, *Spanish Texas, 1519–1821* (Austin: University of Texas Press, 1992), pp. 233–37; Richard W. Gronet, "The United States and the Invasion of Texas, 1810–1814," *The Americas,* 25 (January, 1969): 281–306. Gronet argues that the Magee expedition was less a filibuster than part of a U.S. government plot to overthrow the Viceroyalty of New Spain and establish an independent Mexico.

23. Rembert W. Patrick, *Florida Fiasco: Rampant Rebels on the Georgia-Florida Border, 1810–1815* (Athens: University of Georgia Press, 1954), pp. 1–8, 14–15, 46, 49, 53–57, 95–96, 100–101, 106–107, 111, 121, 127–37, 164–65, 258; Julius W. Pratt, *Expansionists of 1812* (New York: Macmillan, 1925), pp. 74, 78–81, 100, 106, 238–46; Weber, *Spanish Frontier,* p. 298.

24. Warren, *Sword Was Their Passport,* pp. 146–72, 233–54; Chipman, *Spanish Texas,* 238–40; Margaret Swett Henson, *Juan Davis Bradburn: A Reappraisal of the Mexican Commander of Anahuac* (College Station: Texas A&M University Press, 1982), pp. 30–33; Henderson, *Congress, Courts, and Criminals,* pp. 131–32; Rembert W. Patrick, *Aristocrat in Uniform: General Duncan L. Clinch* (Gainesville: University of Florida Press, 1963), p. 39. Spanish and American officials received reports of other filibusters throughout this period, including one expedition to Puerto Rico. See Cox, *West Florida Controversy,* pp. 155, 440–52; Henderson, *Congress, Courts, and Criminals,* pp. 56, 150; Harris Gaylord Warren, "Southern Filibusters in the War of 1812," *Louisiana Historical Quarterly,* 25 (April, 1942): 291–300; Warren, "Pensacola and the Filibusters, 1816–1817," *Louisiana Historical Quarterly,* 21 (July, 1938): 806–22; Steward, "John Smith T.," 61–72.

25. Paul D. Lack, *The Texas Revolutionary Experience: A Political and Social History, 1835–1836* (College Station: Texas A&M University Press, 1992), pp. 114–15, 122–23, 125–28, 134; Alwyn Barr, *Texans in Revolt: The Battle for San Antonio, 1835* (Austin: University of Texas Press, 1990), pp. 1–4, 8, 17–18, 35, 37–38; Joseph Milton Nance, *After San Jacinto: The Texas-Mexican Frontier, 1836–1841* (Austin: University of Texas Press, 1963), pp. 16–17, 18, 28–29; Robert E. May, *John A. Quitman: Old South Crusader* (Baton Rouge: Louisiana State University Press, 1985), pp. 76–89; Kimberly Ann Lamp, "Empire for Slavery: Economic and Territorial Expansion in the American Gulf South, 1835–1860" (Ph.D. diss., Harvard University, 1991), pp. 71–72, 77–84. Lack also notes that of the soldiers serving in Texan revolutionary forces other than Houston's army in March–April 1836, about a third were recent American arrivals. Lack, *Texan Revolutionary Experience,* p. 128. The Jackson administration in Washington assumed an official stance of neutrality during the Texas Revolution and instructed district attorneys to prosecute persons violating U.S. neutrality laws. However, federal officials were either unwilling or unable to enforce these orders. Robert V. Remini, *Andrew Jackson and the Course of American*

Democracy, 1835–1845 (New York: Harper & Row, 1984), p. 357; John M. Belohlavek, *"Let the Eagle Soar!": The Foreign Policy of Andrew Jackson* (Lincoln: University of Nebraska Press, 1985), pp. 230–31.

26. Kenneth R. Stevens, *Border Diplomacy: The* Caroline *and McLeod Affairs in Anglo-American-Canadian Relations, 1837–1842* (Tuscaloosa: University of Alabama Press, 1989), pp. 7–17, 20–21, 36–41; Howard Jones, *To The Webster-Ashburton Treaty: A Study in Anglo-American Relations, 1783–1843* (Chapel Hill: University of North Carolina Press, 1977), pp. 22–27; Oscar A. Kinchen, *The Rise and Fall of the Patriot Hunters* (New York: Bookman Associates, 1856), pp. 16–17, 20–61; Albert B. Corey, *The Crisis of 1830–1842 in Canadian-American Relations* (New Haven: Yale University Press, 1941), 35, 38–39, 41, 70–75; Reginald C. Stuart, *United States Expansionism and British North America, 1775–1871* (Chapel Hill: University of North Carolina Press, 1988), 135–38; Harwood Perry Hinton, "The Military Career of John Ellis Wool, 1812–1863" (Ph. D. diss., University of Wisconsin, 1960), pp. 151–54; Major L. Wilson, *The Presidency of Martin Van Buren* (Lawrence: University Press of Kansas, 1984), p. 159.

27. John F. Crampton to Lord Clarendon, September 25, 1853, in James J. Barnes and Patience P. Barnes, eds., *Private and Confidential: Letters from British Ministers in Washington to the Foreign Secretaries in London, 1844–67* (Selinsgrove: Susquehanna University Press, 1993), p. 84. I have already briefly treated post–Mexican War U.S. filibustering's cultural manifestations in "Young American Males and Filibustering in the Age of Manifest Destiny: The United States Army as a Cultural Mirror," *Journal of American History* 73 (December, 1991): 857–64, and have a more comprehensive treatment of this theme in progress. See also Tom Chaffin, "'Sons of Washington': Narciso López, Filibustering, and U.S. Nationalism, 1848–1851," *Journal of the Early Republic* 15 (Spring, 1995): 79–108.

28. There is a vast literature on the López and Walker filibusters. Brown, *Agents of Manifest Destiny*, pp. 42–88, 267–455, provides a useful one-volume account of the two movements.

29. Nelson Reed, *The Caste War of Yucatan* (Stanford: Stanford University Press, 1964), pp. 110–14; Edward O. Fitchen, "Self-Determination or Self-Preservation?: The Relations of Independent Yucatán With the Republic of Texas and The United States, 1847–1849," *Journal of the West*, 18 (January, 1979): 33–40. Americans had also filibustered to Yucatán in 1844. See David M. Pletcher, *The Diplomacy of Annexation: Texas, Oregon, and the Mexican War* (Columbia: University of Missouri Press, 1973), p. 151.

30. Helen Chapman to her mother, June 13, 1848, in Caleb Cocker, ed., *The News from Brownsville: Helen Chapman's Letters from the Texas Military Frontier, 1848–1852* (Austin: Texas State Historical Association, 1992), pp. 49–50; Washington *Daily National Intelligencer,* August 2, November 10, 1848, July 6, August 27, 1849, September 25, 1851; *Charleston* (South Carolina) *Courier,* September 21, 1848; Earnest C. Shearer, "The Carvajal Disturbances," *Southwestern Historical Quarterly* 55 (October, 1951): 201–30; Justin Harvey Smith, "La República De Río Grande," *American Historical Review* 25 (July, 1920): 660–75; Nance, *After San Jacinto,* pp.

142–377; John Moretta, "Jose Marie Jesus Carvajal, United States Foreign Policy and the Filibustering Spirit in Texas," *East Texas Historical Journal* 33 (Fall, 1995): 3–22.

31. Joe A. Stout, *The Liberators: Filibustering Expeditions into Mexico, 1848–1862, and the Last Thrust of Manifest Destiny* (Los Angeles: Westernlore Press, 1973), pp. 37–48.

32. Eugene Keith Chamberlin, "Baja California After Walker: The Zerman Enterprise," *Hispanic American Historical Review* 34(May, 1954): 175–89.

33. Ronnie C. Tyler, "The Callahan Expedition of 1855: Indians or Negroes?," *Southwestern Historical Quarterly* 70 (April, 1967): 574–85; Kevin Mulroy, *Freedom on the Border: The Seminole Maroons in Florida, the Indian Territory, Coahuila, and Texas* (Lubbock: Texas Tech University Press, 1993), pp. 78–80.

34. "Execution of Colonel Crabb and Associates," *House Executive Documents*, 35th Cong., 1st Sess., no. 64; San Francisco *Daily Alta California*, May 14, November 6, 1857; Cornelius C. Smith, Jr., *William Sanders Oury: History-Maker of the Old Southwest* (Tucson: University of Arizona Press, 1967), pp. 93–96. Crabb and his men claimed that they entered Sonora as invited colonizers rather than as conquerors. See Stuart V. Voss, *On the Periphery of Nineteenth-Century Mexico: Sonora and Sinaloa, 1810–1877* (Tucson: University of Arizona Press, 1982), pp. 92, 136–40; James E. Officer, *Hispanic Arizona, 1536–1856* (Tucson: University of Arizona Press, 1987), pp. 300–302; Joe A. Stout, Jr., "Henry A. Crabb: Filibuster or Colonizer?," *American West* 8 (May, 1971): 4–9.

35. Walter Prescott Webb, *The Texas Rangers: A Century of Frontier Defense* (2nd. ed., Austin: University of Texas Press, 1965), pp. 189–90, 192; Robert E. May, *The Southern Dream of a Caribbean Empire, 1854–1861* (Baton Rouge: Louisiana State University Press, 1973), pp. 148–55; Sam Houston to John B. Floyd, February 13 [2 letters], February 15, 1860, in Amelia W. Williams and Eugene C. Barker, eds., *The Writings of Sam Houston, 1813–1863*, 8 vols. (1938; reprint ed., Austin: Jenkins Publishing Company, 1970), vol. 7, pp. 474–76, 478; John Hoyt Williams, *Sam Houston: The Life and Times of the Liberator of Texas, an Authentic American Hero* (New York: Simon & Schuster, 1993), pp. 314–24.

36. Mark J. Van Aken, *King of the Night: Juan José Flores and Ecuador, 1824–1864* (Berkeley: University of California Press, 1989), pp. 243–45; Brown, *Agents*, pp. 164–67; Lawrence A. Clayton, "Steps of Considerable Delicacy: Early Relations with Peru," in T. Ray Shurbutt, ed., *United States-Latin American Relations, 1800–1850: The Formative Generations* (Tuscaloosa: University of Alabama Press, 1991), pp. 81–82.

37. May, *Quitman*, pp. 270–95; James T. Wall, *Manifest Destiny Denied: America's First Intervention in Nicaragua* (Washington, D.C.: University Press of America, 1981), pp. 49–70; Tampa (Florida) *Peninsular*, June 30, 1855; San Francisco *Daily Alta California*, May 30, 1858.

38. Malcolm W. Mearis to John M. Clayton, October 16, 1849, Despatches from Special Agents of the Department of State, RG 59 (reel 9, M 37).

39. N. S. Reneau to James Buchanan, Janurary 6, 1859, James Buchanan to John B. Blake, Jan. 7, 1863; James Buchanan Papers, Historical Society of Pennsylvania,

Philadelphia; Memphis *Daily Appeal,* December 29, 1858; Memphis *Daily Avalanche,* October 21, 1859; New York *Herald,* February 6, 1859.

40. James Buchanan to Robert Rantoul, June 23, 1848, in John Bassett Moore, comp. and ed., *The Works of James Buchanan,* 12 vols. (Philadelphia: J. B. Lippincott, 1908–1911), vol. 8, pp. 105, 159–60; *Galveston* (Texas) *Weekly News,* May 22, 1855; Malcolm W. Mearis to John M. Clayton, August 10, 1849, Despatches from Special Agents of the Department of State (reel 9, M 37); Philadelphia *Public Ledger,* December 29, 1855; *New York Herald,* February 14, 1858.

41. Savannah *Daily Morning News,* June 3, 1850; *Our Times,* 1 (October, 1852): 115; Washington *Daily National Intelligencer,* November 24, 1852; *New York Herald,* February 1, 1850, quoted in Alejandro Bolaños-Geyer, *William Walker: The Gray-Eyed Man of Destiny,* vol. 2: *The Californias* (Lake Saint Louis: Privately Printed, 1989), pp. 39–41; Theodore Poesche and Charles Goepp, *The New Rome; Or, The United States of the World* (New York: G. P. Putnam, 1853), pp. 12–13; Donald S. Spencer, *Louis Kossuth and Young America: A Study of Sectionalism and Foreign Policy, 1848–1852* (Columbia: University of Missouri Press, 1977), p. 167.

42. Lord Tenterden, "The Fenian Brotherhood: An Account of the Irish Revolutionary Society in the United States from 1848 to 1850," in Kenneth Bourne and D. Cameron Watt, eds., *British Documents on Foreign Affairs: Reports and Papers from the Foreign Office Confidential Print,* vol. 3: *The Irish Problem and Immigration, 1848–1870* (Frederick, Md.: University Publications of America, 1986), pp. 64–70; *United States* v. *Lumsden et al.,* case no. 15,641 in *The Federal Cases, Comprising Cases Argued and Determined in the Circuit and District Courts of the United States,* 30 vols. (St. Paul: West Publishing Company, 1894–1897), vol. 26, pp. 1013–20; Philadelphia *Public Ledger,* January 12, 1856. One of the defendants was discharged prior to the case coming before U.S. district court judge H. H. Leavitt for a preliminary hearing. In that hearing, Leavitt dismissed all charges on the grounds that there was not enough proof to hold over the suspects for a grand jury investigation.

43. San Francisco *Daily Alta California,* October 21, 1855.

44. Richard Tansey, "Southern Expansionism: Urban Interests in the Cuban Filibusters," *Plantation Society in the Americas,* 1 (June, 1979): 227–51; William O. Scroggs, *Filibusters and Financiers: The Story of William Walker and His Associates* (New York: Russell & Russell, 1916).

45. Henry E. McCulloch to Elisha M. Pease, October 17, 1855, Elisha M. Pease Papers, Austin History Center, Austin Public Library, Austin, Texas; Persifor F. Smith to R. Jones, July 18, 1852, *Senate Exec. Doc.,* 32nd Cong., 2nd Sess., no. 1, Serial Set 659, p. 15; W. J. Hughes, *Rebellious Ranger: Rip Ford and the Old Southwest* (Norman: University of Oklahoma Press, 1964), p. 100; Tyler, "Callahan Expedition," pp. 574–79.

46. Washington *Daily National Intelligencer,* September 29, 1851.

47. John S. Brenizer to "Dear Brother in Law," July 24, 1856, John S. Brenizer Papers, Tennessee State Library and Archives, Nashville; John W. Fleener to John A. Quitman, August 17, 1854, John Quitman Papers, Mississippi Department of Archives and History, Jackson; William Frank Stewart, *Last of the Filibusters; Or,*

Recollections of the Siege of Rivas (Sacramento: Henry Shipley and Company, 1857); Antonio Rafael de la Cova, "Ambrosio Jose Gonzales: A Cuban Confederate Colonel" (Ph.D. diss., West Virginia University, 1994), pp. 12, 165, 178–79, 191. In using expeditions as a means to travel, filibusters followed the precedent of Mexican War volunteers. See Robert W. Johannsen, *To the Halls of the Montezumas: The Mexican War in the American Imagination* (New York: Oxford University Press, 1985), pp. 146–64.

48. John Rapier Diary [reminiscence], p. 153, Rapier Family Papers, Moorland-Spingarn Research Center, Howard University, Washington, D. C.; [F. M. Boggess], *A Veteran of Four Wars: The Autobiography of F. C. M. Boggess* (Arcadia: Champion Job Rooms, 1900), p. 8; Martha A. Sandweiss, Rick Stewart, and Ben H. Huseman, *Eyewitness to War: Prints and Daguerreotypes of the Mexican War, 1846–1848* (Washington, D.C.: Smithsonian University Press, 1989), p. 9; John S. Slocum to Albert Tracy, June 27, 1849, Albert H. Tracy to Albert Tracy, Aug. 13, 1849, Albert Tracy Papers, New York Public Library, New York City; Anna Pashall Hannum, ed., *A Quaker Forty-Niner: The Adventures of Charles Edward Pancoast on the American Frontier* (Philadelphia: University of Pennsylvania Press, 1930), pp. 328, 372–73.

49. John Henderson to John A. Quitman, November 6, 1850, in J. F. H. Claiborne, *Life and Correspondence of John A. Quitman*, 2 vols. (New York, 1860), vol. 2, pp. 70–71; John T. Pickett to John A. Quitman, March 20, 1854, John Quitman Papers, Mississippi Department of Archives and History.

50. B. F. Dill to John A. Quitman, June 7, 1854, John A. Quitman to B. F. Dill, February 9, 1854 [1855], Robert O. Love to John A. Quitman, May 24, 1854, John Quitman Papers, Mississippi Department of Archives and History, John A. Quitman to B. F. Dill, June 18, 1854 [draft], John A. Quitman Papers, Houghton Library, Harvard University; May, *Southern Dream*, pp. 30–34, 48–53.

51. May, *Southern Dream*, 106–35; Frederic Rosengarten, Jr., *Freebooters Must Die! The Life and Death of William Walker, the Most Notorious Filibuster of the Nineteenth Century* (Wayne: Haverford House, 1976), p. 47; *New York Times*, October 19, 1857, p. 2; New York *Herald*, July 21, 1858; William Walker, *The War in Nicaragua* (1860; reprint ed., Tucson: University of Arizona Press, 1985), pp. 254–80; R. Raub to John A. Quitman, January 18, 1858, John A. Quitman Papers, Harvard University.

52. May, *Southern Dream*, 149–51; Walter L. Buenger, *Secession and the Union in Texas* (Austin: University of Texas Press, 1984), pp. 156–57.

53. *Blackwood's Magazine*, quoted in *Littell's Living Age*, 49, no. 621 (Apr. 19, 1856): 129.

54. Weinberg, *Manifest Destiny*, pp. 100–11; Merk, *Manifest Destiny and Mission*, pp. 29–31; Norman Graebner, ed., *Manifest Destiny* (Indianapolis: Bobbs-Merrill, 1968), p. xxxi.

55. Chaffin, "'Sons of Washington,'" pp. 88–89, 98, 101–103; T. S. Anderson to John A. Quitman, April 24, 1854, James Madison Miller to Quitman, September 17, 1854, John Quitman Papers, Harvard University, Cambridge, Mass.; John A. Quitman to William Walker, November 22, 1856, in T. Harry Williams, *P. G. T. Beauregard: Napoleon in Gray* (Baton Rouge: Louisiana State University Press, 1955), p. 42; P. G. T. Beauregard to Persifor F. Smith, January 24, 1856 [1857], Persifor Frazer Smith Papers, Historical Society of Pennsylvania, Philadelphia.

56. Weinberg, *Manifest Destiny*, pp. 160–83; Reginald Horsman, *Race and Manifest Destiny: The Origins of American Racial Anglo-Saxonism* (Cambridge, Mass.: Harvard University Press, 1981), pp. 208–209, 229–48; Thomas R. Hietala, *Manifest Destiny: Anxious Aggrandizement in Late Jacksonian America* (Ithaca: Cornell University Press, 1985), pp. 133–34, 152, 155–59.

57. Appleton Oaksmith to James Neal, June 14, 1856, Appleton Oaksmith Papers, William R. Perkins Library, Duke University, Durham, North Carolina; *El Nicaraguense,* enclosed in John H. Wheeler to William Marcy, July 15, 1856, in Manning, comp., *Diplomatic Correspondence,* vol. 4, pp. 544–45; "Address of President Walker, to the People of the United States," November 30, 1853, in Arthur Woodward, ed., *The Republic of Lower California, 1853–1854* (Los Angeles: Dawson's Book Shop, 1966), pp. 31–33; San Juan del Norte *Central American,* September 15, 1855; Leo Wheat, "Memoir of Gen. C. R. Wheat," *Southern Historical Society Papers,* 17 (1989): 50–51; *Fayette* (Mississippi) *Watch Tower,* September 4, 1857; Sam Houston to John B. Floyd, April 14, 1860, in Williams and Barker, eds., *Writings of Sam Houston,* vol. 8, p. 18.

58. New Orleans *Daily Creole,* October 28, 1856; New York *Daily Times,* December 15, 1854.

59. John S. Brenizer to "Dear Brother in Law," July 24, 1856, Brenizer Papers; Flavel Belcher to his father, June 30, 1856 [quotation], November 27, 1857, Flavel Belcher Papers, Bancroft Library, University of California, Berkeley; John C. Reid, *Reid's Tramp: Or, A Journal of the Incidents of Ten Months Travel Through Texas, New Mexico, Arizona, Sonora, and California* (Selma: John Hardy & Co., 1856), pp. 36, 194–97, 220.

60. Weinberg, *Manifest Destiny,* p. 115; William J. Cooper, Jr., *Liberty and Slavery: Southern Politics to 1860* (New York: Alfred A. Knopf, 1983); George M. Fredrickson, *The Black Image in the White Mind: The Debate on Afro-American Character and Destiny, 1817–1914* (New York: Harper & Row, 1971), pp. 59–62; Chaffin, "'Sons of Washington,'" p. 97.

61. Harris, "O'Sullivan," pp. 53–54, 270, 275–76; Merk, *Manifest Destiny,* p. 58; John L. O'Sullivan to John A. Quitman, June 26, 1850, John Quitman Papers, Mississippi Department of Archives and History; Mike Walsh to John A. Quitman, October 3, 1853, John Quitman Papers, Harvard University.

62. *Congressional Globe,* 35th Cong., 1st Sess., p. 293; George M. Dallas to Francis Markoe, May 9, 1854, Galloway-Maxcy-Markoe Papers, Library of Congress, Washington, D.C.; May, *Southern Dream,* pp. 53, 55–63.

63. "Central America—The Late War In Nicaragua," *Democratic Review,* New Series, 40 (July, 1857): 10; Albert Z. Carr, *The World and William Walker* (New York: Harper & Row, 1963), p. 84.

64. Manuel Diez de Bonilla to James Gadsden, November 15, 1853, Gadsden to Diez, November 18, 1853, Gadsden to William L. Marcy, November 19, 1853, September 2, 1854, Draft treaty antifilibustering provision, in Manning, comp., *Diplomatic Correspondence,* vol. 9, pp. 663–64, 664–65, 666, 728–30, 694n; James Gadsden to "the Officer of the U.S. Navy Commdg any Squadron or vessel of war in the Pacific," October 22, 1853, Letters Received, Squadron Letters, Records of the

Secretary of the Navy, RG 45, NA (reel 36, M 89). Gadsden's request to the Navy derived not only from concerns about Walker's expedition, but also the Sonoran filibusters, from California, of French count Gaston de Raousset-Boulbon. See Nancy Nichols Barker, *The French Experience in Mexico, 1821–1866: A History of Constant Misunderstanding* (Chapel Hill: University of North Carolina Press, 1979), pp. 131–40; Rosengarten, *Freebooters Must Die!*, pp. 29–33; Brown, *Agents of Manifest Destiny*, p. 171.

65. Paul N. Garber, *The Gadsden Treaty* (Philadelphia: University of Pennsylvania Press, 1923), pp. 91–92. Gadsden's negotiating instructions, conveyed to him verbally by courier Christopher M. Ward, suggested six possible boundary lines as terms, the most coveted of which envisioned Mexico's ceding all of Lower California and other areas of northern Mexico not included in the final settlement for $50 million—considerably more than the Gadsden Treaty's sum of $10 million.

66. John Forsyth to Lewis Cass, April 24, 1857, in Manning, comp., *Diplomatic Correspondence*, vol. 9, pp. 915–16.

67. Samuel McLean to John M. Clayton, July 2, 1850, Despatches from United States Consuls in Trinidad, Cuba, General Records of the Department of State, RG 59, NA (reel 2, T 690); Daniel M. Barringer to Daniel Webster, September 18, 25, 1851, Angel Calderón de la Barca to Clayton, January 19, 1850, in Manning, comp., *Diplomatic Correspondence*, vol. 11, pp. 613, 616, 473–74; James W. Cortada, *Two Nations Over Time: Spain and the United States, 1776–1977* (Westport, Conn.: Greenwood Press, 1978), pp. 66–68, 72–76.

68. Lester D. Langley, *The Cuban Policy of the United States: A Brief History* (New York: John Wiley and Sons, 1968), pp. 35–36; Luis Martínez-Fernández, *Torn between Empires: Economy, Society, and Patterns of Political Thought in the Hispanic Caribbean, 1840–1878* (Athens: University of Georgia Press, 1994), pp. 26–28, 55; Barker, *French Experience in Mexico*, p. 143; Gustave A. Nueremberger, "The Continental Treaties of 1856: An American Union 'Exclusive of the United States,'" *Hispanic American Historical Review* 20 (February, 1940): 32–55.

69. "Message of the President of New Granada on the Opening of Congress Bogota, Feb. 1857" [trans.], enclosed in Philip Griffith to Earl of Clarendon, Great Britain, Foreign Office, F. O. 55/131 [microfilm]; E. Bradford Burns, *Patriarch and Folk: The Emergence of Nicaragua, 1798–1858* (Cambridge, Mass.: Harvard University Press, 1991), p. 213; Marc Edelman and Joanne Kenen, eds., *The Costa Rica Reader* (New York: Grove Weidenfeld, 1989), p. 8.

70. R. C. Wyllie to David L. Gregg, November 13, 1854 [copy], David L. Gregg to R. C. Wyllie, October 28, November 13, 22, 1854 [copies], Gregg to William L. Marcy, November 14, 1854, Thomas A. Dornin to Gregg, November 14, 1854 [copy], Despatches, Hawaii (reel 5); Proclamation of King Kamehameha, December 8, 1854, Wyllie to Gregg, January 30, 1855, Gregg to Marcy, May 16, 1855, ibid. (reel 6).